REFORMATION
CELEBRATION

REFORMATION
CELEBRATION

THE SIGNIFICANCE OF SCRIPTURE, GRACE, FAITH, AND CHRIST

Gordon L. Isaac & Eckhard J. Schnabel, editors

HENDRICKSON
PUBLISHERS

Reformation Celebration: The Significance of Scripture, Grace, Faith, and Christ

© 2018 by Gordon L. Isaac and Eckhard J. Schnabel
Hendrickson Publishers Marketing, LLC
P. O. Box 3473
Peabody, Massachusetts 01961-3473
www.hendrickson.com

ISBN 978-1-68307-183-9

Printed in the United States of America

First Printing — September 2018

Library of Congress Cataloging-in-Publication Data

A catalog record for this title is available from the Library of Congress
Hendrickson Publishers Marketing, LLC ISBN 978-1-68307-183-9

CONTENTS

INTRODUCTION

In 2015, plans were set in motion for a Reformation Celebration at Gordon-Conwell Theological Seminary. We wanted this conference to be strategically placed close to the five-hundredth anniversary of Martin Luther's posting of the Ninety-Five Theses on October 31, 1517. From the beginning, our intention was to involve as many of our faculty colleagues as possible, for in this way the celebration would represent numerous vantage points and thus enrich the experience for all. The assignment given to each was simple: address the genius of Reformation theology from your own particular discipline. As a result, historians, New Testament scholars, ethicists, Old Testament scholars, homileticians, systematicians, counselors, and other practical theologians all contributed. The set of collected essays before you represents reflections on Scripture, grace, faith, and Christ from these different voices on our faculty. Here you will find Reformation insights of ongoing significance for the sake of ministry in the church.

The conference took place October 26–28, 2017, on the South Hamilton Campus in Massachusetts of Gordon-Conwell Theological Seminary. Although the majority of the attendees were local, there were many who traveled from various distances to hear the lectures and to celebrate and reflect on the Reformation. In addition to the crowd that gathered in the Kaiser Chapel, thousands joined the proceedings via live streaming. On the first night of activities, more than four thousand watched from their computers in places as far away as Puerto Rico, China, and India, and as nearby as the student residence halls. The wide reach of this conference was appropriate, given the world-historical significance of the Reformation. Interspersed with the lectures, Daniel Jay McKinley—minister of music, organist, and choirmaster of Christ the Redeemer Anglican Church in Danvers, Massachusetts—led us in singing select Reformation-era hymns, some even with sixteenth-century syncopation. The Reformation Celebration Conference was a time for old friends to reunite and for new friendships to be forged, and to consider again the heritage of faith that has come to us through the religious shift that took place in the sixteenth century.

The Reformation

Five hundred years ago, Europe was on the threshold of change. No sector of society remained unaffected by the seismic shifts that altered political structures, technology, and religious expression. Certainly, the world-shaping nature of the new technologies of gunpowder, the printing press, and emerging national identities meant that the medieval structures could not remain unaffected. Tremendous pressures were also building in the area of religion. The increasing demands of the penitential system of the church obscured the saving work of Christ, placing the conscience of the average believer in a tenuous position. Even voices within the hierarchy complained that the abiding problems of the church emanated from the curia itself. The Reformation movements emanating from Wittenberg (Luther), Geneva (Calvin), and Zurich (Zwingli) were all attempts to see Western Christianity reform itself under the guidance of the word of God. These reform efforts contributed a new energy in the church that touched on at least three areas: a new religious outlook, fresh and practical expressions of the faith, and a driving sense of mission.

While both Protestants and Roman Catholics use the same terminology, they mean very different things by it. Take, for instance, the term "faith." Luther was fond of saying that "we are justified by faith alone and not by works." The fact that this became the hallmark of various streams of Reformation thought is well known. But perhaps what is not so well known is that Christian salvation of the Middle Ages, at least since the twelfth century, had emphasized love instead of faith as the key element. Strictly speaking, medieval Roman theology could say that faith was not saving. It was thus an epoch-making event when Luther, struggling through the biblical text, came to realize that the righteousness of God is revealed apart from the works of the law (Rom. 3:21–28). The fact that we are saved by grace through faith moved Luther to the place where he could, along with Scripture, grant faith that new defining content that allowed it to supersede the medieval centrality of love (*caritas*) and its works (*opera*).[1]

The term "grace" in Roman Catholic nomenclature refers to the aid granted the believer to do the next work of love. The task of the believer is to add works of love to faith so that it might be saving. This was conceived along the lines of an Aristotelian system that says a person becomes good by doing good deeds. The problem with this system is that it can never be determined how many good works one must do to be saved, thus always putting one's conscience in doubt. A reformational reading of Scripture focuses on the promise of right standing with God through Christ as a completed state. As Luther puts it in his treatise *Two Kinds of Righteousness*, "Through faith in Christ, therefore, Christ's righteousness becomes our righteousness and all that he has becomes ours; rather, he himself becomes ours."[2] Thus "grace" from the point of view of the Reformation is not an aid for the accumulation of good works but the declaration of a new relationship and a new reality. Good works flow out of this new reality.

The term "Christ" also takes on new dimensions in Reformation theology. Under the increasingly oppressive penitential system, the good favor of Christ was increasingly hidden, which is one reason for the increase in the devotion of Mary. If Christ is not favorable, then there is no one better to get his attention than his mother. Mary, in the minds of many, was more merciful than Christ, so petitioning for her intercession made sense. Luther's own experience in the monastery ran along these lines. Christ was consistently portrayed as the judge of the Last Day. Luther was terrified at the prospect of falling into the hands of the God of justice without the benefit of a mediator. It was not until Luther realized through meditation on the text of Scripture that the justice of God is not the philosophical or the formal justice required of the believer, but the justice given through faith in Christ who came to save the lost. When he realized this, his fears were allayed and he found peace.[3]

Reformation theology, in addition to a new religious outlook, provided fresh and practical expressions of the faith. Two of the many changes that took place came in the area of approach to the poor and in the area of sex and marriage. First, medieval notions of piety viewed poverty as a particular virtue. The rich could give alms to the poor as a work pleasing to God. But in this schema, the primary purpose of charity was not to alleviate the plight of the poor but to assure that the giver could achieve merit before God. The doctrine of justification by faith cut the nerve of this idealization of poverty. Since righteousness before God is gained by grace alone, and since salvation is the source of life rather than the achievement of life, poverty and the plight of the poor certainly cannot be construed as a peculiar form of blessedness. Reformers took steps to establish the community chest. Out of these gifts, microloans were extended to needy artisans, and daughters of the poor were provided with appropriate dowries and given in marriage. The begging of the monks and mendicants was prohibited. These actions established the saying, "No one should go begging among Christians."

Second, the Reformation view of vocation dramatically altered medieval life in the area of sex and marriage. According to Stephen Ozment,

> No institutional change brought about by the Reformation was more visible, responsive to late medieval pleas for reform, and conducive to new social attitudes than the marriage of Protestant clergy. Nor was there another point in the Protestant program where theology and practice corresponded more successfully.[4]

The Reformers vigorously criticized the Roman imposition of celibacy on the clergy, monks, and nuns. Luther argued that it went against nature and that celibacy did not contribute to salvation as a good work. In addition, through these vows, men and women were removed from service to their neighbor, and the divine order of marriage and the family were contravened.

Consequences of Reformation theology also extended to the area of mission. The first two martyrs for the evangelical faith were the Augustinian monks who preached salvation solely by faith (*sola fide*) in the Netherlands. The authorities demanded that Johann Esch and Heinrich Voes recant their convictions or be burned at the stake. When they refused to recant, they paid the ultimate price for their "Lutheran" beliefs on July 1, 1523. Olof Persson (Olaus Petri) studied theology at the University of Leipzig and ultimately at the University Wittenberg, completing a master's degree in 1518. After returning to his native Sweden, he took up various posts and became instrumental in introducing Reformation theology to his country. In 1541, the monumental completion of the Gustav Vasa Bible helped to codify the Swedish language. Johannes Bugenhagen, pastor of the St. Mary's church in Wittenberg, wrote church orders (*Kirchenordenungen*) for Braunschweig (1528), Hamburg (1528/29), Lübeck (1530–31), the Duchy of Pomerania (1534), East Frisia (1534/35), Schleswig-Holstein (1542), Brunswick-Wolfenbüttel (1543), and Denmark/Norway (1537), where he crowned Christian the III. Through these redoubtable efforts, Bugenhagen gained the title "Apostle of the North." The evangelical faith also flourished in Prussia by its introduction and instruction by Dr. Johann Briesmann. Later on, the evangelical faith of the Reformation was extended by the work of the Pietists of the eighteenth century.

It was under their ministry that John Wesley was converted while hearing Martin Luther's introduction to the book of Romans.

Reformation Celebration

The Reformation with its distinctive theology, innovations in piety, and commitment to mission is the source of the essays in this book. They are gathered in an initial historical section followed by sections on four of the five *solas* of the Reformation: *sola scriptura* (Scripture alone), *sola gratia* (grace alone), *sola fide* (faith alone), and *solus Christus* (Christ alone).

In the opening section titled "Martin Luther and the Reformation in 1571," these first essays explain significant aspects of the theological emphases that were foundational for Luther and the Protestant Reformation in the sixteenth century. To begin, Gordon Isaac tells the story of Luther's approach to Scripture in three parts. Part one outlines Luther's dissatisfaction with Scholasticism's dependence on philosophical categories, which prompts Luther to move to a more Bible-centered approach. Part two shows how Luther understood the Bible as a book that witnesses to Christ; in this way, Christ is the center and meaning of all Scripture. Part three sets out Luther's conviction that Scripture is a book like no other, having the power to produce faith and thus proving its authority. This makes it possible for Luther to say that Scripture is self-authenticating, needing no outside source to establish its authority.

Eckhard Schnabel then explains how Luther came to a renewed understanding of the grace of God. Luther rediscovered that grace is the work of the Triune God alone, that God's unconditional grace granted to the sinner is possible only on account of the person of Jesus Christ who lived and died "for us" (*pro nobis*), and that works do not contribute to grace, not because all works are sinful, but because of the corruption of the human heart. From 1517 until his death in 1546, in hundreds of publications Luther promulgated his conviction that salvation is the justification of the sinner as God's free gift of pure grace.

Lastly, Gwenfair Adams traces how Luther moved from the fear of Christ to the love of Christ. Her account begins with Luther being terror-stricken by the divine majesty as he says his first Mass. The long course of Luther's wrestling with this issue took him through difficult times. Lecturing through the Psalms and the advice of his confessor, Johannes Staupitz, brought Luther to a new understanding of Christ. Luther viewed Christ not as judge but as wounded Savior, willing to save. Preaching this Christ became Luther's single focus to the very end of his career.

In the second section titled "*Sola Scriptura:* By Scripture Alone," three essays explain the foundational significance of the Bible as the authoritative word of God in the context of the Old Testament, the spiritual formation of believers, and the demographics of global Protestantism.

First, Seong Hyun Park explores the significance of Psalm 119 and its statements on the word of God. The longest psalm in the Scriptures—exquisite in its artistry as an acrostic composition in twenty-two strophes, each associated with one of the twenty-two letters of the Hebrew alphabet—celebrates the Torah, the law of God expressed in commandment, judgment, stipulation, regulation, saying, word, and statute. The experience of God's Torah involves the whole person: heart, hands, feet, mouth, and eyes. As Park shows us, Luther turned to Psalm 119 for a description of the fundamentals of studying theology that take place in the context of prayer, meditation, and the struggle against the flesh and Satan.

Next, David Currie explains the role of Luther's *sola scriptura* emphasis for spiritual formation. Rejecting the misconception that a new openness to practices associated with Roman Catholic piety unfailingly leads to an abandonment of the central role of Scripture, and the misconception that an emphasis on "Scripture alone" is bibliolatry that favors the "dead letter" to the "living Lord," Currie explains Luther's call for reform as a vision of the spiritual life shaped by the word, emphasizing Scripture as the central and primary foundation of spiritual formation and resulting in believers becoming increasingly conformed to the image of Christ, which ensures a life in step with the Spirit who breathed out the Scriptures.

Todd Johnson begins his essay by stating that while historical descriptions of the Reformation in the sixteenth century focus on Germany, today the majority of Protestant believers live in Africa, Asia, and Latin America. He explains how Protestantism has expanded globally through the translation of the Bible and the principle and practice of the priesthood of all believers. Luther was personally active in the first, translating the Bible into German so that individual believers could have direct access to the biblical message. And he strongly emphasized the second, resulting in the convincing of Protestants that all Christians are capable of sharing their faith. Citing Adoniram and Ann Judson as examples, Professor Johnson traces the

Protestant movement over its five-hundred-year history, highlighting how Protestants adapted with thousands of cultures and languages.

The third section, "*Sola Gratia:* By Grace Alone," is the longest of the book with six essays. These essays explain the meaning and significance of grace in both the Old and New Testaments, in systematic theological thinking about sanctification, in social ethics, in counseling, and in missionary outreach to Muslims.

First, Walter Kaiser relates grace—understood as "the unmerited favor of God toward men and women"—to Abraham and his descendants; that is, Israel and the Jewish people. He explains Paul's emphasis in his letter to the Romans: even though the Jewish people in general had not accepted Jesus-Yeshua as the Messiah, often rejecting God's offer of grace, nevertheless God did not renege on his promise of his gracious gift of an heir from Abraham's seed. Kaiser argues that theologians who advocate a replacement theology need to come to terms with God's eternal promise granted to the patriarchs with Paul's understanding of Israel's election and with Paul's explanation of the role of Israel's rejection of Yeshua.

Aída Besançon Spencer then explores the relationship between grace and works in Paul's letter to the Ephesians in the context of John Calvin's theology. Calvin stressed that salvation is not a human work, while emphasizing that good works flow from God's grace in human regeneration. As he does in his letter to the Romans, Paul emphasizes in Ephesians that righteousness—which is a quality of God synonymous with holiness, goodness, and truth—becomes a quality of the new believer, granted to Jews and Gentiles as a gift. The good works for which salvation was accomplished "in Christ Jesus" are not meritorious but rather are the fruit of God's work in the believer through the Spirit.

In his essay, Richard Lints explains that grace alone constitutes the means by which God reconciles sinners to himself, and that it is by grace that sinners retain their only hope of eternal life, a hope that cannot be placed partially in God and partially in the good works of the believer. Considering the view of Charles Hodge that the hallmark of sanctification is real moral progress, Lints argues that we need to take seriously Paul who, in Romans 4, depicts faith in contrast to works: faith is hoping and trusting in Christ, outside of oneself, while works belong to the one who does them. Both Luther and Calvin recognized that works performed by believers do not constitute a process in which graces increases and sin decreases: works are always tinged with sin, obedience filled with mixed motives, and neither are ever devoid of self-centeredness. Faith in Christ resists rewards as its motivation; it continues, through the life of the believer, to cling to the God who redeems the sinner, and this alone satisfies the heart.

Next, Dennis Hollinger explains how grace, in the theology of the Reformers, pertains not only to salvation but also to ethics, and that virtuous character and actions are the result of God's grace. Surveying the views of Luther, Melanchthon, and Calvin regarding the third use of the law (that is, the role of the law as a guide for the life of the believer), Hollinger points to Calvin's conviction that, while it is only God's grace that produces true works of righteousness, unbelievers are able to do some good things in the world, such as justice, moderation, and kindness. The questions that believers, whose actions are the result of divine grace, can expect from sinners who have not experienced regeneration through Christ results in different models for understanding social ethics in the context of larger society. Hollinger surveys the approaches of Luther's "two kingdoms," Calvin's "transforming culture," the Anabaptists "radical separation," and the Roman Catholic Counter-Reformation's "natural law." He concludes that while the church should always be distinct from the surrounding culture, we are called to be salt, light, and leaven within the world, embodying the Christian ethic in our personal lives and in the Christian community and seeking to influence culture from within.

Then, on a different note, Karen Mason explores how Christian counselors understand their delivery of mental health services to unbelievers. After surveying the Reformers' definition of common grace, the biblical basis of God's compassion for all his creation, and Reformed perspectives on viable occupations for Christians, she describes and explains the theological praxis of counseling. When Christian counselors work with unbelievers, they participate in God's intentional pouring out of his common grace on all of his creatures, work to alleviate human suffering, seek the peace of the city in which they live, demonstrate what the kingdom of God looks like, help maintain the moral order that may prevent abuse and crimes, and make orderly life possible when a depressed person returns to work and family.

Next, Paul Martindale compares grace and works in Christian theology and practice with Islam's theology and practice. Muslims believe that Christians who emphasize salvation by grace and not by works indulge in an easy grace that seems to give them carte blanche for sin in their lives after conversion, since sin can be easily forgiven without working for it.

If and when Muslims understand that Christians take the role of works seriously—the fruit and evidence of their justification and submission to God—then they can understand that Christians do not believe they have blanket permission for sinning at will. After surveying Islam's understanding of salvation, human nature, sin, and the doctrine of God, Martindale explains the Christian understanding of the role of grace, concluding that justification is a costly grace that perfectly meets all the requirements of divine justice, and fully takes into account humanity's depravity and rebellion against God and the power of God's grace leading to works done by the power of the Holy Spirit. In Islam, Allah's mercy is applied unevenly to some and not to others, quite apart from the satisfaction of divine justice and righteousness.

In the fourth section, "*Sola Fide:* By Faith Alone," the essays explore the conviction that salvation and life as a Christian depend on faith in Jesus Christ, which was a central hermeneutical conviction of Luther's.

Roy Ciampa explores the meaning of *pistis*, the Greek word for "faith," which has been of critical importance not only during the Reformation but also since the beginning of Christianity. He surveys recent debates on the translation of *pistis Christou* as "faith in Christ" or "Christ's faithfulness," considers the understanding of *pistis* as faith or allegiance/loyalty and as both faith and faithfulness, and then he reflects on the question of translation. He concludes by stating that it may part of the genius of the evangelical tradition that its emphasis on faith is closely tied to its emphasis on the importance of having a personal relationship with Christ.

Next, Donald Fairbairn presents the Nicene background to the Reformation in the context of the distinction between *fides quae creditur*, "the faith which is believed," and *fides qua creditur*, "the faith by which it is believed," in the context of the significance of the historical creeds of the church. He demonstrates that the ancient creeds were not meant as descriptions of *what* we believe, but as an affirmation of our allegiance to God the Father, Son, and Spirit *in whom* we believe and to whom we belong. The Nicene Creed—which states the truth that we could not rise up to God and so instead God came down to us—explains this in the very center of the paragraph about Jesus the Son, thus affirming justification by faith alone without using this precise formulation.

In the third essay of this section, Scott Gibson emphasizes faith as the foundation of preaching. God uses preachers to communicate his word, to

show listeners the evidence of God's grace toward them and that there is
hope for life in the God who gives justifying faith. Faith is foundational in
preaching in that the preacher has faith even in the face of being troubled
with unbelief, as the preacher's life matches his or her faith foundation, as
the preacher has faith in the Bible, and as the preacher is faithful.

Jeffrey Niehaus then connects the doctrine and reality of justification by
faith alone with the institution of the Adamic covenant, the new covenant,
and the life of the church. Understanding faith in light of the statement in
Hebrews 11, Niehaus explains that faith agrees with who God is and what
he does, which is explored in the light of Jesus' encounter with the Roman
centurion who pleads for the healing of his servant. Sin is whatever is not of
faith: the problem is not with our behavior, but with ourselves. Sinners can
be saved by faith, which means they are saved by agreeing with who Jesus
was and is and what God did and offered and still offers in and through him.

In the final section, "*Solus Christus:* By Christ Alone," three essays explain the centrality of Jesus Christ, whose significance for the salvation
of the sinner and for the life of the Christian was at the heart of Luther's
Reformation discovery.

First, Eckhard Schnabel explains the centrality of Jesus Christ in Paul's
ethics as seen at work in Paul's first letter to the Corinthians. Paul connects
Jesus the Messiah with divine functions and divine actions: Jesus makes holy,
he grants grace and peace, the day of God's judgment is the day of the Lord
Jesus Christ, the Spirit of God is the Spirit of Jesus Christ, the judgment
of God takes place when Jesus comes again, and Jesus died as our paschal
lamb inaugurating the new era of salvation. Paul's exhortations demonstrate
that Jesus Christ is the basis and the authority of Christian behavior, the
indispensable and foundational content of missionary proclamation, the
causal basis of the unity of the church, and centrally relevant for legal disputes among believers for questions related to sexual ethics, such as visiting
prostitutes, for social ambition, and for the exercise of the gifts of the Spirit.

Next, William Spencer explains the controversy over the significance
of Jesus Christ in the theology of Athanasius and Calvin. In a close reading
of a historical controversy, Spencer shows how and why Calvin defended
his conviction that whatever can be said concerning God the Father may
also be said of Jesus the Son, basing his proof of the equality of the Father
and the Son on the titles shared between God and Jesus. Since some recent
evangelical formulations of the relationship between God the Father and

Jesus the Son echo a low Christology, we need to learn from the Reformers who reached back and retrieved authentic Christian doctrine that had become obscured.

Finally, John Jefferson Davis evaluates recent ecumenical discussions on justification by faith in Jesus Christ in the context of the "Petrine Error" in Antioch, as described in Galatians 2, and its significance for Christian unity. Paul grounds the unity of the believers in their confession that Jesus is Lord and in their faith that God raised Jesus from the dead. Surveying Protestant and Roman Catholic barriers to intercommunion (that is, celebrating the Lord's Supper together), Davis emphasizes that Protestants should not insist on specific verbal formulations of traditional formulas before celebrating the Lord's Supper together. He notes the irony in how the church that emphasizes the primacy of Peter adds conditions other than a confession of faith in Jesus Christ as Lord and Savior. Protestant Christians must be willing to invite all who confess Christ to the Communion table, which not only acknowledges the centrality of Jesus Christ for salvation and the Christian life but also takes seriously the spirit of *sola scriptura* of the Reformers.

It is our hope that you will join us not only in celebrating the past monumental events of the Reformation, but also as we look together to the future and to the continued importance of Scripture, grace, faith—and especially Christ—alone. *Soli Deo gloria*. To God alone be the glory!

Gordon L. Isaac
Eckhard J. Schnabel
Gordon-Conwell Theological Seminary
South Hamilton, Massachusetts

Martin Luther and the
Reformation in 1517

1

THINKING IN THE MANNER OF SCRIPTURE: LUTHER ON *SOLA SCRIPTURA*

Gordon L. Isaac

On October 31, 1517, a solitary figure approached the wooden doors of the castle church in the little town of Wittenberg, Germany. The thirty-five-year-old Augustinian friar held in his hand a set of theses written for the purpose of inviting a disputation on the power and efficacy of indulgences. Martin Luther had asked his printer, Johann Rhau-Gruenenberg, to run off a few copies for his personal use. As disputations were extremely common in academic circles, this action by Luther was hardly attention-getting. It is likely that there was no one there to witness the printed copy being nailed to the door of the Schlosskirche. The Ninety-Five Theses were written in Latin and intended for other academics to consider an unresolved element of church doctrine.

Luther did not craft the theses thinking that he was beginning a movement or that he was initiating a controversy that would reshape Western Christianity. He had no aspirations to become the head of a renewal movement, and he was no moral crusader. He simply knew that his parishioners were suffering under the weight of medieval theological constructions that obscured the bright light of the gospel of Jesus Christ. He wanted nothing more than to care for the people in his charge and by thinking theologically on their behalf.

Luther directed these theses against the system of indulgences that were in place in the church at the time. The common laity would often purchase letters of indulgence, thinking they were reducing the time their departed loved ones would have to spend in purgatory. Others would purchase them for themselves, thinking they were relieving the temporal punishments exacted by the church. At worst, the laity thought they were purchasing the forgiveness of sins with a few coins. Luther was infuriated at the corruption of church doctrine and, more importantly, the deception it produced among the laity. The first thesis states, "When our Lord and Master Jesus Christ said 'Repent!' (Matt. 4:17), he willed the entire life of believers to be one of repentance." Luther knew that the true treasure of the church is not letters of indulgence but the gospel of God's glory and grace shown in Jesus Christ.

What happened next was nothing short of extraordinary. Without authorization, a few of Luther's students translated the Ninety-Five Theses into German from Latin and had them published and distributed. They were reprinted in Leipzig, Nuremberg, and Basel. What would have normally been merely academic ephemera now entered the bloodstream of the European intellectual community. Barely two weeks later, the theses had circulated all over Germany. Finally, they made their way to England where Thomas More received a copy sent from his friend Desiderius Erasmus, another distinguished Roman Catholic man of letters. With the aid of the newly invented printing press, Luther and his cause had become an overnight sensation![1] It was not the Ninety-Five Theses themselves, however, that had such a revolutionary effect on posterity. The decisive event was the subsequent debate on the questions of the fallibility of councils, the supreme power of the pope, and the right to admonish the church on scriptural grounds to change its ways. In short, the Reformation raised the question of the nature of the gospel and how that gospel is to be preached.

In fact, if I were to hazard a brief definition of the central importance of the Reformation that we celebrate today, I would say it this way: Evangelical theology, as articulated in the Augsburg Confession of 1530, is an ecumenical proposal to the church universal regarding the critical criterion by which gospel-speaking properly takes place.[2] The content of evangelical theology embraces both Old and New Testaments, because the God of Israel is the Father of Jesus. This Jesus—in his life, ministry, death, and resurrection—is the person of final destiny, who is at once the fulfillment of Jewish hope and Gentile need, proclaimed to all people by the church. It could be put in this direct manner:

> Jesus the Israelite is risen, and has death behind him. Therefore, nothing can now overcome his will for you; what will come of the human enterprise, and of your participation in it, is in the hands of this man of hope, and no other. There is reason for all your struggles.[3]

This gospel is an unconditional promise that is conveyed through the preached word and the sacraments of the word. In the time of the Reformation, as in our own time, gospel-preaching breaks through the spent thought forms of culture to create a new reality. Just as the word was spoken by God in Genesis, "Let there be light and there was light," so in the preaching of Christ there is a death and a resurrection, a new birth that establishes a new creation—a creation that is based on Jesus' unconditional self-giving. In the time of the Reformation, evangelical theology rejected the assertion of the medieval church that tended to assume human continuity with God and its ability to relate to God through works. In its place, the Reformation was an attempt to think according to the gospel word that creates life along a different structure—namely, from a discontinuity with God and an inability to relate to God through works. In the Bible and in the Reformation, this structure or way is called "faith."

The heart of Reformation theology, at least since the nineteenth century, has been summarized by the four *solas*—the organizing principle of this conference—by grace alone, by faith alone, by Christ alone, and by scripture alone.[4] It is my task to say a few words here about Luther's view of scripture alone (*sola scriptura*). I will show that Luther was anxious to promote the primacy of Scripture in such a way that it can, on the one hand, challenge and tear down whatever stands opposed to the gospel and, on the other hand, build up whatever promotes the centrality and preeminence of Jesus Christ. *Sola scriptura* becomes a christological formula in Luther's hands in such a way that the Word of God is the fountain and source for the church's salvation, life, and action.[5] Thus we anticipate something of our findings by noting that each of the *solas* is contained or implied in the other *solas*.[6] We see this as Luther correlates these four things: the power of Scripture to create faith in those who read and study it, grace that overcomes human/divine discontinuity, Christ as the person of destiny who gathers his church, and faith that is the new pattern for existence in the world.

We will proceed in three stages to set out Luther's approach to *sola scriptura*: First, we must follow Luther's move away from Scholastic theology toward a Bible-centered approach to theology that he established as the norm at the University of Wittenberg. Second, we must take up what Luther means as he asserts that Christ is the sole content of Scripture, and finally we will consider Luther's conviction that Holy Scripture authenticates itself.

A Bible-Centered Approach

First, Luther's move away from Scholastic theology to a Bible-centered approach is one that developed over time but is critical to understanding the Reformation. Since the twelfth century, teachers such as Lombard and Abelard had adopted Aristotelian principles as a means of clarifying biblical thinking and engaging thinkers from outside the Christian framework. It was a blend of biblical teaching with a Neoplatonic philosophical perspective, which was part of Augustine's legacy as well as that of Aristotle.

By Luther's time, a number of "schools" or "ways" existed within the theological forum: chiefly, "Realists" who believed reality lies in divine ideas that form the patterns for the shadows of that heavenly reality on this earth (*via antiqua*), and "Nominalists" who sought to know reality on the basis of the experience of individual creations of God on this earth (*via moderna*). Within each existed various factions.

As it turns out, Luther actually retained certain aspects of his Scholastic training, but he had a sharp reaction to the view of human nature that was set out by Gabriel Biel, one of the foremost Nominalists. Biel had attempted to balance the teaching of God's grace and human performance by insisting that "out of purely natural powers" sinners could "do that which is in them" (*facere quod in se est*). By doing their best, they could win "congruent merit," a worthiness or righteousness before God that is not truly worthy but nonetheless accepted by God as the basis for receiving his grace. Biel followed the Aristotelian tradition and placed at the center of his description of salvation the gift of a "habit"—a disposition. It supplied power to perform acts that are truly worthy or righteous in God's sight.

It was this view that Luther reacted against. In his Romans commentary, he states:

> The Scholastic theologians have not spoken sufficiently clearly about sin and grace, for they have been under the delusion that original sin, like actual sin, is entirely removed. . . . The ancient fathers Augustine and Ambrose spoke entirely differently and in the way Scripture does. But those men speak in the manner of Aristotle in his *Ethics* when he bases sin and righteousness on works, both their performance or omission.[7]

There are many other passages in this commentary where Luther urges against an undue reliance on the wisdom of philosophy, preferring instead the kind of wisdom that Scripture imparts. The point for Luther is this: Philosophy will yield earthly knowledge, but Scripture brings heavenly knowledge. That is the difference between thinking *ad modem Aristotle* and *ad modem Scriptura*—thinking in the manner of Aristotle or thinking in the manner of Scripture.

Luther's determination to think in the manner of Scripture led him to question the Scholastic approach to theology. This opposition becomes quite pointed, as illustrated by a string of comments Luther made in his *Disputation against Scholastic Theology*. Theses 43 and 44 read, "It is an error to say that no man can become a theologian without Aristotle. This in opposition to common opinion. Indeed, none can become a theologian unless he becomes one without Aristotle."[8] And as if this were not compelling enough, he sums up in thesis 50 by saying, "Briefly the whole of Aristotle is to theology as darkness is to light. This in opposition to the scholastics."[9]

Luther's theological insights also have a pastoral focus: "The greatest part of my cross is to see brothers, with brilliant gifts, born for good studies, and yet compelled to spend their life and waste their achievement in these follies."[10] But in Wittenberg, developments had been moving in a different direction. In May 1517, he wrote:

> Our theology and St. Augustine are going ahead, and reign in our University, and it is God's work. Aristotle is gradually going down, perhaps into eternal ruin. It is wonderful how the lectures on the *Sentences* are out of favor. Nobody can hope for an audience unless he professes this theology, i.e., the Bible or St. Augustine, or some doctor of real authority in the Church.[11]

Luther's devotion to Scripture and the theology that emerges from it led to a major change in the curriculum at the University of Wittenberg, which was put to the test at the Leipzig Disputation in 1519. Its initial significance is that the Leipzig Disputation was the first public dispute over the Reformation. Further, it is important in that Johann Eck provoked Luther's first public challenge to the idea of the divine right of papal authority. But it also inaugurated a new way of arguing cases such as these. The debate took into account the methods used by the biblical humanists. Instead of arguing exclusively on the basis of the Scholastic theologians, Luther argued from the church fathers and Scripture. In addition, Luther argued from history. For example, he had asserted that the Roman Church did not have authority over the Greek Church, for the Greeks were never subject to the pope. He argued from papal decretals and conciliar decrees, subjecting all to the authority of Scripture. He went further to say that the pope did not have the authority to promulgate any new doctrine that cannot be shown from Scripture. The disputation is important for this new way of arguing doctrine in the church.

What we need to see is this: for Luther, *sola scriptura* is not something that can be reduced to a doctrine about Scripture as it is in itself; but in his case and the case of the Reformation, *sola scriptura* embraces an overhaul of university curriculum *and* it initiates a new way of adjudicating theological questions in the church. In short, it is the mobilizing of a renewal movement within the church catholic (the church universal) that takes seriously the approach of the early church, which always sought to read the Holy Scriptures in light of the *regula fidei* (rule of faith).

Christ as the Sole Content of Scripture

Second, we take up what Luther means by saying that Christ is the sole content of Scripture. Luther is well aware of the manifold character of Holy Scripture. He makes note of the difference in the way the Gospel writers set out the life of Christ, and he notes how the apostle Paul sets out Christ without dealing in the historical details of the Gospel writers. His translation and exposition of the Old Testament puts him into contact with the law, wisdom literature, prophecies, and poetry that are found there. On this level, the Bible is a collection of diverse literary genres. However, taken theologically (which means in terms of what the Bible promotes), Luther sees the Bible as a great unity. For him there is only one author and it has only one subject—that is, Christ. As Luther says, "There is no doubt that all the Scripture points to Christ alone."[12] Or again, "Take Christ out of the Scriptures and what more will you find in them?"[13] "The universal testimony of Scripture deals only with Christ. . . . [A]ll Scripture finds its meaning in Christ."[14] The relationship between Christ the incarnate Word of God and Scripture as the written word of God is intimate and mutually corroborating. The function of Scripture, its goal, is to make known and promote Jesus Christ to all who read and all who hear it exposited.

We find Luther teaching this approach to Scripture to the laity in his prefaces to the Bible. Now, Luther had full confidence in the power of the

Bible to tell its own story. But he wrote the prefaces because there had been so many misleading comments in the past. In light of this situation, he wanted to set the record straight regarding the purpose and the proper way to read Holy Scripture. Luther suggested that there is a twofold manner in which the works of Christ are grasped. The first and most important is receiving Christ as gift. Being joined to the living Christ through faith is the essence of the gospel. The second is receiving Christ as example. In this way we see how he prays, helps people, and shows them love. In this way, we know how to order our lives.

Holy Scripture is not to be viewed as a book of laws or commandments, for its chief purpose and end is to set forward the gospel. It is thus not a fixed repository of unchanging eternal truths by which the believer and the world is to be measured. Rather, the purpose of Scripture is to convey the chronicle, the story, the narrative about Christ. Seen in this light, Scripture is "a book of divine promises in which God promises, offers, and gives us all his possessions and benefits in Christ."[15] The Bible is read rightly when it sets forward Christ in this way.

But as Luther likes to point out, Christ is not simply a gift for us; he is also an example. Receiving Christ as gift sets faith in motion and begins to produce works of obedience as a result:

> Therefore, make note of this, that Christ as a gift nourishes your faith and makes you a Christian. But Christ as an example exercises your works. These do not make you a Christian. Actually they come forth from you because you have already been made a Christian. As widely as a gift differs from an example, so widely does faith differ from works, for faith possesses nothing of its own, only the deeds and life of Christ. Works have something of your own in them, yet they should not belong to you but to your neighbor.[16]

Scripture as both law and gospel finds its source in Christ. Understood in this way, Scripture is a unity with Christ as its sole content.

Holy Scripture Is Self-Authenticating

Third, we consider Luther's idea that Holy Scripture authenticates itself. We have already seen that Luther argues the priority of Scripture on the basis of its content. It is a book like no other because it drives home Christ to the believer and has the power to create faith. For Luther, the authority of Scripture is material and content driven. It is the voice of its author and is able to make one wise unto salvation. This is what Luther means when he says, "*Sacra scriptura sui ipsius interpres*—Holy Scripture interprets itself."[17]

Luther goes on to say that Scripture authenticates itself precisely in its ability to convey its message and to create faith. This stands as a strong argument against the Roman Catholic insistence that through the process of canonization the church actually guarantees the authenticity of Scripture. On this view the church stands above Scripture and is less likely to be reformed by it. Luther points out that this makes little sense. It would be like saying that John the Baptist is greater than Christ because he pointed to him at the Jordan River. And on the basis of what Paul says in Galatians 1:9, Luther further argues that Holy Scripture is the queen who rules, and everyone—including the pope, Luther, Augustine, Paul, or an angel from heaven—must be subject to her and be witnesses, disciples, and confessors of Scripture.[18] This is a rather powerful way of saying that no one is in a position to validate Scripture; it is Scripture that validates itself.[19] The church's attitude toward Scripture can only be that of placing itself in a position of obedient listening and recognition of the witness Scripture bears to itself as God's word.

That's precisely what Luther did. "For some years now," the doctor said, "I have read through the Bible twice every year. If you picture the Bible to be a mighty tree and every word a little branch, I have shaken every one of these branches because I wanted to know what it was and what it meant."[20]

> Therefore dismiss your own opinions and feelings, and think of the Scriptures as the loftiest and noblest of holy things, as the richest of mines which can never be sufficiently explored, in order that you may find that divine wisdom which God here lays before you in such simple guise as to quench all pride. Here you will find the swaddling cloths and the manger in which Christ lies, and to which the angel points the shepherds [Luke 2:12]. Simple and lowly are these swaddling cloths, but dear is the treasure, Christ, who lies in them.[21]

Conclusion

Clearly there is much more that could be said of Luther's view of Scripture, but what we have attempted here is a good beginning. Luther was a man who immersed himself in the message of the Bible, and he spent time reading and rereading the text to determine what the Holy Spirit was saying. He allowed the words of Scripture to cascade over his intellect in life-changing ways, and it gave him resolve to also change what was out of line with the gospel message of his age. He spent a lifetime translating the Scriptures into the vernacular of his German people with such success that the *Luther Bibel* helped to codify the German language itself. His prayerful approach to the text is one to celebrate and one to emulate as we honor the five-hundredth anniversary of the Reformation and the establishment of evangelical theology.

2

Sola Gratia: The Foundational Significance of Grace in Luther's Early Theology

Eckhard J. Schnabel

"Grace to you and peace from God our Father and the Lord Jesus Christ"—this is how the apostle Paul greets the believers in the churches in southern Galatia, in Corinth, Rome, Philippi, and in the province of Asia.[1]

Grace is the gift of God's own righteousness, holiness, and love to human beings who are mired in unrighteousness, sin, and greed. The grace that God gives, the grace which sinners need and which they can receive by faith as the result of Jesus' death on the cross is at the heart of Luther's life and theology.[2]

Introduction: Grace in Contemporary Late Medieval Theology and Praxis

Luther's view and experience of God's grace was formed by three interrelated traditions: the nominalism of his university education (*via moderna*), the Scholastic tradition based on the anthropology and ethics of Aristotle, the theology of Thomas Aquinas, and the tradition of Augustine's theology.[3] The late medieval Ockhamists, the Nominalist tradition, believed that God's divine gifts of reason and conscience were not eradicated by the Fall; in accordance with God's gracious goodness, human beings who do their best in a state of nature receive grace as a fitting reward (*meritum de congruo*); when we do the best we can "on the basis of natural moral ability" (*facere quod in se est*), God infuses his grace "as an appropriate reward," which leads to moral cooperation with God where we do the best we can "with the aid of grace," which leads to the "reward of eternal life as a just due."[4] The Augustinian tradition understood God's grace as an effective power that enters the Christian at baptism and empowers the Christian to do what is good and live a life of righteousness that is worthy of salvation. The internally formative infusion of grace at baptism is the initial justification of the sinner (*gratia habitualis*); assisted by this habitual grace, the Christian becomes progressively more righteous during the journey of sanctification, which effectively renders the believer acceptable to God (*gratia gratum faciens*) for the day of judgment.

The church and its earthly representatives are essential in the reception of divine grace.[5] God established the church through Christ as a force against the power of sin, as a bulwark against the devil, and as a community in which Christ continues to live and work, showing the way to a life pleasing to God. Divine grace is mediated by the priests as the consecrated representatives of the church who officiate at baptism and at the sacraments, particularly confession and the Eucharist. The justification of the sinner begins with the infusion of grace at baptism and continues during the entire life of the Christian. Final, definite justification is possible only when there is no longer the possibility of a relapse into sin—that is, on the day of judgment. This means that Christians can never be certain whether they will actually receive justification: they can hope, and the pledge of this hope is the church as the earthly form of Christ's presence. The uncertainty of God's ultimate verdict, the uncertainty of successfully living righteously, and the uncertainty of the value of one's personal life bind the Christian to the church, which protects from total despair, which compensates sinful actions, and which alone guarantees the possibility of divine grace.

Grace in Luther's Personal Experience and Exegetical Lectures

Luther abandoned the system of merit taught and practiced in the Church of Rome. He rejected the belief that God gives his grace to those who at least attempt to live a godly life and thus prove themselves worthy of receiving God's grace. He rejected the concept of grace as a substance or quality poured into the soul of the sinner. He rejected the image of the Christian life as a journey with an uncertain outcome.

Formative was his life as a monk in the order of Augustinian hermits in the monastery in Erfurt, coupled with the study of theology suggested by his order, and his pursuit of the degree of *Doctor sacrae scripturae* at the University of Wittenberg (granted on 18/19 October 1512), which provided him with the education, methodological tools, and factual knowledge that allowed him to research, think through, preach, and lecture on the fundamental question of ultimate and final salvation before God and by God. Two factors contributed to Luther's reevaluation of how sinners receive God's grace.[6]

The first factor was Luther's active participation in the praxis of the church and his personal experience. In his life as a monk he experienced the religious elitist forms of the strictest ascetic self-inspection in terms of continuous repentance. His supreme concentration on gaining salvation in the context of the grace offered by the church took him into deepest despair; despite all active, honest, and extreme efforts, the means of grace offered as constituted by the church were incapable of removing the uncertainty of salvation.

The second factor was Luther's study of and lectures on the Psalms from 1513–1515,[7] on Galatians in 1516,[8] on Hebrews in 1517/1518,[9] and on Paul's letter to the Romans, delivered at six o'clock in the morning on Mondays and Fridays in 1515/1516.[10] The date of what is often called the "Reformation breakthrough" is disputed; some date the breakthrough to the autumn of 1514, some to the spring of 1515, and others to the year 1518.[11] In his March 5, 1545, preface to an edition of his Latin works, Luther writes,

> Meanwhile, I had already during that year returned to interpret the Psalter anew. I had confidence in the fact that I was more skillful, after I had lectured in the university on St. Paul's epistles to the Romans, to the Galatians, and the one to the Hebrews. I had indeed been captivated with an extraordinary ardor for understanding Paul in the Epistle to the Romans. But up till then it was not the cold blood about the heart, but a single word in Chapter 1[:17], "In it the righteousness of God is revealed," that had stood in my way. For I hated that word "righteousness of God," which, according to the use and custom of all the teachers. I had been taught to understand philosophically regarding the formal or active righteousness, as they called it, with which God is righteous and punishes the unrighteous sinner. Though I lived as a monk without reproach, I felt that I was a sinner before God with an extremely disturbed conscience. I could not believe that he was placated by my

satisfaction. I did not love, yes, I hated the righteous God who pun-
ishes sinners, and secretly, if not blasphemously, certainly murmuring
greatly, I was angry with God, and said, "As if, indeed, it is not enough,
that miserable sinners, eternally lost through original sin, are crushed
by every kind of calamity by the law of the decalogue, without having
God add pain to pain by the gospel and also by the gospel threatening
us with his righteousness and wrath!" Thus I raged with a fierce and
troubled conscience. Nevertheless, I beat importunately upon Paul at
that place, most ardently desiring to know what St. Paul wanted. At
last, by the mercy of God, meditating day and night, I gave heed to the
context of the words, namely, "In it the righteousness of God is revealed,
as it is written, 'He who through faith is righteous shall live.'" There I
began to understand that the righteousness of God is that by which the
righteous lives a gift of God, namely by faith. And this is the meaning:
the righteousness of God is revealed by the gospel, namely, the passive
righteousness with which merciful God justifies us by faith, as it is
written, "He who through faith is righteous shall live." Here I felt that I
was altogether born again and had entered paradise itself through open
gates. There a totally other face of the entire Scripture showed itself to
me. Thereupon I ran through the Scriptures from memory. I also found
in other terms an analogy, as, the work of God, that is, what God does
in us, the power of God, with which he makes us strong, the wisdom of
God, with which he makes us wise, the strength of God, the salvation
of God, the glory of God.[12]

Here the Reformation breakthrough is linked with the discovery of what is
meant by the righteousness of God (*iustitia Dei*): Luther understood that
the righteousness of God is a *iustitia passiva*, a "passive" righteousness in
which the sinner is not actively attempting to live a righteous life that God
will eventually honor and reward in the final judgment, but in which the
sinner passively receives God's gift of grace who pardons the sinner on account of his mercy through Jesus' death on the cross.

In his lecture on Genesis 48:20–21, delivered in 1545, Luther mentions
what was new in his reformational discovery:

For formerly, under the papacy, when I was a monk, it was by no means
customary to speak of a promise. And I give thanks to God that I may
live at this time, when this word "promise" resounds in my ears and in

the ears of all the godly. For he who hears the Word easily understands the divine promise, which was obscure and unknown to all the theologians throughout the papacy.[13]

Here the breakthrough is linked with the promise (*promissio*) of God, which is the trustworthy word of God (*verbum Dei*) as God's effective word (*verbum efficax*) that, performatively, forgives sin and constitutes assurance of salvation.

The focus on the word of God who alone forgives sin and grants grace, rather than the works of penance imposed by the church, is found in the Ninety-Five Theses of the *Disputation on the Power of Indulgences* (*Disputatio pro declaratione virtutis indulgentiarum*), sent on October 31, 1517, to Albert of Brandenburg, the archbishop of Mainz, and printed in December 1517 in Nuremberg, Leipzig, and Basel.

1. When our Lord and Master Jesus Christ said, "Repent" (Mt 4:17), he willed the entire life of believers to be one of repentance.

2. This word cannot be understood as referring to the sacrament of penance, that is, confession and satisfaction, as administered by the clergy.

54. Injury is done the Word of God when, in the same sermon, an equal or a longer time is spent on pardons than on the Word.

62. The true treasure of the Church is the most holy Gospel of the glory and grace of God.[14]

This focus on the effective word of God is more explicit in Luther's fifty theses in the disputation *For the Investigation of Truth and for the Comfort of Troubled Consciences* (*Pro veritate inquirenda et timoratis conscientiis consolandis*),[15] written in the early summer of 1518.

1. Between these two remissions of punishment and guilt of the church, the remission of guilt excels by far.

2. The remission of guilt calms the heart and takes away the greatest of all punishments, namely the consciousness of sin.

The word of absolution "is not a judgment, which merely establishes that something is true already," referring to an absent reality, but it is the effective word of God that constitutes a present reality—the reality of the forgiveness of sins and liberation from a guilty conscience. At the end of these theses, Luther uses Romans 1:17 as a "summa" of his emphasis of how God forgives sins and grants grace.[16]

Priests absolved people from the guilt of their sin but not from the punishment of sin, the latter being the reason for purgatory and the cause for the sale of indulgences, which were said to reduce the length of time of God's punishment. Luther challenged both in the ninety-five and in the fifty theses the notion that Christ's death deals only with one's guilt on account of sin but not with God's punishment for sin.

Grace as the Work of God

As a result of his study of Scripture and his courage to reject hundreds of years of theological exposition, Luther abandoned the connection between grace and the actions of human beings, whether these are the participation in the sacraments or good works more generally.[17] Luther realized that if grace—which is the forgiveness of sin, the removal of guilt, the liberation from the wrath of God, justification by God, and acquittal on the day of judgment—co-depends on what human beings do, then there can never be an assurance of salvation. Luther understood passages in the Psalms, and in particular Romans 1:17, which state that in the gospel "the righteousness of God is revealed through faith for faith; as it is written, 'The one who is righteous will live by faith,'" to say that grace depends only on what *God* does, radically and consistently—what he *did* in and through Jesus' death on the cross, and what he *does* in saying that sinners are forgiven if and when they believe in God's word, which is effective on account of the power of God and on account of Jesus Christ's life, death, and resurrection.

Luther rejected the system of merit taught and practiced in the church—that is, the notion that grace is the result of a *quid pro quo:* God gives grace to those who prove worthy of it. He writes in the *Treatise on Good Works* (*Von den guten Werken*), published in early June 1520, that there are no good works apart from those commanded by God himself, that the first and supreme good work is faith in Christ, and that the ecclesial system of human merit turns God into a huckster, a cheap salesman of goods.

X. Now you see for yourself that all those who do not at all times trust God and do not in all their works or sufferings, life and death, trust in His favor, grace and goodwill, but seek His favor in other things or in themselves, do not keep this Commandment, and practice real idolatry, even if they were to do the works of all the other Commandments, and in addition had all the prayers, fasting, obedience, patience, chastity, and innocence of all the saints combined. For the chief work is not present, without which all the others are nothing but mere sham, show and pretense, with nothing back of them; against which Christ warns us, Matthew vii: "Beware of false prophets, which come to you in sheep's clothing." Such are all who wish with their many good works, as they say, to make God favorable to themselves, and to buy God's grace from Him, as if He were a huckster or a day-laborer, unwilling to give His grace and favor for nothing. These are the most perverse people on earth, who will hardly or never be converted to the right way.[18]

Luther rejects the traditional notion of instrumental reciprocity, the "placement of grace within a system of gift of return that is given with a view to a counter gift."[19] God's grace has been given in the life, death, and resurrection of Jesus Christ once and for all, a reality that makes it not only unnecessary but also impossible for human beings to elicit grace as a result of good works now or at the future judgment. In his comments on Galatians 3:2, Luther writes:

It seems to be exceedingly inadequate to say that the Holy Spirit is granted solely through hearing with faith and that nothing at all is demanded of us but that we refrain from all our works and just listen to the Gospel. The human heart neither understands nor believes that such a great prize as the Holy Spirit can be granted solely through hearing with faith; but it thinks this way: "The forgiveness of sins, deliverance from sin and death, the granting of the Holy Spirit, of righteousness, and of eternal life—this is all something important. Therefore you must do something great to obtain these inestimable gifts." The devil approves of this opinion and magnifies it in the heart. Therefore when reason hears "You cannot do anything to obtain the forgiveness of sins except only to listen to the Word of God" it immediately exclaims: "Oh no! You are making the forgiveness of sins too meager and contemptible!" Thus the greatness of the gift is responsible for our not accepting it. Because such a treasure is being offered freely, it is despised. But we must learn by all means that forgiveness of sins, Christ, and the Holy Spirit are granted—and granted freely—only when we hear with faith. Even our huge sins and demerits do not stand in the way. We must not consider how great the thing is that is being given and how unworthy we are; otherwise the greatness both of the thing and of our unworthiness will frighten us away.[20]

For Luther, the Christian life is not a journey of ceaseless good works and a constant infusion of divine grace through the sacraments and yet a journey with an uncertain outcome. Rather, God's unconditional grace is a structural characteristic of the Christian life, because the righteousness of the believer always remains the righteousness of Jesus Christ secured for sinners at the cross.[21] True, effective righteousness is "another's righteousness" (*iustitia aliena*), bestowed from outside the sinner by God through Christ and the Spirit, which is thus a "passive righteousness" (*iustitia passiva*), not actively earned by human beings but bestowed by God as the unconditional forgiveness of sin. Luther writes in his *Sermon on Two Kinds of Righteousness* (*Sermo de duplici iustitia*), which was a sermon on Philippians 2:5–6 evidently delivered on Palm Sunday, March 28, 1518:

> Christians have two kinds of righteousness, just as there are two kinds of sins in humans. The first is alien and infused from outside of oneself (*aliena et ab extra infusa*). This is the righteousness by which Christ is righteous and by which he justifies others through faith. . . . The Apostle therefore dares to say in Gal. 2[:20], "I live, though not I, but truly Christ lives in me"; and in Eph. 3[:17]: "that Christ may resideth in your hearts through faith." Therefore this alien righteousness, infused in us without our works by grace alone—while the Father, to be sure, inwardly draws us to Christ—is set opposite original sin, likewise alien without our works, inherited and caused by birth alone. . . . The second kind of righteousness is our proper righteousness, not because we alone work it, but because we work with that first and alien righteousness. This is that manner of life spent profitably in good works.[22]

Luther's use of the term "infused" here is different from the concept of "imputation," which proved to be the more significant concept for Luther and Lutheranism with regard to the notion of "alien righteousness."

The justification of the sinner takes place once and for all when God's effective word that conveys his unconditional grace and mercy reaches and is grasped by the sinner. God's grace that forgives sin, removes guilt, and reconciles the sinner with God does not need to be expanded or deepened. The sinner whom God has justified is always justified—throughout the sinner's life and then also on the day of judgment. Final justification is no longer postponed to the day of judgment, but it happens in history when the sinner receives God's grace by faith. The uncertainty of justification in the final judgment is transformed into the joyful assurance of salvation here and now as well as in the future. Since it is God alone who grants grace, the role of the church—which herself has been created by the word of God—is radically focused on the preaching of the word of God.

Grace and Christ's Death on the Cross

God's unconditional grace granted to the sinner is possible only on account of the person of Jesus Christ who lived and died "for us" (*pro nobis*). In the treatise *The Freedom of a Christian* (*Von der Freiheit eines Christenmenschen*), printed on November 20, 1920, Luther asserts:

> The third incomparable benefit of faith is that it unites the soul with Christ as a bride is united with her bridegroom. By this mystery, as the Apostle teaches, Christ and the soul become one flesh [Ephesians 5:31–32]. And if they are one flesh and there is between them a true marriage—indeed the most perfect of all marriages, since human marriages are but poor examples of this one true marriage—it follows that everything they have they hold in common, the good as well as the evil. Accordingly the believing soul can boast of and glory in whatever Christ has as though it were its own, and whatever the soul has Christ claims as his own. Let us compare these and we shall see inestimable benefits. Christ is full of grace, life, and salvation (*Christus plenus est gratia, vita, et salute*). The soul is full of sins, death, and damnation. Now let faith come between them and sins, death, and damnation will be Christ's, while grace, life, and salvation will be the soul's; for if Christ is a bridegroom, he must take upon himself the things which are his bride's and bestow upon her the things that are his. If he gives her his body and very self, how shall he not give her all that is his? And if he takes the body of the bride, how shall he not take all that is hers? Here we have a most

pleasing vision not only of communion but of a blessed struggle and victory and salvation and redemption. Christ is God and man in one person. He has neither sinned nor died, and is not condemned, and he cannot sin, die, or be condemned; his righteousness, life, and salvation are unconquerable, eternal, omnipotent. By the wedding ring of faith he shares in the sins, death, and pains of hell which are his bride's. As a matter of fact, he makes them his own and acts as if they were his own and as if he himself had sinned; he suffered, died, and descended into hell that he might overcome them all. Now since it was such a one who did all this, and death and hell could not swallow him up, these were necessarily swallowed up by him in a mighty duel; for his righteousness is greater than the sins of all men, his life stronger than death, his salvation more invincible than hell. Thus the believing soul by means of the pledge of its faith is free in Christ, its bridegroom, free from all sins, secure against death and hell, and is endowed with the eternal righteousness, life, and salvation of Christ its bridegroom. So he takes to himself a glorious bride, "without spot or wrinkle, cleansing her by the washing of water with the word" [cf. Ephesians 5:26–27] of life, that is, by faith in the Word of life, righteousness, and salvation. In this way he marries her in faith, steadfast love, and in mercies, righteousness, and justice, as Hosea 2[:19–20] says.[23]

Luther formulates this conviction perhaps most clearly in the *Commentary on Galatians* (*In epistulam S. Pauli ad Galatas Commentarius*) of 1531 (1535) in his comments on Galatians 3:13:

Therefore we should not imagine Christ as an innocent and private person who is holy and righteous only for Himself; this is what the sophists and nearly all the fathers, Jerome and others, have done. It is, of course, true that Christ is the purest of persons; but this is not the place to stop. For you do not yet have Christ, even though you know that He is God and man. You truly have Him only when you believe that this altogether pure and innocent Person has been granted to you by the Father as your High Priest and Redeemer, yes, as your Slave. Putting off His innocence and holiness and putting on your sinful person, He bore your sin, death, and curse; He became a sacrifice and a curse for you, in order thus to set you free from the curse of the Law.[24]

Christ's substitution means, specifically, that he takes upon himself our sins:

> For he does not say that Christ became a curse on His own account, but that He became a curse "for us." Thus the whole emphasis is on the phrase "for us." For Christ is innocent so far as His own Person is concerned; therefore He should not have been hanged from the tree. But because, according to the Law, every thief should have been hanged, therefore, according to the Law of Moses, Christ Himself should have been hanged; for He bore the person of a sinner and a thief—and not of one but of all sinners and thieves. For we are sinners and thieves, and therefore we are worthy of death and eternal damnation. But Christ took all our sins upon Himself, and for them He died on the cross.[25]

Jesus' death is not an external compensatory action. Rather, his substitution for the sinner requires that he becomes the person of the sinner—and this was the mission that Jesus had been given by God.

> In short, He has and bears all the sins of all men in His body—not in the sense that He has committed them but in the sense that He took these sins, committed by us, upon His own body, in order to make satisfaction for them with His own blood.[26]

Because Christ becomes us, fulfilling God's mission—which means that he bears our sin and dies for our sin in the name of God—he conquers death, a reality that loses its power:

> In short, sin is a great and powerful god who devours the whole human race, all the learned, holy, powerful, wise, and unlearned men. He, I say, attacks Christ and wants to devour Him as he has devoured all the rest. But he does not see that He is a Person of invincible and eternal righteousness. In this duel, therefore, it is necessary for sin to be conquered and killed, and for righteousness to prevail and live. Thus in Christ all sin is conquered, killed, and buried; and righteousness remains the victor and the ruler eternally.[27]

As Christ died as our substitute, taking our person with all our sin upon himself, conquering sin and death, he makes us a new person:

By this fortunate exchange with us He took upon Himself our sinful person and granted us His innocent and victorious Person. Clothed and dressed in this, we are freed from the curse of the Law, because Christ Himself voluntarily became a curse for us.[28]

It is in this context that Luther understands justification by God's grace in terms of recreation: just as in the beginning the Word of God created everything out of darkness, the new life of the justified sinner is given by God. Both creation and the recreation of justification are categorical gifts of God, both given *sola gratia.*[29] In the Small Catechism (*Der kleine Catechismus für die gemeine Pfarrherr und Prediger*), composed in the early months of 1529, Luther writes in the first article (on creation):

I believe in God, the Father almighty, Creator of heaven and earth. What is this?

Answer:
I believe that God has created me together with all that exists. God has given me and still preserves my body and soul: eyes, ears, and all limbs and senses; reason and all mental faculties. In addition, God daily and abundantly provides shoes and clothing, food and drink, house and farm, spouse and children, fields, livestock, and all property—along with all the necessities and nourishment for this body and life. God protects me against all danger and shields and preserves me from all evil. And all this is done out of pure, fatherly, and divine goodness and mercy, without any merit or worthiness of mine at all! For all of this I owe it to God to thank and praise, serve and obey him. This is most certainly true.[30]

In his lecture on Genesis 45:7, Luther writes:

For we believe in that God who is the almighty Creator, produces all things from nothing, the best things from those that are evil, and salvation from what is despaired and lost. In Rom. 4:17 this is attributed to Him when it is stated that He "calls into existence the things that do not exist." And 2 Cor. 4:6 speaks of God who ordered light to shine out of darkness—not a spark from a coal but light out of darkness, like life from death, righteousness from sin, the kingdom of heaven and the liberty of the children of God from enslavement to the devil and hell.[31]

Grace and Works

Luther contrasts grace and works, not because all works are sinful but because of the corruption of the human heart. For Luther, the root of sin is "arrogant self-reliance, a self-interestedness whereby humans 'turn in' on themselves and thereby turn away from God," which, essentially, is a violation of the first commandment, a form of idolatry that "refuses to acknowledge, in gratitude, the work of God."[32] Luther criticizes the contemporary ecclesial praxis for understanding good works as the necessary means of salvation, for performing them not to please God or benefit one's neighbor but for the irreligious motivation of obtaining one's salvation, and for performing them in a spirit of presumption in one's own righteousness or in anxiety, fear, and doubt. Luther insists that one is a Christian if one lays hold of Christ as a gift given for sinners and that everything else follows. He writes in *A Brief Instruction on What to Look for and Expect in the Gospels* (*Ein klein Unterricht, was man in den Evangeliis suchen und gewarten soll*), published in March 1522,

> The chief article and foundation of the Gospel is that before you take Christ as an example, you accept and recognize him as a gift, as a present that God has given you and that is your own. This means that when you see or hear of Christ doing or suffering something, you do not doubt that Christ himself, with his deeds and suffering, belongs to you. On this you may depend as surely as if you had done it yourself; indeed as if you were Christ himself. . . . Now when you have Christ as the foundation and chief blessing of your salvation, then the other part follows: that you take him as your example, giving yourself in service to your neighbor just as you see that Christ has given himself for you. See, there faith and love move forward, God's commandment is fulfilled, and a person is happy and fearless to do and to suffer all things. Therefore make note of this, that Christ as a gift nourishes your faith and makes you a Christian. But Christ as an example exercises your works. These do not make you a Christian. Actually they come forth from you because you have already been made a Christian. As widely as a gift differs from an example, so widely does faith differ from works, for faith possesses nothing of its own, only the deeds and life of Christ. Works have something of your own in them, yet they should not belong to you but to your neighbor.[33]

Luther was criticized by his contemporary and later opponents that his radical emphasis on God's grace in obtaining salvation, conveyed once and for all through faith in Jesus Christ on account of Jesus' substitutionary and atoning death on the cross, did not consider the merits of the sinner. The first point of criticism was that Luther's view of grace amounts to salvational egotism and social quietism, which eliminates the significance of personal behavior. The second criticism accuses Luther of fostering an amoral ethics and personal laziness—if divine grace and the faith of the sinner is everything, then there are no norms for personal behavior.[34] These are important and complex questions. Suffice it here to say that Luther countered such accusations with different argumentative strategies. He often used the image of the tree and its fruit. In *The Freedom of a Christian*, Luther writes:

> No good work helps justify or save an unbeliever. On the other hand, no evil work makes him wicked or damns him; but the unbelief which makes the person and the tree evil does the evil and damnable works. Hence when a man is good or evil, this is effected not by the works, but by faith or unbelief, as the Wise Man says, "This is the beginning of sin, that a man falls away from God" [cf. Sirach 10:14–15], which happens when he does not believe. And Paul says in Hebrews 11[:6], "For whoever would draw near to God must believe. . . ." And Christ says the same: "Either make the tree good, and its fruit good; or make the tree bad, and its fruit bad" [Matthew 12:33], as if he would say, "Let him who wishes to have good fruit begin by planting a good tree." So let him who wishes to do good works begin not with the doing of works, but with believing, which makes the person good, for nothing makes a man good except faith, or evil except unbelief.[35]

Another argument, arguably more cogent in the context of Luther's theology, posited that believers can generate new decalogues by faith, meaning that authentic faith leads to normative principles of behavior that have divine value, while here the "lawgiver" and those subject to the law are one and the same. In the *Second Disputation against the Antinomians*, which took place on January 12, 1538,[36] Luther writes,

> 52. For if we have Christ, we can easily establish new laws and we shall judge all things rightly.

53. Indeed, we would make new decalogues, as Paul does in all the epistles, and Peter, but above all Christ in the gospel.

54. And these decalogues are clearer than the decalogues of Moses, just as the countenance of Christ is brighter than the countenance of Moses [II Corinthians 3:7–11].[37]

Luther recognizes the need for rules of conduct but insists on the priority of grace and faith. He does not clarify the relationship between the laws and rules of Scripture, including those formulated by Jesus and the apostles, and these new decalogues, which he quite certainly did not understand in terms of a situational ethics in which the only norm is the perceived needs of the individual believer. For Luther, the gift of grace in and through Jesus Christ is always, radically and consistently, paramount. He formulates in the twenty-eighth and final theological thesis of the *Heidelberg Disputation* (*Disputate Heidelbergae habita*), which took place on April 26, 1518,

> *Amor Dei non invenit sed creat suum diligibile.*
> The love of God does not find, but creates that which is pleasing to it.[38]

Conclusion

For Luther, salvation is always the justification of the sinner as God's free gift of pure grace. He would agree that grace is the gift of God's own life, love, and light to human beings "who have neither the right to them nor a claim on God."[39] Luther promulgated this conviction, from 1517 until his death in 1546, in hundreds of publications in an unsurpassed wide variety of genres—in programmatic writings such as the various *Theses*, or the texts *The Babylonian Captivity of the Church* and *The Freedom of a Christian*; in his disputations (fifty disputations between 1516 and 1545), such as the *Heidelberg Disputation*; in polemical writings such as *The Misuse of the Mass* or *On Eck's New Bull and Lies*; in devotional writings, such as the *Theologia Deutsch* or his *Meditation on Christ's Passion*; in catechisms, such as his Small Catechism and Large Catechism; in sermons, such as his *Sermon on Indulgence and Grace, Ten Sermons on the Catechism*, or his *Sermons on the Gospel of St. John* (more than two thousand in *WA*); in lectures, always on Old Testament and New Testament books, based on the Hebrew and Greek text; in letters[40] (about thirty-six hundred letters, in twelve volumes in *WA Br*); in table talks[41] (in six volumes in *WA TR*); in his Bible translation[42] (*WA DB*, twelve volumes); in liturgical and hymn compositions, writing both text and music; and in fables and collections of proverbs. His convictions on God's grace as a gift for sinners drove his translation of the Bible into German.[43] In the first sentence of the preface to Paul's letter to the Romans, he writes:

> This letter is truly the most important piece in the New Testament. It is purest Gospel. It is well worth a Christian's while not only to memorize it word for word but also to occupy himself with it daily, as though it were the daily bread of the soul.[44]

In his most well-known hymn "Our God He Is a Castle Strong" (or "A Mighty Fortress Is Our God")—which became the national hymn of Protestantism worldwide and was probably written between 1527 and 1528 and then printed in 1529[45]—Luther does not use the word *grace*, but the hymn makes sense only in the context of his emphasis on the efficacy of grace. The first verse emphasizes the incontrovertible power of God whose help never fails, even in the face of attacks from the devil.

> A mighty Fortress is our God / A Bulwark never failing / Our Helper He amid the flood / Of mortal ills prevailing / For still our ancient foe / Doth seek to work us woe / His craft and power are great / And, armed with cruel hate / On earth is not his equal.

The second verse focuses on the gracious power of Jesus Christ who has been sent by God, who is God himself, and whom we can and must trust because he never changes and because he has won and will always win the battle against sin and the devil.

> Did we in our own strength confide / Our striving would be losing / Were not the right Man on our side / The Man of God's own choosing / Dost ask who that may be? / Christ Jesus, it is He / Lord Sabaoth His Name / From age to age the same / And He must win the battle.

The third verse celebrates God's triumph over the prince of darkness and over all fear that threatens to destroy our life in view of the assurance of salvation now and always on account of the gracious will of God.

And though this world, with devils filled / Should threaten to undo us / We will not fear, for God hath willed / His truth to triumph through us / The Prince of Darkness grim / We tremble not for him / His rage we can endure / For lo! his doom is sure / One little word shall fell him.

The fourth verse celebrates the word of God which is the word of God's truth, the Spirit of God and his gifts, and Jesus who is with us and who guarantees for us the reality of the kingdom of God.

That word above all earthly powers / No thanks to them, abideth / The Spirit and the gifts are ours / Through Him who with us sideth / Let goods and kindred go / This mortal life also / The body they may kill / God's truth abideth still / His Kingdom is forever.

3

Solus Christus: Luther's Journey to the Singular Focus[1]

Gwenfair Walters Adams

It was his first Mass as a priest: May 2, 1507. His father, rather critical at the best of times, was present, together with a retinue of family members. And Martin Luther, to put it colloquially, freaked out. He had prepared diligently for this day. He had scoured Gabriel Biel's eighty-nine chapters on the Mass, which went, painstakingly, through every aspect of the liturgy. It had not been an easy read emotionally for Luther. He said later of Biel's book, "When I read in it, my heart bled."[2] And now he was in the midst of carrying out what he had learned about this service. What had shaken his heart was now shaking his hands.

The Mass was of paramount importance to medieval life. The church was central to society, the liturgy was central to the church, and the Mass was central to the liturgy. And what was central to the Mass was the moment of consecration. The church taught that in that moment, when the priest lifted the Host (a sacred wafer of unleavened bread), something miraculous happened: the bread changed into the body of Christ. And when the chalice of wine was elevated, the wine became the blood of Christ. The key words were *Hoc est corpus meum*: "This is my body." It was the priest who said the words; and it was in his hands, while he was still holding the host, that this miracle called "transubstantiation" took place. The substance—the essence—of the Host and wine turned into the body and blood of Christ. This meant that suddenly Christ was *really* present.

Who was this Christ who was suddenly present? What did he mean to Luther? Was he the affectionate child in the arms of the statues of the Blessed Virgin Mary? Was he the figure, clad in suffering and blood, on a wooden crucifix or in crimson glass? For Luther, Christ was not primarily these things. Rather, Christ was first and foremost the Holy Judge depicted in scenes of the Last Judgment that were often painted above the western door of the church. So, as you left the church each Sunday morning, a dramatic depiction of judgment confronted you. You can imagine how terrifying it would be to see Christ primarily this way, sending people on his left—vulnerable in their nakedness—to hell. And although he was also sending the people on his right to heaven, you could never be sure where he was going to send *you*.

This Judge was the one who set the bar high for priests who celebrated the Mass. He required priests to make sure that their vestments were all in order, that they read the words of Institution perfectly, that they were in a state of purity, having confessed all their sins in detail.[3] Luther was highly cognizant of these exacting standards—and he was terrified of violating them. So, given all this, when he came to the moment in the liturgy when he had to say, "We offer unto thee the living, the true, the eternal God," terror touched down. This line found its home in the Prayers for the Living, which was only a page away from what Luther knew was coming: that moment of consecration, when Christ would suddenly be in his lifted hands. Luther said later:

> At these words I was utterly stupefied and terror-stricken. I thought to myself, With what tongue shall I address such majesty, seeing that all men ought to tremble in the presence of even an earthly prince? Who am I, that I should lift up my eyes or raise my hands to the divine majesty? The angels surround him. At his nod the earth trembles, and shall I, a miserable little [person], say, "I want this, I ask for that"? For I am dust and ashes and full of sin, and I am speaking to the living, the eternal, and the true God.[4]

So Luther turned to the prior assisting him and said he had to leave the altar. But the prior said, "Go ahead, faster, faster."[5]

It wasn't the last time Luther's fear would overcome him. Because a priest was meant to be in a state of purity before offering up a Mass, Luther, plagued by scrupulosity, was often in a state of consternation during the Mass. One time, during the Mass itself, he asked a confessor to come and hear his confession in the middle of it! He sometimes had a hard time going for a couple hours without confessing. Such was the intensity of his fear of Christ the Judge.[6]

Luther's First Steps

How did Luther move from *this* to the doctrine of *solus Christus?* To answer that question, we will examine Luther's journey to what we could call the "singular focus"—singular in the sense of *solus*, as well as of being one without peer or equal. I suggest that when we trace Luther's pilgrimage to *solus Christus*, we are not just observing a shift in theology; we are watching someone move from being terrified of Christ to being utterly enthralled by Christ, to the point where he becomes willing to *die* for him.

We will start first with Luther turning to the saints. They were more approachable than Christ, and his favorites were Saint Thomas and Saint Anne. Saint Anne was the one to whom he had made the vow when caught in the thunderstorm, "Save me, St. Anne, and I'll become a monk!" Fulfilling this vow is what made him a monk.

After earning a doctorate in theology and adding university professor to his monastic and priestly roles, between 1513 and 1514, Luther took his first foray into lecturing on a biblical book, plunging himself and his students into the Psalms for a year. As an Augustinian monk, it was perhaps particularly apropos that Luther used a similar hermeneutic to Augustine's. Augustine had taken a christological approach to the Psalms. In his preface to his lectures, Luther showed that he too was using a christological lens, explaining that "every prophecy and every prophet must be understood as referring to Christ the Lord, except where it is clear from plain words that someone else is being spoken of."[7]

Bernhard Lohse points out that Luther, however, did something unusual with Augustine's method.[8] Unlike Augustine, he applied the christological lens not only to the passages that connoted majesty but also to those that dealt with humility. If this is the case, it's very interesting. It may be where we start to see Luther's theology of the cross emerging—a theology where Christ needs to be sought not primarily in his power and glory, but in his humility. If my theory is correct that Luther moves from fear of Christ to love of Christ as he discovers the doctrine of *solus Christus*, then it is intriguing that he may be doing so through the process of focusing on Christ's humility rather than his glory. It would make sense, for Christ's judgeship belongs more to his glory than his humility, and it was therefore perhaps Christ's humility that enabled Luther to start to overcome his fear.

Another point Lohse makes is that Luther also started to differentiate between literal and spiritual interpretations, and that this prepares the way for his later theology of the letter relating to divine judgment and the spirit referring to grace: the "spirit is concealed in the letter."[9] Again, we have an early form of something that will lead to a shift of focus from judgment to grace, pointing away from fear toward love.

It is in these lectures that, as far as I've been able to discover, we find our first *solus Christus* reference.

> The heretics, however, do the same thing the Pharisees did: For though they believe that sins are removed *through Christ alone*, and though they believe in Him, yet because they do not have Him truly, in that they uphold His plan, they remain in sin.[10]

Although it is not yet being used as a deliberate contrast to Catholic teaching, it does relate to the forgiveness of sins, and it shows up in the lecture series that seems to be starting to change Luther's attitude toward Christ.

Now, his time in the Psalms doesn't seem to have fully brought him round, as seen in his reaction to the consecrated Host while participating as a priest in a Corpus Christi procession in 1515. The feast of Corpus Christi involved the priests processing out from and back to the church carrying the consecrated Host for the townspeople to venerate. Luther felt horror again at the thought of the presence of Christ in the monstrance that loomed ahead of him, carried about by a fellow priest.[11] He still seemed to see Christ primarily as a Judge, at least when he believed he was in the presence of the Real Presence.

But here is where Johannes Staupitz seems to have played a major role in Luther's transition. Staupitz was Luther's confessor and a key leader in the Augustinian order, and he was the one who had sent Luther to study the Scriptures at the doctoral level. Now he gently explained to Luther that when conducting a Mass, one should not try to aim at perfection. Rather, one should turn to Christ for forgiveness when one fell short.[12]

Revelations in Romans and Galatians

Luther's next lectures were on Romans, given between 1515 and 1516. Here one sees a major transition happening, for now Luther was dealing directly with the gospel rather than tropologically. That is, whereas the Psalms foreshadowed Christ and presented types for him, Romans could speak *directly* about Christ as the one who had already entered time and space. Paul, living after Christ's time on earth, could speak head on, literally, about him.

It is here, in his comments on Romans 2:12 as far as I've been able to find, that we have the term *solus Christus* being used by Luther for the first time in conjunction with the term "salvation." He raises the question of whether Gentiles who are not in Christ can gain salvation, if they have fulfilled the law that has come to them via their consciences. He indicates that they cannot. It is here that he uses the clause: "For salvation is given through Christ alone."[13]

For the next academic year (1516–17), Luther lectured on the book of Galatians. Students took notes, which Luther turned into a book, a version of which was published in 1520. In that text, I found *sola fide, sola gratia*, and one use of the term *solo* with Christ (*Christo solo*), which comes in the context of Galatians 2, where Luther writes that "we by Christ alone, by grace are justified by faith."[14] In the 1530s, Luther would lecture again on Galatians, and by then "in Christ alone" would be throughout the entire text. But we're getting ahead of ourselves.

The Ninety-Five Theses and Luther's Shift

It was in the next academic semester (fall 1517), while lecturing on Hebrews, that he posted the Ninety-Five Theses. The theses did not include the *solus Christus* language or concepts, but they radically changed Luther's circumstances. Translated into numerous languages, the theses were printed and disseminated throughout Europe.

When people started accusing him of attacking the pope, he wrote a defense of the Ninety-Five Theses in 1518. He then asked his confessor, Staupitz, to send them to the pope. Here, in his letter to Staupitz (Day of Holy Trinity, 1518), we catch a glimpse of Luther's transformed heart toward Christ. He reminded Staupitz that he had taught him how true penitence begins with the love of God and of righteousness:

> This word of thine stuck in me like a sharp arrow of the mighty, and from that time forth I began to compare it with the texts of Scripture which teach penitence. Lo, there began a joyous game! The words frolicked with me everywhere! They laughed and gamboled around this

saying. Before that there was scarcely a word in all the Scriptures more bitter to me than "penitence," though I was busy making pretences to God and trying to produce a forced, feigned love; but now there is no word which has for me a sweeter or more pleasing sound than "penitence." For God's commands are sweet, when we find that they are to be read not in books alone, but in the wounds of our sweet Saviour.[15]

"The wounds of our sweet Savior." Such a difference in his attitude toward Christ.

After discussing the controversy over the Ninety-Five Theses, Luther concluded his letter with additional loving language toward Christ: "Enough for me is the most sweet Saviour and Redeemer, my Lord Jesus Christ, to Whom I shall always sing my song."[16]

He seems to have come quite a distance from his terror over Christ, which is why I was initially surprised by something he wrote the next year (1519), titled "A Meditation on Christ's Passion." I was startled to read Luther writing that we should be terrified when we meditate on Christ's Passion. When I first saw that, I thought Luther had slipped back into his old way of viewing Christ through a lens of fear. But as I read further, I saw his reasoning and also noted that he didn't get stuck in the terror. He said that contemplating the crucifixion should make us aware of our sinfulness, of God's holiness, and of the severe penalty required to bridge the gap between the two. But Luther did not stay at the foot of the cross. He did not want the reader to be in despair. So he led his readers to Easter:

> But pass beyond that and see his friendly heart and how this heart beats with such love for you that it impels him to bear with pain your conscience and your sin. Then your heart will be filled with love for him, and the confidence of your faith will be strengthened.[17]

Luther was, in effect, guiding his readers through the same transition he had made over the previous three or four years—from terror to love.

In 1520, Luther published three tracts that highly influenced the direction of the Reformation. In August, he published his *Address to the Christian Nobility*. In it, he used the phrase "Christ alone" to refer to the only way in which we can be justified. That is, we can be justified "by Christ alone in heaven."[18] In October, in the second work *On the Babylonian Captivity of the Church*, Luther argued for Christ—rather than the seven sacraments, indulgences, or the papacy—being the way to salvation. When discussing the Mass, he expressed concern that "vestments, ornaments, chants, prayers, organs, candles, and the whole pageantry of outward things" had been added to the Eucharist. What mattered were the words of Christ. Anything else was added invention.[19] When Christ said "Take and eat," he was in effect saying:

> "Behold, O condemned and sinful man. Out of the pure and unmerited love by which I love you, and by the will of the Father of all mercies, I promise you in these words, even though you cannot desire or deserve them, the forgiveness of all your sins and life everlasting. And, so that you may be most certainly assured of this my irrevocable promise, I give my body and shed my blood, thus by my very death confirming this promise, and leaving my body and blood to you as a sign and memorial of this same promise. As often, therefore, as you partake of them, remember me, and praise, magnify, and give thanks for my love and largess toward you."[20]

As Luther tried to put Christ's heart into words, the result is full of love. Note the emotions expressed by Luther as he continued:

> [From this] you will see that nothing else is needed for a worthy holding of mass than a faith that confidently relies on this promise, believes Christ to be true in these words of His, and doubts not that these infinite blessings have been bestowed upon it. Hard on this faith there follows, of itself, *a most sweet stirring of the heart*, whereby the spirit of man is enlarged and waxes fat—that is love, given by the Holy Spirit through faith in Christ—so that he is drawn unto Christ, that gracious and good Testator, and made quite another and a new man. Who would not *shed tears of gladness*, nay well-nigh *faint for the joy* he [has] toward Christ, if he believed with unshaken faith that this inestimable promise of Christ belonged to him! How could one help loving so great a Benefactor, who offers, promises and grants, all unbidden, such great riches, and this eternal inheritance, to one unworthy and deserving of some[thing] far different?[21]

In November 1520, the third tract appeared: *On the Freedom of a Christian.* Here Luther exhorted the reader to study Christ rather than one's own works. We are justified by another's merit, not our own. The merits of Christ alone matter; therefore, we should grow in the knowledge of Christ rather than of works. Luther speaks of the union of the soul with Christ the bridegroom. It is as if the wealthy, honorable bridegroom has married the prostitute, and now she is safe and cared for. He has taken on himself all her sin, death, and damnation and has given her his grace, life, salvation, and righteousness.

Thus it becomes essential that preaching's purpose be to promote Christ and faith in him. It is critical that Christ not simply be Christ, but that he "be a Christ for you and me."[22] How can our response to this consolation be anything other than becoming "sweet with the love of Christ"?[23] It should overflow in our becoming "a sort of Christ" to our neighbor, doing to others what Christ has done for us.[24]

The Gospels and *Solus Christus*

In early 1522, when he was hiding out in Wartburg Castle after his "Here I stand, I can do no other" moment, Luther heard that people were calling themselves Lutherans. He begged his readers not to do this. *He* didn't die for them. *Christ* did. So they should be called Christians. They all, together, have only one master.

In that same year (1522), in his *Brief Instruction on What to Look for and Expect in the Gospels*, Luther explained that a gospel is nothing more or less than a story about Christ. The Gospels may have different details and vary in length, but ultimately they are the story of what Christ "did, said, and suffered."[25] A Gospel is a "chronicle, a story, a narrative about Christ," and the Gospels deliver Christ first as a gift and only later as an example.[26]

A decade later, in 1531, after he was excommunicated from the Catholic Church and became the leader of a rapidly expanding movement, Luther taught Galatians again, this time in the summer and fall. In 1535, students' lecture notes for this class were turned again into a commentary, published, and then corrected and republished in 1538. This edition turned out to be one of the most important sixteenth-century commentaries on Galatians. In his first lectures on the Epistle—before he posted the Ninety-Five Theses— he had used the term *solus Christus* only once. Now it flowed throughout his commentary; the phrase and the concept had become central and *solus Christus* had come into its own.

In his lectures, Luther unpacked the theological implications of this concept. The Father has put everything in Christ's hands. If you have Christ, then you have everything. If you do not have him, then you have nothing. Justification comes only by faith in Christ. The law tells us how to behave properly, but it cannot tell us how to be saved. That's the gospel's role, and the gospel points to Christ. Luther said, "I must listen to the Gospel. It tells me, not what I must do, but what Jesus Christ, the Son of God, has done for me."[27] Christ is our Lord, mediator, Savior, redeemer.[28]

Salvation does not come from observing the law, whether ceremonial or the whole law, or through free will, but through Christ alone. Sacrifices, ceremonies, circumcision, human works, political laws, and traditions cannot save us.[29] We must focus on Christ, the one promised as a blessing to Abraham, the one who gives us grace, the one who is our Savior.[30] It is Christ alone who can bring together the fact that we are sinners and also loved by God, for Christ is the Mediator.[31] He, through his shed blood, is the only "pacifier of God's wrath."[32] Faith without Christ as its object is meaningless: "Faith, therefore, is a certain, steadfast beholding, which looks on nothing else than Christ, the conqueror of sin and death, and the giver of righteousness, salvation, and eternal life."[33] Thus it is critical to keep one's focus on Christ and nothing else, which explains why Paul includes Christ in almost every verse of his writing.[34] For Luther, the bronze serpent lifted in the desert illustrated this: all the Israelites needed to do was to gaze up at the snake; all we need to do is gaze up at Christ. Luther wrote:

> If I would find comfort when my conscience is afflicted, or when I am at the point of death, I must do nothing but apprehend Christ by faith, and say: I believe in Jesus Christ the Son of God, who suffered, was crucified, and died for me, etc. in whose wounds and in whose death I see my sin, and in his resurrection victory over sin, death, and the devil, also righteousness and eternal life. Besides him I see nothing, I hear nothing.[35]

It is Christ alone who "first makes us righteous by the knowledge of himself in his holy gospel, and afterwards he creates a new heart in us" and "gives us that assurance by which we are persuaded that we please the Father for his sake."[36]

Conclusion

As the years unfolded, *solus Christus* would cut a swathe through medieval piety directly to Christ. No longer were the priests the mediators between the believer and Christ. No longer were the saints the mediators between the believer and Christ. In his commentary on John the Baptist's pointing to the Lamb of God, Luther noted that it is, unfortunately, often easier for humans to attach themselves to saints than to Jesus, that the papacy had taught the laity to rely on their merits. This was, of course, what had triggered the Reformation in the first place. Luther had been concerned that the papacy was advocating indulgences that pressured the laity to literally *pay* for merit with money. The money would then draw merits from the Treasury of Merit, which was believed to hold the merits of Christ and the saints. As mentioned above, Saint Anne and Saint Thomas had been Luther's favorites. He also noted that other people ran after Saint James. Here he was referring to the popularity of the pilgrimages to Santiago de Compostella in Spain. People would also pray to Saint Barbara and Saint Christopher to avoid sudden death so that they could receive last rites in time.[37]

In addition to indulgences, the intercession of the saints, and pilgrimages, many people depended on their position as a monk or nun to get them into heaven. Wealthy patrons left money in their wills to fund chantry priests, whose full-time job was to celebrate Masses for the dead to get their souls out of purgatory faster. *Solus Christus* eliminated all of this. And *solus Christus* became Luther's heart cry.

It proceeded to the point where *solus Christus* became a hermeneutic principle for him. It even became a test for inclusion in Scripture's canon. For Luther, the true test for all books of the Bible was whether or not they "preach Christ." He referenced Romans 3:21, arguing that all the Scriptures were meant to display Christ to us and that Paul refused to know anything but Christ.[38] All the Scriptures "point to Christ alone."[39] If you take Christ out of the Scriptures, what else is there? The Holy Spirit is like a lute player who plays only one note or string: Christ.[40] Luther aimed to have the same focus, stating in his preface to Galatians that Christ was the one in whom he wished all his theological thinking to flow. Regarding John 14:6, he wrote that Christ must be our entire salvation: its foundation stone as well as all the others; all the rungs on the ladder to heaven; the beginning, the continuation, and the completion of our lives.[41]

It is interesting to consider what Luther's last words might indicate about his attitude toward Christ at the end of his life. We find them in the biography written by Philipp Melanchthon, Luther's friend and longtime colleague at Wittenberg and in Reformation matters. They provide a window for us into Luther's heart toward Christ in his final moments:

My Heavenly Father, Eternal compassionate God, you have revealed to me your beloved Son our LORD Jesus Christ whom I have known, of whom I have acquaintance, whom I love, and whom I honor as my beloved Savior and Redeemer, whom the Godless persecute, dissipate, and reproach. Take my Soul to you. This he said three times: "Into your hands I commend my spirit, you have redeemed me, God of truth. [And God so loved the world, that he gave his only begotten Son that whosoever believeth in him shall not perish but have everlasting life.]"[42]

"The Lord Jesus Christ . . . whom I love." Gone was the terror. Christ had become his beloved, singular focus.

Sola Scriptura:
By Scripture Alone

4

Torah in Psalm 119

Seong Hyun Park

Introduction

There are three reasons to explore Psalm 119. First, Psalm 119 is such an intriguing chapter in the Bible: the ultimate alphabetic acrostic composition that is the longest in the Bible, taking a good twenty minutes to just recite it. What are the implications of its artistry and length? Second, Psalm 119 is a Torah[1] psalm. While the theme of Torah is prevalent across the entire Hebrew Bible, in this author's opinion, Psalm 119 occupies a special place in the shaping of the Psalms as a collection and also in the shaping of Torah as the written word of God. The third reason is the impetus coming from Luther who noted that in Psalm 119 one finds "a correct way of studying theology."[2]

Acrostics for Torah

As already mentioned, Psalm 119 is the ultimate alphabetic acrostic composition and the longest in the Bible. This psalm consists of twenty-two strophes in which each strophe is associated with one of the twenty-two letters of the Hebrew alphabet, and within each strophe there are eight bicola[3] lines that all start with the same letter of the Hebrew alphabet associated with the strophe.

The phenomenal artistry of acrostics in Psalm 119 extends beyond the psalm itself, when we consider the possibility that Psalm 119 may structurally be connected with the remaining acrostic compositions in the book of Psalms, of which there are seven: 9/10, 25, 34, 37, 111, 112, and 145. The details of the possible structural relationship between Psalm 119 and the other seven have been studied by David N. Freedman[4] and are beyond the scope of the present article, but it comes down to this: If one were to combine all seven remaining acrostic psalms into one psalm, that psalm would be equivalent or comparable to Psalm 119 in terms of the number of lines per strophe (8), cola in the strophe (16), the total number of lines (173/4 versus 176 in Psalm 119), and the total number of cola (364/6 versus 352 to 364 in Psalm 119). What is the implication of such an intricate artistry? In Freedman's words,

> At a minimum, we can say that this group of 8 psalms is more than a haphazard or accidental collection based only on the common use of the alphabet as an organizing principle. . . . The Great Psalm, revolving around the number eight, is a celebration of the Torah (and its seven sister and brother keywords), while the seven lesser psalms celebrate the whole gamut of divine activity and presence in his universe.[5]

One further implication in terms of the scholarship on Psalm 119 is that if Psalm 119 was composed with the seven remaining acrostic psalms in view, then Psalm 119 must be dated as the latest among all the acrostic compositions in the book of Psalms, falling in the same timeline with the process of the final shaping of the Psalms as a collection. Such a dating of the psalm is corroborated by Armin Lange, who observes that Psalm 119 must precede in date the pre-Maccabean texts from Qumran but follow in date the introduction of the Jewish coinage in Jerusalem, which points to the mid-fourth century BC as the time when the psalmist would have penned it.[6]

Torah as Theme

If Psalm 119 was composed at the time that Psalms was being compiled as a collection, could Psalm 119 bear the marks of the perspective at work that gave the book of Psalms its final shape?

Psalm 119 is a Torah psalm. It is peculiar in that it incorporates the language of a wisdom psalm and borrows the elements of a personal lament. But it is a Torah psalm, and the most expansive one at that. In each of the twenty-two strophes, the eight lines that make up the strophe make eight different statements about Torah through various combinations of eight terms that the psalmist has chosen to refer to Torah: law (*tôrâ*), commandment (*miṣwâ*), judgment (*mišpāṭ*), stipulation (*ʿēḏûṯ*), regulation (*piqqûḏ*), saying (*ʾimrâ*), word (*dāḇār*), and statute (*ḥōq*).

The most conspicuous term of the eight is "law"—or *tôrâ* in Hebrew. This is the term that leads the rest of the eight terms, and it is firmly positioned in the opening line of Psalm 119:[7]

1 Blessed are those whose way is blameless,
who walk in the law [*tôrâ*] of the LORD![8]

There is more to the term *tôrâ*, however, in Psalms and the Hebrew Bible as a whole. For example, Psalm 1 opens with lines strikingly similar to Psalm 119:

1 Blessed is the man who walks not in the counsel of the wicked . . .
2 but his delight is in the law [*tôrâ*] of the LORD.

The noted similarity between these two psalms has an implication that is more than mere textual interdependency. Psalm 1 is the psalm that functions as the opening to the book of Psalms, and it adds to the conjecture previously noted that Psalm 119 encapsulates the perspective at work in the shaping of the psalms into a collection. Psalm 119 not only interacts with the seven other acrostic psalms placed in different parts of the book, but it also opens with lines that directly invoke the heading of the book as a whole. And these very opening lines make clear that Torah is the underlying current that reaches and connects the psalms together, like streams that nourish the tree, enabling it to bear fruit (Ps. 1:3). It is often observed that the final shape of the book of Psalms (i.e., Five Books of Psalms) may reflect the structure in which *Tôrâ*—i.e., the Five Books of Moses—has come to be known. This is very probable, given the centrality of Torah as the underlying theme in the Psalms as a whole.

Psalm 1, in addition to serving as the heading for the book of Psalms, also serves as the chapter that opens the third section of the tripartite Hebrew canon of the Old Testament known as *Kǝṯûḇîm* (Writings).[9] This way, the placement of the term *tôrâ* in Psalm 1 has essentially the effect of guiding the readers of the Old Testament to approach the entire third section of the Hebrew canon in the spirit of Torah.

Such an introduction is also given at the start of the second tripartite section of the Hebrew canon: *Nǝḇîʾîm* (Prophets). In this section, the opening chapter is Joshua 1, in which God charges Joshua by saying:

7 Only be strong and very courageous, being careful to do according to all the law [*tôrâ*] that Moses my servant commanded you. Do not turn

from it to the right hand or to the left, that you may have good success wherever you go.

The key term here is *tôrâ* and, as with Psalm 1, Joshua 1 guides the readers of the Old Testament to approach the second section of the Hebrew canon in the spirit of Torah. As Gordon J. Wenham aptly notes, "This way, the second and third parts of the Old Testament canon both point back to the [*Tôrâ*] (the *Law*), the first part of the canon, as foundational for a righteous and successful life."[10]

Torah in Eight Words

Torah is, then, the theme that underlies and connects the Hebrew canon of the Old Testament in its entirety; and within the book of Psalms, the theme reaches a broad place in Psalm 119, where Torah is experienced through multiple scenarios and designations: i.e., law, commandment, judgment, stipulation, regulation, saying, word, and statute. Is such multiplicity really necessary? One should recall that, in addition to the employment of eight terms to refer to Torah, Psalm 119 also employs the acrostic technique—a feature that has often been criticized as a mere mechanistic endeavor needed to fill the content of a lengthy poem.

In Kent A. Reynolds' understanding, however, the author of the psalm "heaps up the Torah terms so that through the accumulation 'the desired expansion of the conceptual sphere would be achieved.' "[11] In other words, the Torah one encounters in Psalm 119 is far more expansive and multifarious than can be captured in the term *tôrâ*, even broader than the sum of the concepts addressed by the eight terms individually.

Similarly, the author's characterization of the speaker in the psalm would be far too complex and multifarious as to be captured in a static portrait. The approach taken by the psalmist is to heap up multiple "snapshots that capture the speaker in different situations and different emotional states," which will result in the construction of a "persona that is far more rhetorically effective."[12] Acrostics, in this sense, serve as the standardized frames within which the writer organizes and portrays the individual snapshots.

In short, Reynolds helps us see Psalm 119 as a repository of standardized portraits in which each scene depicts the speaker's experience of Torah in varying circumstances. As Wenham notes, Torah here "is not just ethical injunctions and rules, but rather the whole of God's revelation. . . . It covers all that helps to link God to his people, from the revelation in the created order (Ps 19:1), to the patriarchal experience of salvation, to the laws given at Sinai, to the teaching of the sages, to the return to Zion."[13]

Torah in the Eye

What is remarkable about the experience of Torah as portrayed in Psalm 119 is that the speaker in the psalm responds to Torah through heart, hands, feet, mouth, and eyes:

- He keeps God's regulations with his whole heart (v. 69).
- He finds God's saying sweet to his taste (v. 103).
- He turns his feet to God's stipulations (v. 59).
- God's word is a lamp to his feet (v. 105).
- With his lips he declares God's judgments (v. 13).
- He lifts up his hands toward God's commandments (v. 48).

It is peculiar, however, that ears are not mentioned in any of the portrayed experiences (see the table below).

Speaker's Channels of Response to Torah in Psalm 119					
Torah term and frequency in Psalm 119	Eyes	Mouth, tongue, or lips	Heart or soul	Hands	Feet
statute (*ḥōq*) x 22		✓	✓		
regulation (*piqqûḏ*) x 21		✓	✓		
word (*dāḇār*) x 22	✓		✓		✓
saying (*'imrâ*) x 19	✓	✓	✓		
stipulation (*ʿēḏûṯ*) x 23	✓	✓	✓		✓
law (*tôrâ*) x 25	✓	✓	✓		✓
commandment (*miṣwâ*) x 22	✓	✓	✓	✓	✓
judgment (*mišpāṭ*) x 23		✓	✓	✓	✓

Should we assume, as Ivana Procházková does, that Torah is first *heard* before the speaker in the psalm responds to it in any particular manner, and therefore we assume that ears are implicitly present in the psalm?[14] The fact is, however, that Psalm 119 does not employ a single word—whether noun or verb—that relates to the auditory channel. Instead, references are given where Torah is engaged through sight, which is an entirely unexpected phenomenon in the Old Testament:

Open my *eyes*, that I may behold
 wondrous things out of your law [*tôrâ*]. (v. 18)

The *unfolding* of your words [*dāḇār*] gives light. (v. 130)

My *eyes* long for your saying [*'imrâ*]. (v. 82; author's own translation)

Torah should certainly be audible when the speaker declares God's judgment (Ps. 119:13) or when he meditates on God's precepts (Ps. 119:15). Psalm 119 entirely overlooks such audible qualities of the Torah, however, giving its attention to the visible qualities of the Torah instead. Instead of hearing—which has always been the primary mode of receiving God's word in the Old Testament (e.g., Deut. 6:4)—one now *sees* the Torah and unfolds it. Given the dating of the psalm embraced in the present study, it would seem that at the time of the composition of Psalm 119, God's Torah was experienced in *written* form rather than by *hearing*, and that the speaker in the psalm is turned from a *hearer* of Torah into a *reader* of it.

Holy Scriptures Alone

In the preface to the 1539 collection of his German writings, Luther wrote the following as "a correct way of studying theology":

I want to point out to you a correct way of studying theology, for I have had practice in that. . . . This is the way taught by holy King David . . . in the one hundred nineteenth psalm. There you will find three rules, amply presented throughout the whole psalm. They are *oratio, meditatio, tentatio*.[15]

While Luther's attribution of the psalm to David is no longer tenable in the contemporary scholarship of the psalm, what makes Luther's work remarkable is that he saw Psalm 119 as a guide for reframing the experience of God's word in daily Christian living. In a time when the encounter with God's word was limited to the religiously privileged in the monastic settings that emphasized "the path of spiritual ascent—from reading, to inward meditation, to contemplation of the divine,"[16] Luther learned in Psalm 119 that the correct reading of the Scripture starts by asking God himself to be the teacher of the word (the rule of *oratio*), by meditating on the word not only in the heart but by the mouth, hands, and feet as well (the rule of *meditatio*), and ultimately directing "one toward the ambiguities and trials of one's external earthly life"[17] (the rule of *tentatio*).

Luther's preface containing Psalm 119's "rules" was soon recognized as worthy of publication in its own right, in 1539 and again in 1540. The "rules" have since then been widely revisited and used by theologians in subsequent periods, even today.[18] Luther wrote elsewhere in the same preface:

> Herein I follow the example of St. Augustine, who was . . . the first and almost the only one who determined to be subject to the Holy Scriptures alone.[19]

Luther turned to Psalm 119 in pursuit of "a correct way of studying theology," and it was ultimately so that he would "be subject to the Holy Scriptures alone," like Augustine. And once the way was found in Psalm 119, Luther bid his readers to "keep to it"[20]—which is a call consistent with the experience of the speaker in Psalm 119, and also with his own efforts to reform the common spiritual practices of Christians on the foundation of the Scriptures alone.[21]

Is reading superior to hearing? Is the written Torah a securer footing for Christian living than an oral dictum? The Torah that the speaker in Psalm 119 experiences is an all-encompassing Torah, for he responds to it with his hands, mouth, lips, tongue, feet, heart, and soul. This is the Torah that he reads; and as he contemplates on it through all that he is, this Torah "prompts a deep yearning for a closer walk with God."[22]

5

Shaped by the Word: *Sola Scriptura* for Spiritual Formation

David A. Currie

If you could transport yourself back five hundred years to Wittenberg and told the good townsfolk you had journeyed to their fair city because you wanted to be spiritually formed, I think I know where they would have sent you. They probably would not have pointed you to the university to listen to Dr. Luther lecture on the book of Romans. Much more likely, they would have directed you to look at Elector Frederick's huge collection of relics, one of the largest in Europe. According to an inventory taken in 1518, the total came to 17,443 items and included such treasures as a thumb from St. Anne, a twig from Moses' burning bush, hay from the Christmas manger, thorns from Christ's crown, and milk from the Virgin Mary. The spiritual potential inherent in these holy objects came to over 1,902,202 years' worth of penance, spiritually forming the observer to a state of holiness that would significantly reduce the pains of purgatory.[1] A decade later, they would have sent you instead to Dr. Luther, who would have handed you a Bible, reflecting his own spiritual journey that led him to affirm the doctrine that has come to be designated *sola scriptura*.

Today, as interest in spiritual formation among evangelicals is growing and there is a new openness to practices associated with Roman Catholicism, some may fear that spiritual formation is incompatible with *sola scriptura*. "First, it's *lectio divina*, next it's contemplative prayer, and before you know it, you're looking for a toenail of the Virgin Mary to get really holy!" Such fears are just as unfounded as are caricatures of evangelical piety as being spiritual formation by *only* Scripture—Bibliolatry—the worship of the word, a preference for the dead letter to the Living Lord. As an alternative to each misconception, let me sketch out a spiritual theology based on *sola scriptura*. At the heart of Luther's call for reform was a vision of the spiritual life shaped by the word. On the one hand, Scripture alone does not suggest that Bible reading is the only truly spiritual practice. On the other hand, Scripture alone does claim that Bible reading is not simply one spiritual practice among many that believers may adopt or reject according to their tastes.

Sola scriptura affirms a priority, indeed even more, a primacy, of the word as the foundation of spiritual formation resulting in believers becoming increasingly conformed to the image of Christ. The Bible alone can provide the first, true note to release believers in the rhythms of authentic spirituality. Without it, we will grow increasingly out of step with the Spirit who breathed out the Scriptures and stumble into spiritual malformation. The rhythms of authentic spirituality always begin with the downbeat of the word—God's own self-revelation—evoking the upbeat of prayer, monitored through reflection, inwardly in self-examination and outwardly in community discernment.

The centrality and primacy of Scripture in the dynamics of spiritual formation are reflected in my working definition of this term:

> Spiritual formation is
>> the lifelong, faith-filled process
>>> of the Holy Spirit transforming
>> the whole person
>>> into the loving likeness of Christ
>> to the glory of the Father
>>> as informed by the whole
>>> word of God,
>> in relationship with the whole
>>> people of God
>> to fulfill the whole mission of God.

This definition also echoes some of the other classic *solas* of the Reformation. Spiritual formation can only begin because of the divine initiative of the Trinity through the Holy Spirit (*sola gratia*); it centers on the Son (*solus Christus*) and ultimately results in bringing greater glory to the Father (*soli Deo gloria*). Human involvement in this process is responsive, not generative, based in trusting acceptance of and cooperation in the work of the Triune God (*sola fide*).

Let me make clear that the spiritual theology of the word that I will now briefly lay out is not directly taken from Luther, though I believe it is a consistent outworking of his formulation of *sola scriptura* and his own spiritual practices.[2] Older alumni of Gordon-Conwell Theological Seminary and students of Reformed biblical theology will recognize that it owes as much to Meredith Kline as to Martin Luther, though I will take full responsibility for the exegetical and theological reservations that both of these students of the word might have with my reformulation of their insights.[3]

Let us begin at the beginning—the beginning of creation and the beginning of the Bible—which strongly emphasizes the uniquely formative character of the Word of God. More specifically, the Word gives form to what was formless and fills up what was empty. "In the beginning God created the heavens and the earth. Now the earth was formless and empty, darkness was over the surface of the deep, and the Spirit of God was hovering over the waters" (Gen. 1:1–2).[4] How might God have transformed this primordial chaos? Because the narrative is so familiar, it is easy to overlook how radical and distinctive Genesis 1:3 is. Theoretically, God could have silently shaped and filled creation, or accomplished the work by direct manual labor as in many extrabiblical creation narratives.

Creation remained "formless and empty" with the *ruach* (spirit/wind/breath) of God hovering over it until the breath of God is formed into the word of God (v. 3): "And God said, 'Let . . .'" The centrality of the Word in forming what was formless and filling up what was empty is emphasized with the repetition of the phrase "God said, 'Let . . .'" to inaugurate each day of creative activity (Day Two, v. 6; Day Three, v. 9; Day Four, v. 14; Day Five, v. 20; and Day Six, v. 24). The implication is that creation would have remained primordial chaos, without shape or content, apart from the Word of God. In a similar way, spirituality detached from the Word is chaotic, formless, and empty.

I would suggest even more specifically that it is a Trinitarian word involved in creation, recreation, and spiritual formation. To adapt Augustine's description of the Trinity as Lover (Father), Beloved (Son), and the Love shared between the Lover and Beloved (Spirit), the act of creation involved the Speaker (Father), the Word (Son), and the Breath that enables the Speaker to utter the Word (Spirit). These relational ways of formulating the Trinity show the inadequacy of substituting functions—Creator, Redeemer, Sanctifier—for names, the most personal kinds of words, in referring to the persons of the Trinity.

The six days of Creation emphasize the formative character of the Word of the Triune God, giving form and filling up what was formless and empty.

Days One, Two, and Three describe the formation of three sub-kingdoms that are then filled up by three sets of sub-rulers in Days Four, Five, and Six. The ruling quality of these sub-rulers filling up these sub-kingdoms is highlighted most clearly in the description of the relationship between "day" and "night" on Day One (v. 5) and the "greater light" (i.e., the sun) and the "lesser light" (i.e., the moon) on Day Four (v. 16). Instead of describing the sun as shining during the day and the moon as shining during the night, filling each realm with light, the unexpected word *govern* is used. By implication, those creatures that fill the realms created on the other days—birds/sky, fish/sea, land/animals—are also "governing."

The particularly formative character of Day Six is highlighted with greater repetition of "God said" and the repetition of the language of new creation ("God said, 'Let . . .'") used to introduce a new day of creation previously, signaling the unique character, potential, and responsibility of human beings to rule over the rest of creation as vice-regents of the Creator King.

> Then God said, "Let us make mankind in our image, in our likeness, so that they may rule over the fish in the sea and the birds in the sky, over the livestock and all the wild animals, and over all the creatures that move along the ground." So God created mankind in his own image, in the image of God he created them; male and female he created them. (Gen. 1:26–27)

While caution should be taken to not reduce the rich, comprehensive character of being created in the image of God to any particular human capacity such as reason or tool making,[5] the *imago Dei* provides the structural capability for spiritual formation, reflected in humanity's distinctive capacity for language. The divine Spirit who spoke, breathing human beings and the rest of creation into existence, is most fully reflected in and reechoed by these unique image-bearers. Although "the heavens declare the glory of God" (Ps. 19:1) and the fish, birds, and animals all give evidence of God's greatness (Ps. 104), they are not capable of reflecting who God is in the way that image-bearing people can. Spirituality is a uniquely human capacity.

Spiritual formation can then be understood as continuing the pattern of creation in giving form and filling up. God's Word is intended to keep forming humans into the image of God's Son and to be the vehicle to keep filling humans with God's Spirit. The end result of spiritual formation is God's glory: "God saw all that he had made, and it was very good" (Gen.

1:31) This glory is reflected and enhanced in the unparalleled and unspoken[6] Day Seven of creation, affirming that God rules over all that had been spoken into creation in Days One through Six. The Creator King has uttered the universe into existence and rests in delighting in the echo of his goodness, resounding in his newly formed and ready to be filled dominion as his image-bearing vice-regents carry out his word. Inherent in the creation of the Sabbath are the foundational rhythms of spiritual formation: revelation/ word, response/prayer, rest/reflection.

The primacy of the word of God for spiritual formation continues in Genesis, positively in chapter 2 and negatively in chapter 3. Formation proceeded well when human words echoed God's word, but humanity became spiritually malformed when detached from God's word. God continued to speak in Genesis 2: breathing his *ruach* into Adam (v. 7), verbalizing his expectations for tending the garden (vv. 16–17), and expressing his loving care and concern for Adam (v. 18). Adam demonstrated that he shared this uniquely divine ability for verbal expression that equipped him for ruling and relationships, first by naming the animals (v. 20) and even more fully in his doxological love poem at the creation of woman (v. 23):

> This is now bone of my bones
>   and flesh of my flesh;
> she shall be called "woman,"
>   for she was taken out of man.

The positive trajectory for spiritual formation launched by the word of God and humanity's faithful response in Genesis 2 comes crashing down in Genesis 3. Not coincidentally, temptation, the dark side of formation, comes in verbal form: "He said . . ." (v. 1). Only God has spoken to humanity thus far, and the only other speech humans have heard has been from one another, divine image-bearers. The Fall narrative is so well known that it is easy to miss the strategic intentionality of using words to lead to sin. Conceivably, the satanic serpent could have tempted in other nonverbal ways, perhaps by pointing toward the forbidden fruit or dangling it in front of Adam and Eve. The repetition of "said/say" in the opening temptation narrative (vv. 1–5) may highlight Satan's desire to displace God by using the divine prerogative of speech.

Ironically and tragically, the evil one recognized the power of words more fully than those created in the image of God. Divine words had the power to bring a good world into existence; demonic words had the power to corrupt this good world with evil by distorting God's word in the ears and mouths of God's vice-regents. Malformation in humanity began when the woman misquotes God—"You must not touch it" (v. 3)—and continues today as people resist and distort the word of God. The narrative could have been different. The woman could have exercised her role as God's vice-regent by rightly quoting God and speaking in his name, and as a result could have cast the serpent out of the garden for usurping the divine prerogative of speech and questioning what God had said. It took the coming of the Seed of the woman (v. 15) to demonstrate how to overcome satanic verbal temptation by the right use of God's word (Matt. 4:1–11; Luke 4:1–13).

If creation and spiritual formation were originally by the Word of God, then recreation and overcoming spiritual malformation are also by the Word of God. "Therefore, if anyone is in Christ, the new creation has come: The old has gone, the new is here!" (2 Cor. 5:17). Humanity's original purpose of glorifying God by reflecting the divine image and echoing the divine word has been restored through Christ. The malformation of sin has been overcome through reconciliation secured through Christ alone by grace alone and appropriated through faith alone.

The priority of verbal revelation remains. "Consequently, faith comes from hearing the message, and the message is heard through the word about Christ" (Rom. 10:17). Spiritual formation flows from faith that must rest on the word. Faith comes preeminently from hearing, not from seeing or from nonverbal mystical ecstasies. Martin Luther himself affirmed the centrality of meditating on Scripture for spiritual growth in the brief treatise he wrote for his barber in 1535, *A Simple Way to Pray*. Later Lutherans expanded on Luther's basic approach that focused on meditating on the Lord's Prayer and the Ten Commandments to include a process for reflecting on all of Scripture for spiritual benefit. Here is how Anglican theologian Peter Toon summarizes the typical steps among Lutherans for what is often called *lectio divina* in other traditions:[7]

- *Preparation:* Set apart at least fifteen minutes every day in a quiet place, preferably in the morning.

- *Reading of Scripture:* Typically the lessons appointed for the day in the daily lectionary.

- *Choice of a short portion:* A phrase or verse, e.g., if John 3 is the Gospel lesson, then John 3:16 might be the focus of reflection and read slowly multiple times.

- *Questions to ask of the text for personal application:* Who, what, where, and why? E.g. for John 3:16: Who has loved the world? What does it mean that he gave his one and only Son? Where did this divine giving take place? Why do people of this world need eternal life? Why am I to believe in God's one and only Son?

- *Recollection:* Recall from memory what is taught in creed and catechism, sermon and liturgy, hymn and prayer, Old and New Testaments, which provides information to answer these questions.

- *Consideration:* Carefully consider what teaching is being received from God, both encouragements and chastisements.

- *Self-examination:* Because the written word of God is a personal word to the reader through the operation of the Spirit of the Lord Jesus, consideration of the text includes self-examination.

- *Prayer and communion with God:* With a heart now warmed and inspired by the love of God and mind illuminated by the truth of the gospel, faithful prayer can begin—loving and adoring God, thanking and praising him, confessing sins to him, and offering petitions and intercession to him in the name of Jesus.

The prologue of John recaps the connections between the Word of God, creation, recreation, and spiritual formation. "In the beginning was the Word, and the Word was with God, and the Word was God. He was with God in the beginning. Through him all things were made; without him nothing was made that has been made" (John 1:1–3). The Word—the eternal Son of God—is reaffirmed as the agent of all creation and recreation: "Yet to all who did receive him, to those who believed in his name, he gave the right to become children of God—children born not of natural descent, nor of human decision or a husband's will, but born of God" (vv. 12–13). Faith alone is essential for recreation, based on the most personal kind of verbal communication, "his name."

John's whole Gospel pays close attention to the person of Jesus, the Word made flesh, and to his words, thereby inviting careful observation of Christ as the model for spiritual formation and trusting reception of and reflection on his words as the primary means of transformation (2:22; 3:34; 4:41; 6:63, 68; 7:40; 10:19; 12:47–48; 14:10, 24; 15:7; 17:8; 18:9). Therefore, it is impossible to know the face and heart of God apart from the Word made flesh: "No one has ever seen God, but the one and only Son, who is himself God and is in closest relationship with the Father, has made him known" (1:18). Natural revelation is not sufficient for fully formed spirituality. Although John has mystical elements, mystical experiences alone are not sufficient either. Verbal content shapes how believers come to know and reflect the holy love of God.

Jesus is clear that there is no division or conflict between himself as the living Word of God and Scripture as the written word of God. The written word uniformly points to the living Word, inviting encounter and faith, as Jesus makes explicit in John 5:39–40: "You study the Scriptures diligently because you think that in them you have eternal life. These are the very Scriptures that testify about me, yet you refuse to come to me to have life." The living Word consistently points back to the written word as well. Jesus' own use of Scripture—indiscriminately interchanging phrases such as "God says," "[the name of a human author of a book of the Bible] says," and "Scripture says"—reflects his core belief that the words of Scripture, like his words, are the words of God.[8]

The formative character of the word of God suggests that verbal—at least spoken, possibly God-breathed written—revelation might still have been foundational for spiritual formation, even if humanity had remained unfallen, and may continue to contribute growth in Christlikeness in the fullness of the new heavens and new earth. How much more foundational for those who have been so malformed by our own self-centeredness and God-deafness, and who have been so prone to confuse the voice of our own flesh/the world/the devil spoken in a loud voice (or a still small one) for God's own. *Sola scriptura* for spiritual formation means that believers are shaped by the word, or more precisely that the living and active Word shapes believers, forming them into the image of Christ and filling them with the Holy Spirit.

6

SOLA SCRIPTURA AND THE RISE OF GLOBAL CHRISTIANITY

Todd M. Johnson

While historical descriptions of the Reformation in the sixteenth century naturally focus on Germany, today, five hundred years later, the majority of Protestants are not German, not European, and not North American. The typical Protestant today is African, Asian, or Latin American. How did a largely European phenomenon go global? While this story is complicated, two features of early Protestantism help to explain how it happened: The first is Bible translation, and the second is the priesthood of all believers. In addition, two movements impacting Protestantism—Evangelicalism and Pentecostalism—help account for the spread of Protestants around the world. Finally, a global demographic profile of changes since the sixteenth century helps frame the past, present, and future of Protestantism around the world.

Bible Translation

The Reformers' strong emphasis on the Scriptures (*sola scriptura*) and their translation into mother tongues was partly responsible for the global expansion of the Protestant faith. Translation of the Scriptures gave individual believers a direct approach to the biblical message. Luther's translation of the Bible into common German empowered German Christians by giving them access to the Scriptures in a new way and deprived priests of sole interpretive right.[1] In translating the Old Testament prophets, Luther wrote, "O God, what a hard and difficult task it is to force these writers, quite against their wills, to speak German."[2] Translation was not a phenomenon unique to the Reformation; it had always been at the core of Christian mission and the primary tool for introducing the gospel to new peoples. In the early centuries of the faith, Christianity spread to cultures in Ethiopia, Armenia, Egypt, Persia,

Central Asia, and China.[3] Mission historian Lamin Sanneh concludes that "Christianity could avoid translation only like water avoiding being wet."[4] As Protestantism grew within and beyond Europe, its leaders eagerly translated the Scriptures into new languages that facilitated growth to new peoples.

Priesthood of All Believers

A second factor in the global expansion of Protestantism was the concept of the priesthood of all believers. All Christians were considered capable of sharing their faith, which democratized the spread of the gospel. Church historian Timothy George writes,

> For Luther, the priesthood of all believers did not mean, "I am my own priest." It meant rather: In the community of saints, God has so tempered the body that we are all priests to each other. . . . Moreover, our priestly ministry does not terminate upon ourselves. It propels us into the world in service and witness.[5]

Thus every Protestant was a potential witness. Furthermore, in principle, European missionaries eventually spread the gospel to faraway places, but in practice, it was local evangelists who did most of the work—a phenomenon known as "indigenous agency." Consequently, although foreign mission work was an expression of the priesthood of all believers, ultimately the main drivers of the global expansion of Protestantism were local evangelistic initiatives.

Nineteenth-Century Example

American missionaries Adoniram and Ann Judson represent this dual dynamic of Bible translation and indigenous agency.[6] A cascade of events transpired in New England in early February 1812. Adoniram Judson and Ann Hasseltine were married on Wednesday, February 5, in Haverhill, Massachusetts. On Thursday, February 6, fifteen hundred people attended the ordination service of the male missionaries at Tabernacle Church in Salem. The young missionaries and their wives were scheduled to sail for India on February 10. Their sailing was delayed due to bad weather until Wednesday, February 19. The trip to India took almost four months, and as they arrived they saw what they thought was their first Hindu, who turned out to be a Muslim. Another year passed before the Judsons finally arrived in Burma.

The Judsons made important strategic decisions in their mission work that set the stage for later indigenization of Christianity. In Burma, Adoniram took a very different approach to indigenous peoples than their fellow missionaries did to Native Americans in the United States. Bible translations were slow to appear among Native Americans, but within a few decades there were already two full Bible translations in Burma, including Judson's Burmese Bible. The Bible made it possible for the Burmese (and other peoples in Burma) to encounter the gospel message directly.

At the same time, Ann Judson was deeply involved with local people. This was important because the primary carriers of the gospel message were to a great extent unknown individual converts from among the indigenous people. One such person was Ko Tha Byu, a reputed thief and murderer, who became the most effective evangelist in spreading the gospel beyond the narrow confines of the missionary community. He was not Burmese but Karen. Today there are hundreds of thousands of Christians among the Karen, tracing their lineage back to Ko Tha Byu. Thus the gospel was effectively spread by what is now termed "indigenous agents."

Between Bible translation and indigenous agency, the kind of Christianity that spread in Burma quickly differentiated itself from that of the colonial missionaries. In essence, foreign missionaries in Burma provided the necessary spark while local evangelists did the work on the ground and produced a culturally relevant version of the Christian faith. As Christian mission scholars Lamin Sanneh and Andrew Walls have shown, this principle of translation eventually changed the balance of power among peoples who embraced Christianity.[7] In many countries in Africa, Asia, and Latin America, this phenomenon repeated itself, so that today the vast majority of Christians (and of Protestants) are found there.

The Demographic Reality of Protestant Expansion

Tracing the Protestant movement demographically over its five-hundred-year history reveals a fascinating story about the adaptation of Christianity in thousands of cultures and languages. The growth of the movement from its European origins to the current majority in the Global South is presented at the end of the chapter (pages 65–70) in a series of charts, tables, and maps.

Protestants in the Context of Christian Traditions

In 1500, Catholics made up two-thirds of all Christians and Orthodox the remaining third. After the Reformation, Protestants (and later Independents)[8] represented an increasing portion of global Christianity. Today, Catholics are half of all Christians but Protestants and Independents together are about 40 percent, with the remaining 10 percent Orthodox.

Protestants by Continent

The graph on page 66 shows that until 1800, Protestants were largely confined to Europe. North America became significant after 1800, but in the mid-twentieth century Africa's share of Protestants was more prominent. Today, 41 percent of all Protestants are Africans. Asians and Latin Americans also represent significant proportions. The shift to the Global South represents the future of Protestantism.

Number of Protestants in 2017

Today there are 560 million Protestants found in a wide array of denominations: Baptists, Lutherans, Methodists, and nondenominational, among others. The map on page 67 shows the dramatic demographic role of Africa today.

Top 10 Largest Protestant Denominations

The shift of Protestantism to the Global South is further illustrated by the fact that China and Brazil have the two largest Protestant denominations. Countries in Africa—such as Nigeria, Uganda, and Ethiopia—also have a prominent place, but Germany, the United Kingdom, and the United States still make the list.

Top 10 Countries and Fastest Growth Countries

From 1910 to 2015, there was a shift from North to South for the largest Protestant population by country, although the US, the UK, and Germany still hold prominent places. Fastest-growing populations are all in the Global South, both over the whole period and in the current period. The rapid growth there is partly the result of Brazilian missionaries.

Evangelicals and Pentecostals

Other factors in the global expansion of Protestants are due to the Evangelical and Pentecostal movements. The diagram on page 70 illustrates the complexity of overlapping identities within these movements. In each of these cases, the movements proved to be major drivers in both missionary work and in on-the-ground evangelism.

Evangelicals as Protestants

Mission historian Gina Zurlo shows that the Protestant Reformation was highly generative in the fragmentation of Christianity. She writes, "Its emphasis on individual reading and interpretation of Scripture, combined with renewed religious freedom, resulted in the development of many new Christian groups, each an attempt to capture a more 'pure' version of the faith. Denominational affiliation became the foundation of Protestant Christian group identity."[9] Zurlo continues,

> Initially, "Evangelical" was simply synonymous with "Protestant," especially in Germany, where even today the German *Evangelische* is better translated as "Protestant" than "Evangelical."[10] Among English speakers, many Lutherans in particular still use the term in this sense, as in the "Evangelical Lutheran Church." Over time the term "Evangelical" largely came to describe the network of Protestant Christian movements in the eighteenth century in Britain and its colonies, the individuals who were associated with those movements, and a larger pattern of theological convictions and religious attitudes.[11]

Evangelical denominations generated mission movements, and vast numbers of missionaries (including the Judsons) emphasized the role of the ordinary believer in evangelism and discipleship. Consequently, much of the work on the ground was done by laywomen (and some men) who went from village to village spreading the gospel. As already observed, their efforts were critical for the expansion of Protestantism around the world.

In 1900, 45 percent of all Protestants were Evangelical. This rose to 46 percent by 2010 and is expected to rise further to over 50 percent by 2050 as Evangelicalism shifts to the South. In 1900, approximately 82 percent of all Evangelicals were Protestants, and most of the rest were Independents and unaffiliated. Today, it remains at 82 percent. Evangelicals currently number 342 million, with projected growth to 581 million by 2050.[12]

Pentecostals as Protestants

Pentecostal Christians are members of Protestant denominations whose major characteristic is a new experience of the energizing ministry of the Holy Spirit, which most other Christians consider to be somewhat unusual.[13] This is interpreted as a rediscovery of the spiritual gifts of New Testament times and their restoration to ordinary Christian life and ministry. Though most scholars accept a polycentric theory of Pentecostal origins, Classical Pentecostalism usually is held to have begun in the United States in 1901.[14] For a brief period, Pentecostalism expected to remain an interdenominational movement within the existing churches, but from 1909 onward its members increasingly were ejected from mainline bodies and forced therefore to begin new organized denominations.[15] Among Protestants are Pentecostal denominations such as the Assemblies of God, the International Church of the Foursquare Gospel, and the Church of God of Prophecy. There are also many subcategories of Pentecostal denominations, including Oneness, Baptistic, Holiness, Perfectionist, and Apostolic.

Pentecostals, like Evangelicals, have a strong mission motivation and an equally strong commitment to lay involvement in evangelism. Pentecostal networks spread rapidly around the world and, like Evangelical ones, are partly responsible for the shift of the Protestant faith to the Global South.

In 2017, there were approximately 669 million Pentecostals/Charismatics globally. This includes large numbers of non-Protestants, mostly Catholics and Independent Charismatics. Nonetheless, there are two kinds of Protestant Pentecostals. The first group, those who belong to Pentecostal denominations such as the Assemblies of God (denominational Pentecostals), numbered just under 100 million in 2017. The second type, individual Protestants who identify as Pentecostals or Charismatics but belong to non-Pentecostal denominations, numbered just under 70 million. Together there were approximately 170 million Protestant Pentecostals/Charismatics in 2017.

Significant overlap exists between Evangelicalism and the Pentecostal/ Charismatic movement. It is important to note that classical Pentecostals are normally considered Evangelicals, whereas Charismatics in mainline churches are usually not. This is because the Evangelical minorities within mainline churches generally are not identical to the Charismatic minorities in terms of self-identification.

Conclusion

Many studies highlight the demographic shift of Christianity from the Global North to the Global South. Global Christianity is already a majority-South tradition and will be, within a short time, an African-majority tradition. Protestantism has followed a similar path. From its localized origins in Western Europe, it has become a global movement with a wide variety of denominations, now well over eleven thousand.[16] Part of the explanation for that expansion has been Bible translation and indigenous agency ("the priesthood of all believers"). In addition, Evangelical and Pentecostal movements have deeply impacted Protestant churches.

Protestants of all kinds continue to grow around the world, taking it far from its Western cultural origins. The five hundredth anniversary of the Protestant Reformation has provided a fitting opportunity to reflect on demographic changes within the movement and how these might impact its future.

Protestants in the Context of Christian Traditions

Roman Catholics · Protestants · Independents · Orthodox

Source: Todd M. Johnson & Gina A. Zurlo, eds. *World Christian Database*. Leiden/Boston: Brill, accessed October 2016. Anglicans are included with Protestants in this analysis.

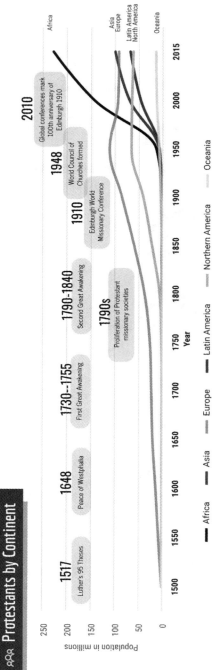

Protestants by Continent

1517 Luther's 95 Theses

1648 Peace of Westphalia

1730–1755 First Great Awakening

1790s Proliferation of Protestant missionary societies

1790–1840 Second Great Awakening

1910 Edinburgh World Missionary Conference

1948 World Council of Churches formed

2010 Global conferences mark 100th anniversary of Edinburgh 1910

Population in millions

Year

Africa
Asia
Europe
Latin America
North America
Oceania

— Africa — Asia — Europe — Latin America — Northern America — Oceania

Source: Todd M. Johnson & Gina A. Zurlo, eds. *World Christian Database*. Leiden/Boston: Brill, accessed October 2016. Anglicans are included with Protestants in this analysis.

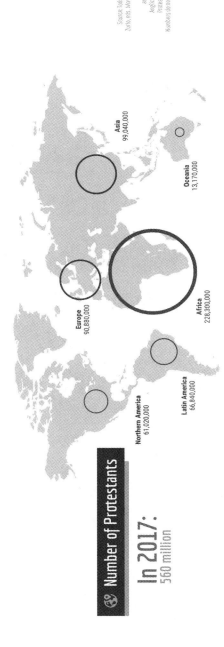

Number of Protestants

In 2017: 560 million

Northern America
61,020,000

Latin America
66,840,000

Europe
90,880,000

Africa
228,300,000

Asia
99,040,000

Oceania
13,170,000

Source: Todd M. Johnson & Gina A. Zurlo, eds. *World Christian Database* (Leiden/Boston: Brill, accessed October 2016. Anglicans are included with Protestants in this analysis. Numbers do not add due to rounding.

TOP 10

Largest Protestant Denominations (in a country) in 2015

1.	Three-Self Patriotic Movement	*China*	26,000,000
2.	Assembléias de Deus	*Brazil*	25,000,000
3.	Evangelische Kirche in Deutschland	*Germany*	24,450,000
4.	Church of England	*United Kingdom*	23,700,000
5.	Anglican Church of Nigeria	*Nigeria*	22,000,000
6.	Southern Baptist Convention	*United States*	20,000,000
7.	Church of Uganda	*Uganda*	14,185,000
8.	World of Life Evangelical Church	*Ethiopia*	8,500,000
9.	United Methodist Church	*United States*	7,094,000
10.	Evangelical Church Winning All	*Nigeria*	6,800,000

Source: Todd M. Johnson & Gina A. Zurlo, eds. *World Christian Database*. Leiden/Boston: Brill, accessed October 2016.

Anglicans are included with Protestants in this analysis. Independents, such as Chinese house churches and African Independent churches, are not included under Protestants.

Countries with the Largest Populations of Protestants

		1910		2015
1.	United States	42,360,000	United States	56,177,000
2.	United Kingdom	35,664,000	Nigeria	53,106,000
3.	Germany	28,351,000	Brazil	34,836,000
4.	Sweden	5,400,000	United Kingdom	29,020,000
5.	Netherlands	3,560,000	China	26,556,000
6.	Canada	3,407,000	Germany	25,430,000
7.	Finland	2,849,000	India	20,994,000
8.	Australia	2,778,000	Kenya	19,249,000
9.	Denmark	2,716,000	Indonesia	18,213,000
10.	Norway	2,383,000	Ethiopia	16,714,000

Countries with the Fastest-Growing Protestant Populations

		Annual Growth Rate 1910-2015			Annual Growth Rate 2005-2015
1.	Rwanda	13.01%	1.	Sao Tome & Principe	11.50%
2.	Burundi	12.62%	2.	Bhutan	10.21%
3.	Cote D'Ivoire	12.44%	3.	Niger	7.14%
4.	Burkina Faso	12.32%	4.	Singapore	5.66%
5.	Chad	11.98%	5.	Iran	5.51%
6.	Viet Nam	11.85%	6.	Benin	5.40%
7.	Central African Republic	11.38%	7.	Azerbaijan	5.31%
8.	Republic of Congo	10.85%	8.	Senegal	5.13%
9.	Philippines	10.82%	9.	Honduras	5.13%
10.	Nepal	10.22%	10.	Laos	5.07%

[in countries > 100,000 in population]

Despite Europe being the birthplace of Protestantism, it is expected that by 2050, less than 10% of Protestants will live in Europe.

Today, Africa is home to 41% of all Protestants. By 2050, it is expected that 53% of all Protestants will live in Africa.

Source: Todd M. Johnson & Gina A. Zurlo, eds. *World Christian Database*. Leiden/Boston: Brill, accessed October 2016. Anglicans are included with Protestants in this analysis.

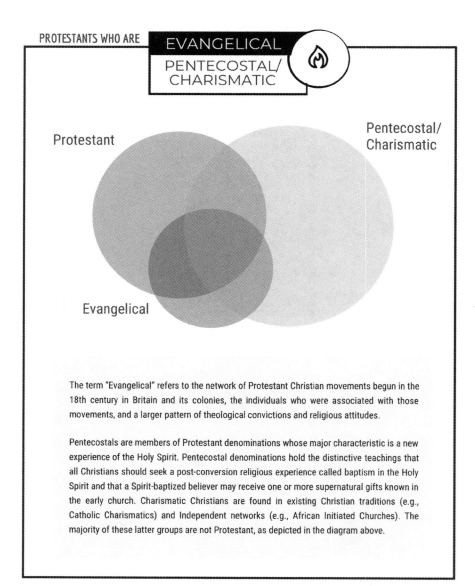

PROTESTANTS WHO ARE

EVANGELICAL
PENTECOSTAL/
CHARISMATIC

Protestant

Pentecostal/
Charismatic

Evangelical

The term "Evangelical" refers to the network of Protestant Christian movements begun in the 18th century in Britain and its colonies, the individuals who were associated with those movements, and a larger pattern of theological convictions and religious attitudes.

Pentecostals are members of Protestant denominations whose major characteristic is a new experience of the Holy Spirit. Pentecostal denominations hold the distinctive teachings that all Christians should seek a post-conversion religious experience called baptism in the Holy Spirit and that a Spirit-baptized believer may receive one or more supernatural gifts known in the early church. Charismatic Christians are found in existing Christian traditions (e.g., Catholic Charismatics) and Independent networks (e.g., African Initiated Churches). The majority of these latter groups are not Protestant, as depicted in the diagram above.

Source: Todd M. Johnson & Gina A. Zurlo, eds. *World Christian Database*. Leiden/Boston: Brill, accessed October 2016. Anglicans are included with Protestants in this analysis.

Sola Gratia:
By Grace Alone

7

SOLA GRATIA: HOW THIS GRACE STILL EXTENDS TO ISRAEL

Walter C. Kaiser Jr.

The word *grace* (*gratia*) in biblical usage can be as broad as embracing the whole of God's activity to mortals, or as limited as focusing on just one piece of the merciful work of God. Thus God's "grace" is most commonly defined as "the unmerited favor of God toward men and women." But this "grace" is also most prominently set forth as the favor God bestowed on Abraham and on his descendants, and through them as God's redemptive program to all the families of the earth. This, then, would be the channel through which the benefits and favor of God in salvation would flow to all humanity.

Never was there a more startling illustration of this grace, however, than this one offered to Abraham and his family. The apostle Paul, a Jewish Christian, writing his letter to the Gentile Christians in the church at Rome (Rom. 11:13), argued most vigorously that—even though in general the Jewish people had not accepted Yeshua (Jesus) as the Jewish Messiah, and even though they had more often than not outrightly rejected his offer of grace—nevertheless, God did not renege on his promise of his gracious gift of an Heir from Abraham's seed, or the patriarch's inheritance of the land of Canaan, or even that the Jewish people would be the channel for the heritage of the gospel to all the families of the earth. As Paul says in Romans 11:28–29 (NIV),

> As far as gospel is concerned, [the people of Israel] are enemies for your sake; but as far as election is concerned, they are loved on account of the patriarchs, for God's gifts and his call are irrevocable.

In fact, the Jewish opposition and rejection of the Christian message amazingly made room for the Gentiles' reception of Jesus as Savior—and that apart from any covenantal observance on their part of the law. In fact, the

Gentiles of this world would experience such "greater riches" (Rom. 11:12), when Israel's "fullness/full [number]" had occurred, that it would be like "life from the dead" when that nation began to accept the Messiah (11:15). At that time, God will show himself powerful through the people of Israel in the eyes of the whole world (Ezek. 36:23). This is some fantastic promise indeed!

The Eternal Promise Granted to the Patriarchs

But despite the general Jewish refusal to accept Yeshua as their own Messiah, God would continue to maintain these very same promises to Abraham and his descendants forever. In the amazing grace of God, the Jewish people had not stumbled merely so as to fall and thus to be disinherited from the promises of God—for God would never abandon his promise to Abraham, Isaac, and Jacob, nor would Israel be disinherited of God's ancient promise! God would not deny himself or lie to them or to us! Here, then, is one of the prime examples of "the wonderful grace of Jesus that is greater than all of [Israel's] sin."

The Rise of Replacement Theology/Supersessionism

Unfortunately, this biblical and apostolic view of the "everlasting" nature of God's ancient promise-plan to the patriarchs Abraham, Isaac, and Jacob would not be firmly retained in the teaching of the Christian church. Only some one hundred years into the Christian era, the church father and apologist Justin Martyr, a Gentile Christian, put forth a different view of the enduring grace of God in his *Dialogue with Trypho*, a Jewish debater with whom Justin Martyr argued, especially in section 119 of his *Dialogue*, which reads:

> We [Christians] shall inherit the Holy Land together with Abraham, receiving our inheritance for all eternity, because by our similar faith we have become children of Abraham. . . . Thus, God promised Abraham a religious and righteous nation of like faith, and a delight to the Father; but it is not you "in whom there is no faith [Deut. 32:20]."

Gentile believers in Yeshua did, of course, become "children of Abraham" (Gal. 3:29). According to Justin, however, the physical benefits of the covenantal promise no longer applied to the Jewish people as it had been given originally to Abraham; for God had instead transferred all these same promises later on over to the Gentile believers in the church, who now replaced Israel as the recipients of the promises. For in Justin's view, the Jewish people were cursed because they had rejected Yeshua as their Messiah. This became known as "Replacement Theology" or "Supersessionism,"[1] in which, presumably, all the promises made to the patriarchs were now given over by the Lord to the believing Gentile church (but not the curses, however, curiously enough!). The church had "replaced" Israel as the new recipient of God's promises according to this Gentile view of the promise of God.

But how did it happen that, in the span of just one Christian century, a new perception of the status of the Jewish people changed so radically from what Paul had taught and what God had promised in the previous two millennia throughout the Old Testament: that the promise made to the patriarchs had been completely transferred to the Gentile believers? Where did the thought originate that God had rejected his people Israel (Rom. 11:1)? Why was it necessary for Paul to declare that he too was a Jew and a descendant of Abraham (11:1b)? What happened to the old promise God gave to Abraham?

The promises God made to Abraham, of course, were numerous: Genesis 12:1–3, 7; 13:14–17; 15:1–6, 18–20; 17:1–21; and 22:15–18. God promised Abraham that he would have an heir, along with countless descendants, who would conqueror the evil one and who would live in the special land of Canaan, and who would be the means of blessing all the families and nations on the earth (Gen. 12:2–3). The mention of this promise to Abraham is not only found within the book of Genesis; these same promises recur throughout the rest of the first testament in at least some two hundred other major passages.[2] Even more important, the land in particular was promised to Abraham's seed as an "everlasting covenant" (Hebrew, *berit 'olam*) in Genesis 13:14–15; 15:18; 17:7, 13, 19; 26:1–4; 28:12–14. How could it be "replaced" if it was an "everlasting" or "eternal" covenant and one promised by God?[3]

Some have argued, however, that the land promise had already been fulfilled long ago according to Joshua 21:43–45. Thus God had affirmed and continued his promise to Israel! As the text reads:

> So the LORD gave Israel all the land he had sworn to give their ancestors.
> . . . Not one of all the LORD's good promises to Israel failed.

The same statement is repeated in Joshua 23:14–15 and Nehemiah 9:8. Therefore, some interpreters conclude that the land portion of the promise had been fulfilled as judged by these passages. That, for instance, was the conclusion of the late Philip E. Hughes, who wrote,

> And so we see how the promises to Abraham of old were, in their externals at least, quite definitively fulfilled, — [and] how his seed . . . [would] inherit . . . the promised land in accordance with the limits which God had foretold. Nor is this a mere personal conclusion, but one that is attested in the plainest possible terms both by Scripture of that time . . . and by those of a later time.[4]

Before such a judgment is rendered all too quickly, however, a distinction must be made between the land being conquered *in principle*, in that all the main objectives had been reached, and a land that hadn't been totally subjugated *in actuality*. Thus there were a large number of "mopping up" operations that had to be completed but that were, as a matter of fact, left as unfinished tasks of conquering the whole land, which are noted in Joshua 13:1 to Judges 3:5–6. Moreover, Israel never really did complete the complete job of conquering the entire land, even though 1 Kings 8:65 would appear to include everything was occupied "from Lebo Hamath [in the north] to the Wadi of Egypt [in the south]." We are told, however, that the Gaza Strip of the Philistines was not as yet under Israel's control, nor were parts of the coastal strip of Phoenicia north of Tyre under Israel's administration (1 Kings 4:21; 2 Chron. 9:26).[5] There was, then, much land yet to be possessed before the promise of the land was to be fully realized!

The Possible Conditionality of the Covenants

Another way often used to deny the continued viability of the promise to Israel and the future restoration of Israel to their land, with an alleged subsequent transfer of the promises from Israel to the Gentile church, is to interpret the Abrahamic and Davidic covenants as being just as "conditional" as the Sinaitic covenant. For example, Professor Oswald T. Allis states the issue this way:

> The claim that the Abrahamic covenant was "unconditional" has dangerous implications; for it suggests an antithesis between *faith* and *obedience*, which is not warranted in Scripture.[6]

But what could this mean? If the covenant was sworn by God alone and not by Abraham, how could that set up an antithesis or suggest some "dangerous implications"? The truth of the matter is that Abram was told to bring the three animals (a heifer, a goat, and a ram, each three years old, along with a dove and a young pigeon) for sacrifice, then cut the larger animals in half and arrange them opposite each other so as to form an aisle, where those taking the covenantal oath were to walk between the pieces. However, Abram fell into a "deep sleep" (15:12), thus only the Lord, as "a smoking firepot with a blazing torch . . . passed between the pieces" without Abram joining him (15:17). If God did not perform what he had said he would do, then the curse of death would fall on him, as death had come on the three animals, along with the dove and the young pigeon. In a bilateral covenant, normally both parties would walk through the cutup sacrifices. In this case, instead of God and Abraham each walking through the pieces, God alone walked down the newly formed aisle by himself, while Abraham slept soundly off to one side. Thus God did not allow Abraham to contribute, or to indemnify himself, in this covenant (cf. Jer. 34:18–20); it was a covenant made by God alone!

Abraham, however, did not personally see the promises made to him fulfilled in his lifetime, for the book of Hebrews tells us that he never received his inheritance and that he was still waiting for it to happen (which means he would need to be resurrected sometime in the future to receive these promises). But the promises were made to him by God without condition. The Abrahamic covenant was "unconditional!"

God's plan for the fulfillment of Abraham's promise becomes more specific and elaborate as it continues through the promises made to David in 2 Samuel 7:8–9, 12–13, and 15–16. It is important to recognize that the covenant made with David is directly related to the one given to Abraham. The Davidic covenant also has no condition attached to it. This is shown by the fact that many of the same promises made in the Abrahamic covenant are repeated in the Davidic Covenant. It further adds, though, that this promise-plan will involve a "throne, a dynasty, and a kingdom" for David and the coming rule and reign of Messiah, which would be established forever. What is even more significant is that both the Abrahamic and Davidic covenants use a distinctive and unique *name* for God, otherwise rarely found elsewhere in the first testament, viz., "Adonai Yahweh." It is found twice in Genesis 15:2, 8; and seven times in 2 Samuel 7:18–19 (twice), 20, 22, 28 (twice). Surely this is meant to draw our attention to the fact that the

Abrahamic and Davidic covenants were to be viewed as connected and a continuing part of the one continuous promise-plan of God.

But God gave another key prediction as to how he would bring his promises to fulfillment. It involved his answer as to how he would handle the sinfulness of humanity. Our Lord would not relate to Abraham, David, or their seed, (or to us), based on how they (or we) performed and kept his promises, but by his grace. Instead, he predicted that a time was coming when he would offer to Israel and Judah a new covenant, in which he would write his law on the hearts of mortals (Jer. 31:31–34) and he would put his Spirit into people to empower them to obey (Ezek. 36:26–28). It too would be an "everlasting covenant," which would last forever—as long as the sun and the moon lasted (Jer. 32:40–41)! In fact, this new covenant repeats some 70 percent of the promises found in the Abrahamic and Davidic covenants along with its new elements.

It is little wonder, then, that the case for God's grace accompanied the concept of the covenants and divine election. Both the Old Testament word *hen* ("grace") and the Greek term *charis* ("grace") indicate a real objective relation in which an undeserved and unmerited favor from a superior to an inferior is given. The spirit of the grace of God found in the Abrahamic-Davidic-new covenant promise was God's gift to Israel and to all who believed on Yeshua the Messiah.

The Jewish People and the Development of Reformed Theology

A good deal of what later became known as Reformed or covenant theology in the sixteenth century and later was grounded in the earlier fourth-century AD Augustinian doctrine, which emphasized the replacement of Israel with the church, called now the "new Israel." Even though Saint Augustine at first embraced the promises made to the people of Israel as those that had a continuing endurance until the end-times, he later felt that the house of Israel had been cast off by God for their rebellion and refusal to accept Yeshua as Messiah. Due to his prolific writings and large esteem among believers, then and now, his views on a displaced, disowned, and rejected Israel, whose blessings were now made over to the church, thus became almost official church doctrine, especially among Roman Catholic and in many Protestant Reformed traditions descending from the Reformation.

Even more harmful to the vanishing Jewish-Christian relations was the series of eight anti-Jewish messages by the gifted orator, also of the fourth-century church, John Chrysostom. In AD 387, Chrysostom declared that Jewish "Deicide" ("killing God," i.e., Yeshua) was the ultimate Jewish crime. Thus a strong tendency developed in the Reformed tradition to continue the Augustinian theology of excluding the Jewish people from the ancient promises of God. Instead, these promises were given over to the "new Israel," the church!

Not all Reformers followed this pattern; for example, the European Dutch Reformed theologian Wilhelmus Brakel (1635–1711) in Rotterdam took issue with the Augustinian line of interpretation. Nor must one over-look all of the Puritans, for many of them still held the promises given to the patriarchs were operative even to the end times. One such defender was Samuel Rutherford in his book *Lex Rex,* and even John Milton in *Paradise Regained.* Another strong advocate for the centrality of the Jewish people in the cosmic plan of God was the Moravian Movement, started by Count Nicholas von Zinzendorf (1700–1760), and in the theology of the Hussites.

A classic example of Reformed theology[7] is also seen in the distinguished writings of Francis Turretin (1623–87) and in his thirty years of teaching at Calvin's Academy in Geneva. His volume titled *Institutes of Elenctic Theology,* in which he quotes Augustine copiously, is a text that continued to be used all the way into the nineteenth century by early theologians at Princeton Theological Seminary. Turretin argues this way:

> The expressions [about Israel's return to the land of Canaan in the end days] are not to be pressed literally, because they are symbolical, not proper; typical not literal; to be explained spiritually and not carnally. Israel is to be restored, not according to the flesh and letter, but according to the promise and spirit (Rom 9); the holy city, not Jerusalem, but the Church.[8]

All the while, Paul's letter to the Romans urges believers to understand that the theme of his great masterpiece in the redemptive plan of God for sinners has the same theme as announced in Romans 1:16: "For I am not ashamed of the gospel, because it is the power of God that brings salvation to everyone who believes: *first to the Jew* and then to the Gentile"(italics added). God had distinctly set a priority, both in chronological time and in his redemptive program strategy, for giving to the Jewish people a priority in hearing the message and in sharing it with others! Likewise, in John 4:22, Jesus taught that "salvation is from the Jews." But even more dramatically, Romans 9–11 was specific and dealt with the problem of how the Jewish people fit into the program of God.

God's Election of the People of Israel (Romans 9–11)

Our point now is not to wrestle with the alleged Calvinistic or Arminian views of individual salvation in Romans 9–11. Rather, we are here more concerned about this text's wider usage as it applies to the "election" of the people of Israel. The apostle Paul's concept of election in Romans 9–11 is about an elect people and an elect nation, not primarily about individuals at this point! Paul's message was not just about Gentile conversions to Yeshua, but he declared Israel's king and ruler had appeared already once in the person of Yeshua of Nazareth, and both Jewish persons and Gentiles should submit to King Jesus as Savior and Lord over all.

In Romans 9–11, Paul answered the real dilemma that was troubling all too many: How could Yeshua be the king of Israel, if at the same time Israel was continually rejecting him as Lord and sovereign over their lives. To meet this dilemma, Paul had to answer two top objections if Israel is (or we are) to grasp what he was saying in these chapters: (1) This rejection by Israel was not new, for it had happened all through Israel's past history (that point is more than obvious!); and (2) Israel, however, remained the "elect" of God, even if she continued in her unbelief, for the promise of God remained true and available, even if the people for whom it was meant did not respond as yet!

This did not mean that God had not elected Israel as a people, nor did it mean that he only elected *individuals* to salvation; this just was not the purpose he had in mind in this section. Israel had a distinctive redemptive purpose and calling as a whole, and Paul was deeply burdened about the election of the people in that nation to receive God's redemptive program. In fact, he received this burden for his people from his being "in Christ," not from some academic or emotional source, as he pointedly affirms in Romans 9:1. Moreover, he was not exaggerating or lying, for both his conscience and the Holy Spirit bore witness to the fact that Israel's refusal to accept this "election" in the plan of God had caused Paul "great sorrow and unceasing anguish and pain in [his] heart." He was telling the truth; their rejection had caused a huge amount of emotional, mental, and physical pain for him. Had Paul's angst ended, as some want to argue, with the church being the "new Israel" in God's revised redemptive purpose, then Paul could have been relieved of his anguish of heart and soul. But such a redefinition of "Israel," which made the church God's "New Israel" never happened in God's plan, as Romans 9:4–5a immediately tells us. Look what the people of Israel still had in their present and future gifts, in spite of their rebellion and intransigence:

> The people of Israel. Theirs is the adoption to sonship; theirs the divine glory, the covenants, the receiving of the law, the temple worship, and the promises. Theirs are the patriarchs, and from them is traced the human ancestry of the Messiah.

The promises, covenants, the line of the Messiah, and more, Paul argued, were still being traced, not to the church or to the Gentiles, but to the elect nation of Israel; it all still belonged to Israel. But if that was so, then Paul still had two very difficult points with which to wrestle: (1) If Israel was still the elect people of God, then why did she not presently enjoy the benefits of her election? (2) Had the word of God then failed? If that was so, how then could Paul invite the Gentile nations to submit to a Jewish king who has failed thus far to bring salvation to Israel—indeed, to those who had been offered this status originally? What would the Gentiles think about this if God had, as the argument seems to argue, totally failed to effect what he had promised? It just didn't make sense! To make these points, however, Paul quickly adds,

> It is not as though God's word had failed. For not all who are descended from Israel are Israel. Nor because they are his descendants are they all Abraham's children. On the contrary, "It is through Isaac that your offspring will be reckoned." (Rom. 9:6–7)

Paul now makes the amazing statement that it is possible to be a descendant of Israel and yet be cut off from the benefits of being part of God's present-day Israel. True, all descended from Jacob are called Israel, but not all those so descended from Jacob are, or will, participate in the kingdom of God. Paul shows that it is possible to be an Israelite and yet to be cut off from the benefits of being part of those who are the elect of God.

Illustrations That Help Us Make a Proper Comparison

Paul invites us to make a comparison, so he calls us to see what happened to Abraham's sons, when Ishmael rejected God's choice of Isaac in God's plan. True, both of Abraham's sons were later blessed: Ishmael was divinely promised to be made a large nation, because he was one of Abraham's offspring (Gen. 21:13), but he would not recognize God's election and choice of his younger brother Isaac for God's redemptive program, for he "mocked" Isaac (Gen. 21:8–10). Therefore, what happened in Abraham's day when Ishmael rejected Isaac as God's choice in his redemptive purpose is still happening today: Israel's sons are born for blessing, but they lose their position of blessing when they reject God's election in his redemptive purpose. They end up being "children of the flesh" and not "children of the Spirit." When God called Isaac, that did not invalidate God's calling of Ishmael. He too would be blessed through Isaac's seed, just like the rest of the world would be, if he and they believed by faith. Thus Paul was not speaking of God's decision to personally save Isaac or Ishmael at this point; rather, it was God's election of Isaac for the special redemptive purpose in God's plan for all the world. Unfortunately, in the Arab world today, all too many continue to reject God's calling of Isaac for this divine purpose; for example, the Islamic Arabs say that it was Ishmael, and not Isaac, that Abraham offered up as sacrifice on Mount Moriah in Genesis 22! That twisting of the facts is tantamount to rewriting history and the original plan of God.

The crisis Israel faces today is the fact that they have continued, for the most part, to reject Yeshua as their Messiah. Even though the promise of the second coming of Messiah and his ancient promise has divided the nation, nevertheless, God made a solemn and holy promise that there is a day coming when he will bring the whole nation of Israel into salvation and fulfill the destiny he set for them millennia ago. Israel's rejection of Yeshua will not invalidate their calling, their restoration, or their experience of the wonderful grace of Jesus, which is still greater than all their sin or even ours! True, such a failure by the people of Israel will cause many individuals to suffer an enormous loss in that particular generation, but it will in no way invalidate the certainty of the covenantal promise of God given originally to Abraham, David, and their seed. Just as Ishmael's descendants suffered, because they failed to recognize Isaac's election, in like manner has Israel suffered enormously because she too has failed to recognize Yeshua's election. This is why the apostle Paul is in such anguish (Rom. 9:1–3), but mark this well: God will yet one day still fulfill his promise (Rom. 9:26).

After Paul had used the illustration of Ishmael and Isaac, he next went to the illustration of Jacob and Esau (Rom. 9:9–13). Esau is obviously the older of the twins and seems to be more qualified in many ways, for Jacob is weak and in some ways a flawed character—whose name, meaning "supplanter," which tends to emphasize the same point. But God selects Jacob for his own reasons so that the purpose of election might stand. To miss this purpose is to miss Paul's point in this text. Surely as Creator, God can do as he pleases, but that is not what Paul was getting at here. Instead, it was that God's purpose of election was to demonstrate that all are unworthy and no better qualified to be chosen as God's elect people than any other. God chose what was weaker so all of us could know that his love and grace to any of us is without regard to what we might offer to him. God's choice is for his own redemptive purpose.

Paul's argument in Romans 9 was not primarily to discuss individual salvation, for he had already done this in Romans 1 to 8. But now in Romans 9, he is more concerned with a very different question. If God is faithful to his word, then the sixty-four-thousand-dollar question is this: How is it that the Jewish Messiah has appeared, yet most of Israel has rejected him? There is the enigma of enigmas!

Of course, Israel's election has been divisive and it has been painful, as similar times in Israel's past history have shown. So Paul now explains for a Gentile audience why Israel has rejected the Messiah. In fact, Yeshua himself also wept in anguish over Israel's rejection of him in Matthew 23:37, "How often would I have gathered you . . . but you were not willing!" Nevertheless, Israel's election remains intact only because of God's promise.

The Surprising Result of Israel's Rejection of Yeshua

But Paul has one more startling aspect of Israel's election to share. In Romans 11, he boldly argues there is also a redemptive side to Israel's rejection of Yeshua. Paul straightforwardly states that we Gentiles owe our access to the gospel directly because of the fall of Israel. Paul carefully declares that Israel's fall resulted in the knowledge of God being shared with the Gentile nations. Thus the exact purpose for which Israel was called was now happening, even though she still was disobedient. Amazing! How could this be? Here is how Paul said it:

But if [Israel's] transgression means riches for the world, and their loss means riches for the Gentiles, how much greater riches will their full inclusion bring! (Rom. 11:12)

He adds,

For if [Israel's] rejection brought reconciliation to the world, what will [Israel's ultimate] acceptance be but life from the dead? (Rom. 11:15)

And,

I do not want you to be ignorant of this mystery, brothers and sisters, so you may not be conceited: Israel has experienced a hardening in part until the full number of the Gentiles has come in, and in this way all Israel will be saved. (Rom. 11:25–26)

That is enough to blow our minds! Even when Israel tried to avoid the election of God, even her disobedience was used by God to bring blessing and a light to the Gentiles. But when the "full number" of the gathering in of the Gentile believers has happened, that will be one of the ways God will spark a massive salvation of the Jewish people in the final days of this era. Gentile believers are warned not to be arrogant toward the Jewish people, nor should we avoid sharing the gospel with them. For after all, we Christians have been blessed by them, so why should Gentile believers not turn around and aid in our contemporary world the salvation of the Jewish people? Isn't this a fair turnabout for those of us who have been so blessed by the redemptive purpose of God?

Conclusion

Gentile believers must see to it that their mission strategies have a priority to "the Jew first." If that mission is to enjoy the blessings of God, then it must follow the strategy set by our Lord and the apostle Paul, who went to the people of Israel "first."

Gentiles must also recognize that the Jewish righteous remnant are full brothers and sisters with us. Gentile believers must also take special care not to be arrogant toward the Jewish branches of the olive tree we have replaced, thus all forms of anti-Semitism are out of place and should be repented.

We must likewise recall that we Gentiles are not the ones who support Israel, but it is they who support us in the roots and trunk of the olive tree. The Christian church would otherwise just float in the ethereal air with no anchor, grounding, or roots in space or time, if we were not attached to the Jewish olive tree. Yes, Israel has been largely broken off from the trunk of the tree because of their unbelief, but we are not to become proud; we are to fear lest we too might be cut off (Rom. 11:18–22).

Moreover, our systematic and biblical theologies must include Israel once again if we are to get our theology right. Often Israel is conspicuously missing in our systematic theologies. Finally, our prayer must be for the "peace of Jerusalem" (Ps. 122:6) and the salvation of her people, for they too are loved by God. Thus the Christian church is called not only to take the gospel to Israel, but also to stand with the remnant of Israel, who are saved, and to stand with Israel in crises as a nation as well. We must not misunderstand the scourging of the Lord as evidence that he has totally rejected and forever abandoned them. Instead, God's promise-plan is still on course, and he will complete it as he said.

8

UNDERSTANDING THE RELATIONSHIP BETWEEN GRACE AND WORKS: EPHESIANS 2:8–10 AND JOHN CALVIN

Aída Besançon Spencer

"Grace" is an important theme for John Calvin. Book 3 of his *Institutes of the Christian Religion* is titled "The Way in which we receive the Grace of Christ," and book 4 covers the means of grace. Calvin fills the *Institutes* with scriptural proof. According to numerous commentators, Calvin called the Letter to the Ephesians his favorite Epistle.[1] One particularly important text for Calvin was Ephesians 2:8–10. It was also important to the early church. Ephesians 2:5, 8–9 was cited as early as AD 155–160 by Polycarp, bishop of Smyrna: "You believe (in Christ Jesus) . . . knowing that by grace you have been saved, not because of works, but by the will of God through Jesus Christ" (Polycarp to the Philippians 1.3). Calvin cites Ephesians 2:8–10 at least ten times in eight sections of the *Institutes of the Christian Religion*, mainly in book 3.

Following is a summary of the points that he derives from these citations: The Lord poured his grace upon us in order that we praise the Lord's righteousness (III.13.2); we attain salvation by God's grace alone, not by works (III.14.5); grace saves not just at the beginning but to the very end of life (III.14.11; two references); all good works come from our second creation (III.3.6; two references); we are God's handiwork (III.3.21); our first capacity for well-doing flows from regeneration (III.14.5); no good comes forth from us except insofar as we have been regenerated (III.15.7); and we are called for good works (III.23.13).

Ephesians 2:8–10 is also crucial in Calvin's harmonizing James 2:21–24 with Romans 4:2–3ff., even though he does not cite Ephesians 2:8–10 in that section (*Inst.* III.17.11–12). He says that Christ teaches through the *same* Spirit in Paul as in James:

The Spirit declares through Paul's mouth that Abraham attained righteousness through faith, not through works [Rom. 4:3; Gal. 3:6]. We also teach that by faith all are justified apart from the works of the law. The same Spirit teaches through James that the faith both of Abraham and of ourselves consists in works not only in faith. It is sure that the Spirit is not in conflict with himself. (III.17.11)[2]

Calvin adds that James contends with those who "vainly pretended faith as an excuse for their contempt of good works." Rather, "an empty show of faith does not justify, and a believer, not content with such an image, declares his righteousness by good works" (III.17.12).

Calvin thus, while stressing that salvation is in no way humanly derived, also stresses that good works flow from God's grace in human regeneration. I think one important criticism of the doctrine "by grace alone" today in the global church is the publicity of those who claim to be Christians who have been discovered *not* living in a righteous manner. Such examples are prominent in the news and on the Internet, so I do not think I have to cite examples (you can probably think of someone yourself!). And such lapses have wreaked enormous damage not only on those involved but also on their families, churches, presbyteries, and others in the larger society. How can we believe in such "cheap grace"? Ephesians 2:8–10, however, correctly ties together salvation and good works:

For by means of grace you have been saved, through faith; and this is not from you, it is God's gift; not from works, lest anyone might boast. For we are his creation, having been created in Christ Jesus for good works, which God prepared beforehand, that in them we might walk.[3]

First, briefly, I will give an overview of the letter and the passage. Then I will discuss specific aspects of the passage, such as the significance of "saved," "grace," "gift," the prepositional phrases, "boast," "for good works," "prepared beforehand," and "walk." Finally, I will summarize the passage by relating it to the letter's historical context and a synonymous theme in the letter, and end with a brief application.

The Letter of Ephesians is written to Gentiles,[4] fellow-heirs of the Jews, by Paul while he is under house arrest in Rome, to encourage them to lead a life worthy of God's gracious calling.[5] The letter may be divided into three sections: (1) God's grace provides an inheritance (1:3–2:22); (2) for this reason, Paul is a prisoner for Gentiles, fellow heirs (3:1–21); and (3) therefore, Paul, a prisoner, urges readers to live a life worthy of their calling (4:1–6:20). Our text here fits in the first section: The Gentiles' heritage is salvation given by God's grace (2:1–22). Ephesians 2:8–10 explains what is God's grace in kindness toward us (2:7).

Paul has explained that being dead in sins, "all of us," Gentiles and Jews, have been made alive by the superlative glorious riches of God's generous grace (2:1–5). If we are dead, then we cannot boast that we have saved ourselves! Salvation by means of grace is mentioned twice in this paragraph, in 2:5 and 2:8. Grace is the foundational act.[6] Grace is the atmosphere in which faith breathes and grows. God, and God alone, has to recreate us if we are dead! But "faith" is our response. It is the agent by which salvation is attained (*dia*, 2:8*)*. "By grace you are saved" is God's gift.[7] It is not our own work (2:9). Even as God created Adam and Eve (*poiēma*) in Genesis, and God creates each of us at our own birth, God has *re*created us at our salvation[8] in two ways: "in Christ Jesus" and "for good works" (2:10). Calvin explains,

> Now seeing we are created in Jesus Christ, it is the same as saying that all the righteousness, all the wisdom, all the virtue, and all the goodness that is in us we draw from that source, and God . . . has put the fullness of all things belonging to our salvation into Jesus Christ.[9]

Even these good works are ones God prepared beforehand that we might walk in them, in contrast to the evil works in which we used to walk when we were dead, following the ruler of this world (2:2, 10). The "good works" reflect the character and action of the good God,[10] as opposed to the evil works of the evil one.

Being made alive occurred at a point in time (2:5, aorist), but the state of salvation follows. Our salvation (as the perfect tense) looks to the past, but it has ongoing effects (2:8). The readers of Ephesians are Gentiles, who were not so concerned about blood sacrifice for atonement, but rather becoming heirs of God's promises along with the Jews. Therefore, Paul uses a verb for "salvation" (*sōzō*), rather than the verb for "justification" (*dikaioō*). However, he describes salvation with the periphrastic perfect—the verb "to be" plus the participle, hence the translations "you have been saved" and "you are saved." The perfect tense unites the present and aorist. It is the "continuance of completed action." It is both punctiliar and durative, a completed state or condition. (The participle is durative.)[11] Thus in Ephesians 2:5 and 8, the reader is described as having been saved at some point in time and having a salvation that continues its state over time.

This use of "salvation" is similar to Paul's use in Romans 10:9–13 when he writes those readers, Jews and Gentiles, that they will be saved if they call on the Lord. In Romans 10:9 and 13 he uses "salvation" in a punctiliar sense, "you will be saved," and in 10:9 "justification" (*dikaiosunē*) and "salvation" (*sōtēria*) appear to be synonyms:

> If you declare with your mouth, "Jesus is Lord," and believe in your heart that God raised him from the dead, you will be saved. For it is with your heart that you believe and are justified, and it is with your mouth that you profess your faith and are saved. (Rom. 10:9–10 NIV)

But earlier in Romans, Paul focuses on the terms for justification (*dikaioō* and *dikaiosunē*) because his goal is to convince the Jews that the Gentiles have the same criteria for salvation: faith (Rom. 2:17; 3:28–29). He writes to Jews to explain atonement through blood that results in salvation from God's wrath (Rom. 5:9). There he explains that obedience to the law is not sufficient for justification (Rom. 3:20). Jew *and* Gentile are both justified by God's grace as a gift through the redemption that is in Christ Jesus, and the sacrifice of atonement is by Christ Jesus' blood, effective through faith (Rom. 3:24–25).

Paul thus states the same basic concept in Romans 3 as he does in Ephesians 2, but the different verbs clarify different emphases to different readers in the two letters. However, in both letters, "righteousness" (*dikaiosunē*) is a quality of God, synonymous with holiness, goodness, and truth,[12] which becomes a quality of the new believer.[13] F. F. Bruce explains that in Ephesians "salvation" is "something accomplished and experienced; it has much the same force as justification" in Romans. "You have been saved" in Ephesians 2:5, 8 is "equivalent to 'you have been justified.'"[14]

"Grace" in Ephesians is wonderful. It is glorious and rich, operant in salvation, and in our lives as Christians.[15] This is a point that Calvin has stressed:

> [Grace saves] to the very end of life, believers have no other righteousness than that which is there described. For Christ ever remains the Mediator to reconcile the Father to us; and his death has everlasting

efficacy: namely, cleansing, satisfaction, atonement, and finally perfect obedience, with which all our iniquities are covered. And Paul does not say to the Ephesians that we have the beginning of salvation from grace but that we have been saved through grace, "not by works, lest any man should boast" (Eph. 2:8–9). (*Inst.* III.14.11)

"Gift" (*dōron*) in Ephesians 2:8 is a significant word for Paul to use here. The majority of the Pentateuch references to *dōron* refer to gifts humans give to God in the tabernacle, such as whole burnt offerings to make atonement, sacrifices, offerings for voluntary sins, transgressions, consecration, and peace.[16] The priest cannot offer blemished gifts. Sometimes *dōron* is used in the Old Testament of gifts offered from one human to another in order to be accepted by the receiver.[17]

What we have in Ephesians, as in the other Bible examples, is something offered to God in order to be well received. Even more specifically, it appears to be a gift for atonement or transgression.[18] In contrast to most other examples in the Old Testament tabernacle, in Ephesians *God* gives the gift, a perfect unblemished gift,[19] implied to God, but then returned to humans. Paul specifies that the gift is not from humans and therefore one cannot boast about it.

The prepositional phrases "not from you" and "not from works" (Eph. 2:8, 9) are parallel. Both refer to some act that originates from within (*ek*) one's own self. "Work" (*ergon*) is used negatively in verse 9 but positively in verse 10. By itself, "works" (*ergon*) is not wrong. So what is the difference? Salvation is not granted because of human good works, but good works are God's goal for saved humans.

"Boast" (*kauchaomai*, 2:9) is a frequent word for Paul. It can be used negatively or positively. Paul considers that humans should not boast of an action that is not true,[20] but Christians should boast in God's gifts and truths,[21] as he tells the Corinthians, citing Jeremiah 9:24: "Let the one boasting—in the Lord—boast" (1 Cor. 1:31; 2 Cor. 10:17). The point in Ephesians 2:9 is that arrogance about salvation is false, therefore the Gentiles, together with the Jews, have no excuse to boast about their part in being saved.

Salvation was accomplished "in Christ Jesus" "for good works" (Eph. 2:10). "Good works" are embedded in the larger sentence. We are God's good work or creation (*poiēma*), having been created in Christ Jesus. The "good works" were "prepared beforehand" (2:10). Paul uses the preposition *epi* ("*for* good works"), which may refer to basis, ground, aim, or purpose. Its root idea is "resting upon."[22] "We might walk" is aorist subjunctive referring to will (that in these good works, we might choose to walk) or anticipation (that in these good works, we will choose to walk).[23] The subjunctive mood communicates doubt. Should we imitate Jesus ("in Christ Jesus") or obey God's intentions for our salvation?

Calvin presupposes that *epi* refers to basis or ground: Paul, Calvin says, "intends to shew [sic] that we have brought nothing to God, by which he might be laid under obligations to us; and he shews [sic] that even the good works which we perform have come from God."[24] They were "prepared beforehand." He is fighting those Roman Catholics who infer from this passage that "half of our justification arises from works." In other words, we were created in Christ Jesus "on the basis of our good works." Calvin claims that "papists" "possess the heavenly life" "partly by God's grace" "and partly by our own free will."[25] But, for Calvin, the "good works which God prepared beforehand" refer to the good works prepared by God "before we were born . . . meaning, that in our own strength we are not able to lead a holy life, but only so far as we are formed and adapted by the hand of God."[26]

The grammarian A. T. Robertson concludes that *epi* is a dative of purpose,[27] which Arthur Patzia explains, "believers are created with a view *toward* good works." "Good works" are the "outcome, not the cause, of salvation." The whole context "prohibits one from taking *good works* in any meritorious way."[28]

Martin Luther separates life into two parts: (1) waiting for "the blessed hope and appearing of our Lord Jesus Christ," mentioned in Titus 2:13–14, or knowledge of our Savior Jesus Christ; and (2) learning "what good works are, namely, those which proceed from faith in the office entrusted to us according to God's command and Word." Luther further explains that good works are *not* things people make up and choose from their own devotion, but rather "what God has bidden . . . here on earth." For example, he explains that a maid "does good works when in faith she carries out her calling and does what the lady commands her to do, when she sweeps the house, cleans and cooks in the kitchen." A servant does "good works when he fears God, believes in Christ, and walks in the obedience of his lord." Luther argues against "good works" as entailing the ascetic contemplative life apart from a worldly vocation.[29]

N. T. Wright appears correct in relating Ephesians 2:1–10 to 2:11–22, suggesting that the "good works" God prepared is the unity between Jew and Gentile (the united church is "itself *part of the reality of the gospel*")[30] or, as Paul says, Christ is "our peace; in his flesh he has made both groups into one and has broken down the dividing wall, that is, the hostility between us" (Eph. 2:14 NRSV). It is because we have been recreated in Christ Jesus that we can and should end hostility between redeemed but divided groups. John MacPherson summarizes:

[God's] workmanship should produce good works. This will be the best evidence that the work is His who Himself is good, that the creation is wrought in Him who went about doing good. . . . These good works performed by the believer are fruits of his new creation, the proper products of that new nature which the presence of Christ's Spirit has begotten in us.[31]

Harold Hoehner agrees that we are "to walk," not "to work" in them:

God has prepared beforehand good works for believers that he will perform in and through them as they walk by faith in his power. It is not doing a work *for* God but God doing a work *in* and *through* the believer.[32]

Lynn Cohick adds that Ephesians 2:10 gives believers "a purpose, divinely given and divinely empowered: to function as God's agents of goodness in the world."[33] Thus to imitate Jesus is to obey God's intention for our salvation.

Both Paul and Jesus use the phrase good "work" or "works" (actions or deeds)[34] elsewhere in the New Testament. Jesus tells the Jewish leaders who plan to stone him, "Many good works, I have shown you from the Father" (John 10:31–32). They reply, "Concerning any good work, we are not stoning you, but concerning blasphemy, and that you, being a human, make yourself God" (John 10:33). Jesus also taught his disciples to let their light shine before others so that they may see "your good works and give glory to your Father, the One in the heavens" (Matt. 5:16).[35]

Paul exhorts the Colossians, at about the same time he wrote to the Ephesians, to "lead lives worthy of the Lord, fully pleasing to him, as you bear fruit in every *good work* and as you grow in the knowledge of God" (Col. 1:10 NRSV).[36] The same concept is expressed in Ephesians 1:4: God chose us "to be holy and blameless before him in love." Paul exemplifies "good works" in Ephesians 3:8–9. He received grace "to bring to the Gentiles the news of the boundless riches of Christ, and to make everyone see what is the plan of the mystery" (Eph. 3:8–9 NRSV). To have "good works," he says, is to "live a life worthy of the calling you have received. Be completely humble and gentle; be patient, bearing with one another in love. Make every effort to keep the unity of the Spirit through the bond of peace" (Eph. 4:1–3 NIV) and to "equip the saints for the work of ministry" (4:12 NRSV).[37] "Good works" include character and action.

Ephesians is like a diamond that as one turns it, its different facets all point to the same brilliance. In Ephesians 2:8–10, we learn one aspect of why readers should lead a life worthy of God: They are saved by God's grace to walk in good works. How does this relate to the historical context? Paul describes the recipients of the letter as faithful (1:1), and yet he also wants them to be more faithful *and* loving. Here are Gentiles who are not fully living the Christian life; rather, in many ways they are living their old life (4:17). Paul wants them to understand the close connection between God's grace and doing good works or faith in God and faithful lives. A synonym for "salvation" in Ephesians is "adoption." The Gentiles have been adopted into the Father's household and, therefore, are citizens and heirs of this new household and kingdom with access to the Father. As exalted heirs, they need to be obedient children imitating their new Father, the living God.[38] Therefore, an analogous group today would be those who call themselves Christians but who may not be living the Christlike life, or believers who do not understand how God's grace relates to one's actions.

In the midst of difficulties today very similar to those in the first century (where people claim to be Christians but are not living like Christians), we need to teach and remember two key and interrelated points. One is that when it comes to salvation, we need to be thankful and humble.[39] God has freed us from perfectionism that is never satisfied. As Calvin summarized: "faith" is "a firm and certain knowledge of God's benevolence toward us, founded upon the truth of the freely given promise in Christ, both revealed to our minds and sealed upon our hearts through the Holy Spirit." He explains that "our salvation is [God's] care and concern." Grace testifies to us that "the Father is merciful" (*Inst.* III.2.7) and the Father is great! If we understand that the God of this universe is a holy God, a devouring fire, and we are sinful in comparison, then how can we ever approach him and not be burned up? However, our merciful God can free us and fully justify us. We're free so of course we should be thankful! But we must receive God's grace through faith. "Faith" is not a work; it is a response of gratitude, a welcoming of a gift, an outstretched palm. A "gift" (*dōron*) in ancient times could be represented by the palm,[40] because the "palm" gives the gift to another. But also a palm may represent faith, the one who receives the gift with the palm because the Giver is trusted and the gift is good. We can rest in God, and we should receive God's recreation of us.

The second key point is that God's recreation of us, of course, will be evident in our actions. Our actions do not save us. Our good actions are the outward evidence of inward change. We need to teach ourselves and the church that God has recreated us so that we develop through God's help (continual grace) character and actions consistent with God's own character and actions. Given all this scriptural truth appropriated by the Reformers, no wonder they saw *sola gratia* as one of the four pillars supporting the tasks of the Reformation!

9

SOLA GRATIA: DOES IT APPLY
TO SANCTIFICATION?

Richard Lints

The gospel is the story of God creating, redeeming, sustaining, and consummating a people for his own possession. In that narrative is embedded the entire Christian life. There is no other story that narrates our reconciliation with God past, present, or future. As a gift from God, the gospel is received by faith alone. The gospel never ceases to be a gift and never ceases to be received by faith throughout the Christian life. Protestant traditions have generally affirmed that this gospel is the sole ground of our salvation. They have spoken with less than a ringing consensus about the gospel as the ground of sanctification. If the gospel is God's redeeming actions past, present, and future, then consistency would suggest that there is essential continuity of grace in justification and sanctification. That is not the case for many Protestants. This essay attempts to get at some of the underlying reasons why this is so.

If the gospel is the narrative of God's creating, redeeming, and consummating work in Christ, then there is no progress beyond the gospel in the Christian life, there is no story beyond the story. The Christian life is about divine grace growing deeper into the human soul and therefore implies living by faith, not beyond faith. The significance of *sola fide* in this context is, quite simply, immense.[1]

Grace alone constitutes the means by which God reconciles sinners to himself and by virtue of which sinners retain their only hope of eternal life. It is vital not to refer to this hope as the result of the collaborative work of God and the sinner, which would wrongly connote that sinners hope partially in God and partially in themselves. Their relationship with God is always based on grace. It is God who graciously reconciles sinners to himself as an act of his divine compassion.

Being reconciled to God is not only initiated by God but continues by virtue of his grace. We may refer to Christian holiness as that ongoing work of divine grace by which reconciliation with God is sustained in the life of the believer. Holiness attaches to the divine declaration that God's people are set apart in Christ. The creaturely counterpart to this divine declaration is faith. Yet in many Protestant traditions, the believer's actions (i.e., their good works) in sanctification come perilously close to being precisely another instrumental ground of their ongoing reconciliation before God.[2] The argument for this theological temptation is straightforward and goes like this: If one downplays the necessity of "good works" in sanctification, then one will be answering Paul's rhetorical question of Romans 6:1—"Are we to continue in sin that grace may abound?"—in the affirmative. Yet, as I shall argue, by emphasizing the necessity of good works in sanctification, the risk is that one's continued reconciliation with our Covenant Lord will be based on a "boast" before God, which Paul expressly denies in Romans 4. The danger of boasting is mitigated only by keeping grace as central to sanctification as it is to justification. As Calvin reminds his readers, "Let us not consider works to be so commended after free justification that they afterward take over the function of justifying man or share this office with faith."[3] Unfortunately, it is the theological place of grace in sanctification that has proven all too confused in many Protestant traditions.

Two Courtrooms?

Protestants have often interpreted Paul's rhetorical question in Romans 6:1 as implying the insufficiency of grace in sanctification.[4] There can be no license to sin in the face of divine grace, so the argument goes. Charles Hodge offers a representative exposition of this framework of sanctification in the light of the fear of antinomianism. "Justification," he writes, "is a forensic act, God acting as judge, declaring justice satisfied so far as the believing sinner is concerned, whereas sanctification is an effect due to the divine efficiency."[5] After justification and by means of the impartation of divine grace, "sinful acts become more infrequent and holy acts more and more habitual and controlling."[6] The Holy Spirit provides the "occasion for the exercise of . . . submission, confidence, self-denial, patience and meekness as well as faith, hope and love."[7] Real moral progress appears to be the hallmark of sanctification.[8] Hodge goes so far as to say, "The best Christians are in general those who not merely from restless activity of natural disposition, but from love to Christ and zeal for his glory, labor most and suffer most in his service."[9]

For Hodge, the scales of divine justice operate according to two different and conflicting principles. From one angle, the justice of God is satisfied by Christ's death as the federal representative of his people and the imputation of Christ's righteousness to them. In this divine courtroom, the innocent one (Jesus) has been declared guilty in the place of the guilty ones (believers), and in turn the guilty ones have been declared innocent in place of the innocent one. But evidently, in another divine courtroom nearby with those very same believers, as Hodge says, "a man shall reap what he sows, and God will reward everyone according to his works."[10]

The reason Hodge backs himself into this corner is straightforward. To avoid any hint of moralism on the one hand, Hodge affirms double imputation with respect to justification. To avoid any hint of antinomianism on the other hand, he affirms the necessity of good works in sanctification. He cites Luther's denunciation of Agricola as the confirming historical evidence that Protestants are committed to the necessity of good works.[11] Good works are not meritorious in justification, but they are "rewarded" and appear to have a judicial function in sanctification according to Hodge.

The problem is twofold. In Hodge's portrayal, justification is grounded in God's imputed grace received by faith precisely because good works are in sufficiently short supply as to warrant condemnation rather than reward. But in sanctification, there appears to be a sufficient supply of good works to warrant blessing. A different kind of grace (infused grace) is apparently the ground for this in sanctification. Second and more importantly, Christ's redeeming work is entirely sufficient for the reconciliation of sinners, but in the courtroom of sanctification the verdict is based on the cooperating good works of believers as well.[12] At the very least this is confusing.

Listen again to the apostle Paul's argument in Romans 4:1–5. Faith has no "boast" (i.e., merit) before God not only because of its causal ancestry in the Holy Spirit, but primarily because its reference point lies outside of itself in the grace of God. The causal conditions of faith appear irrelevant to its meritorious standing (or lack thereof) in Romans 3 and 4. There is no reference to the work of the Holy Spirit producing faith at the critical juncture in Paul's argument against moralism ("having a boast") or against antinomianism ("a license to sin"). Rather, Paul depicts faith in contrast to works, as hoping and trusting in something (Christ) outside of one's self (Rom. 4:3–5, 21–25). It has a fundamental exteriority about it in this respect.

By contrast, works have no such fundamental exteriority about them; they belong to the one who does them. When works are conceptually contrasted to faith, it is the contrast between an action without an external reference and an action with an external reference. Faith takes hold of the grace of God. Or, more accurately, faith has no "boast" because divine grace is its sole object. Calvin pungently reminds us:

> God does not as many stupidly believe once for all reckon to us as righteousness that forgiveness of sins concerning which we have spoken in order that having obtained pardon for our past life, we may afterward seek righteousness in the law. This would be only to lead us into false hope, to laugh at us and mock us.[13]

Simul Sanctus et Peccator

"There is no greater sinner than the Christian Church," said Luther in his Easter Day sermon in 1531.[14] Calvin's rhetorical flourish may be less startling, but his conviction is remarkably similar in this regard:

> The best work that can be brought forward from them is still always spotted and corrupted with some impurity of the flesh and some dregs mixed with it. Let a holy servant of God choose from the whole course of his life what an especially noteworthy character he thinks he has done. Let him well turn over in his mind its several parts. He will somewhere perceive that it savors of the rottenness of the flesh. We have not a single work going forth from the saints that if it be judged in itself deserves not shame as its just reward.[15]

Whatever else may be said about works performed by believers, it is clear that essential goodness is not one of their primary attributes.[16] Sin and grace are never mere "quanta" in process, grace increasing and sin decreasing.[17] The situation in which believers find themselves is always one in which their works are tinged with sin. Their obedience is always filled with mixed motives. Their actions are never devoid of self-centeredness. So it is that there is no such thing as a gradual purification by which their need for the forgiveness of sins would diminish. They remain sinners thoroughly and through and through.[18] They are also, surprisingly, declared holy and sanctified by divine grace.

Both Luther and Calvin affirm that believers are simultaneously sanctified and sinful, but how so?[19] At the very least sanctification must not equate to intrinsic righteousness, or to a notion of inward renewal that implies the (increasing) absence of sin.[20] The simultaneity of sin and sanctification prohibits the interpretation of sanctification as ethical self-improvement, nor can sanctification signal the emergence of self-sufficiency in any form.[21]

When Paul declares the saints at Corinth to be sanctified (1 Cor. 1:2), it is not grounded in their good works; it is by virtue of belonging to Christ that they are declared sanctified. There is also a surprising reversal of this claim later in the very same chapter: viz., that Christ is the sanctification of the saints (1 Cor. 1:30). Paul was making the claim that belonging to Christ was the meaning of their sanctification. The saints are sanctified "in Christ," not "in themselves."

There is no stage in the life of the sanctified believer in which the forgiveness of sins is not absolutely central to their relationship to God. G. C. Berkouwer refers to this as the "constant commerce with the forgiveness of sins" in the life of the believer.[22] In other words, there is no point when Christ ceases to be the representative mediator between them and God. This also is to resist the notion of an infused principle into believers by which they become Christlike and thereby are less in need of divine forgiveness.[23] Grace is not like an antibiotic given to the sick patient to ward off the infection of sin, enabling them to take on a less sinful posture.[24]

If dependence upon divine grace is a hallmark of sanctification, then faith is the primary expression of this orientation precisely because faith orients the believers outside of themselves.[25] In this regard, repentance rather than moral exertion is the appropriate response that flows from this faith. Repentance manifests the ongoing necessity of divine forgiveness and grace. And insofar as divine forgiveness is in view in every act of repentance, it is grounded in the gospel declaration of reconciliation through the death and resurrection of the Son. Salvation is not grounded in the believer being like Christ, but rather being forgiven "in Christ."[26] It is not grounded in any notion of a partial righteousness or holiness in the believer.[27]

Calvin goes so far as to suggest that the works of believers are acceptable to God only because Christ's righteousness has been imputed to these works:

> After forgiveness of sins is set forth, the good works that now follow are appraised otherwise than on their own merit. For everything imperfect in them is covered by Christ's perfection, every blemish or spot

is cleansed away by his purity in order not to be brought in question at the divine judgment. Therefore after the guilt of all transgressions that hinder man from bringing forth anything pleasing to God has been blotted out, and after the fault of imperfection, which habitually defiles even good works is buried, the good works done by believers are accounted righteous, or what is the same thing, are reckoned as righteous [Rom 4:22].[28]

The climax of the story of redemption is Christ's assumption of our full human nature, by which he stands in our place before the judgment of God and by which he suffers on our behalf. By this he makes us holy before God in actual fact. The gift of the Holy Spirit inaugurates that reality not by dispensing divine holiness into believers but simply (!) by being redemptively and locally present in and to the church. Believers are the new temple (1 Cor. 6:19) of the Holy Spirit, which is to say that the Holy Spirit is really and locally present with them.

The Antinomian Accusation?

Paul's claim that justification accrues by faith alone (Rom. 4) leads him to ask the question: "Are we to continue in sin that grace may abound?" (Rom. 6:1). This question arises at the end of Paul's argument in Romans 5 where he has made the case that human disobedience brings death and Jesus' obedience has brought life. There is no mention in Romans 5 of an instrumental role given to a believer's obedience in the matter of salvation. In Romans 4, Paul makes it clear there is no "boast" to be made by Israelites (or Gentiles) before God. As Romans 2 has proven, it is not merely that there is to be no boast in Israel's privileged status as possessors of Torah, but there is no boast because of their inability to obey Torah.[29] In contrast to earlier midrash traditions that understood Abraham to have been justified on the basis of obedience to God and thereby to have a "boast" before God, Paul argues instead that Abraham believed (in contrast to working) and that he was reckoned as righteous.[30] Faith lays no claim to a boast for the one who exercises it because its hope and trust is in another. Neither Abraham nor his natural descendants, the Israelites, were to be counted as righteous on the basis of their obedience, not because obedience was not requisite to righteousness, but because they were in actual fact disobedient sinners, as were the Gentiles.

Having made the case in this fashion, Paul confronts the natural next question: If obedience cannot bring salvation, then should we disobey and thereby have more of God's grace of forgiveness to enjoy? This so-called antinomian accusation of Romans 6:1 (repeated in Rom. 6:15; 7:7; 9:14) addresses the consequences of their union with Christ. Nowhere in Romans 6 does Paul broach the possibility that the believer's obedience sustains their union with Christ. Christ sustains that relationship. His work (the entire messianic mission) and his continuing mediated presence through the Spirit is the sole ground of their assurance of salvation (Rom. 5:5).

The rhetorical question of Romans 6:1 and 6:15 points at the reality that Christ is the answer to the antinomian accusation. Being united to Christ means being united to his rule and reign as covenant Lord. The church's relationship to Christ is such that his presence continues to fulfill the terms of the covenant in her life. The paradox of sin and grace in the covenant becomes clear as Paul writes in the imperative, "Let not sin therefore reign in your mortal body, to make you obey its passions" (Rom. 6:12).[31] Remembering that "sin" is not an external force, but simply another way of speaking of the self, Paul was saying, "Be free from the rule of yourself."[32] But wherein is the "rule of self" broken? In none other than the presence of Christ as mediated by the Holy Spirit, whose temple is now the gathered believers. It is the temple of the Holy Spirit, not as a function of the causal cooperation of the human will, but because in fact the Holy Spirit is dwelling with his people.[33] In other words, the antinomian accusation is answered by an appeal to the ongoing presence of the Holy Spirit. The accusation is not answered by an appeal to greater moral responsibility on the part of the believer. The anti-antinomian is the one who confesses that Christ lives and those who were formerly dead now live because they are near him. "The death he died he died to sin, once for all, but the life he lives he lives to God" (Rom. 6:10). This exchange (death and life) is made present by the Holy Spirit and has become the sum and substance of sanctification.

Accordingly, the law no longer exercises its judicial function over the believer; it no longer accuses nor rewards. As Paul affirms in 1 Timothy 1:9, "The law is not laid down for the just but for the lawless and disobedient."[34] The law loses its power in Christ. Justification has removed the weight of the law upon believers.[35] There can be no return to the forensic character of the law in sanctification, lest the completed work of Christ be undermined.

What is the nonlegal relationship to the law in which believers now stand? It is a sapiential relationship. The law is now the source of wisdom in the life of believers.[36] It is pedagogical rather than judicial in its function.[37] Wisdom is no less normative than forensically oriented law, but its "force" is surely different. Wisdom celebrates that which is good, and thereby draws its adherents to how (theological) reality works rather than uniquely how one is punished or rewarded.[38] The consequences of (dis)obeying wisdom is not (punishment nor) reward, but rather (dissatisfaction or) satisfaction.

Worship as Wisdom and as Command

It is appropriate to speak of worship as wisdom (Ps. 29) and also to speak of worship as commanded (Deut. 6:4). Remembering that humans are constituted as reflections of that which they worship, the worship of the Living God gives rise to a natural delight of the creature in their creator. Humans are made in such a fashion to find their delight in the One who made them.[39] In the language of the psalmist, the "splendor of His holiness" is the sufficient ground for drawing the human agent into the worship of their creator and covenant Lord.

Worship is also a moral command in the covenant that regulates the relationship of the creator and creature. So the command to love the Lord your God with all your heart, soul, and strength is at the center of the covenant between YHWH and Israel, even as Jesus' summary of the whole law begins with the same command (Mark 12:28–34).

As a kind of wisdom, worship celebrates that which is good, and thereby draws its adherents to how (theological) reality works rather than uniquely how one is punished or rewarded. The central consequence of worship is not reward but satisfaction. Though there is a moral character to worship, moral imperatives do not function in our union with Christ as laws that punish or reward, but rather as principles of worship. They function by virtue of how the created order was made and now how it has been redeemed in Christ.

As an act of corrupted worship, idolatry depicts sin along a spectrum of freedom and slavery.[40] Idolatry asserts independence from God and enslavement to the idols. Worship that arises out of the gospel, by contrast, frees one from the idols and makes one a servant of the Living God. The drama of redemption plays out in part as a drama of competing objects of worship in the "eyes" of human persons.[41] "Eyes" function not only as organs by which one perceives the material world, but also as windows into the human heart through which objects of worship are appraised.[42]

The "worship organ" that Scripture speaks of most is the human heart. It is the place where one's treasures are stored (Matt. 6:21). It is that from which flows every kind of evil (Matt. 15:18). Being given a new heart is to be given a properly functioning disposition to worship YHWH rather than the idols (Ezek. 11:19). This promise of a new heart is the promise of the new creation in which God will recreate his people (Deut. 30:6). That new creation takes place "in Christt" (2 Cor. 5:17) by which God's people are recreated in the image of the Son (Rom. 8:29). The image of the Son is not a reference to the moral character of the Son, but rather a reference to the properly functioning dependence of the Son upon the Father.[43] As an act of the new creation, the gift of a new heart is nothing other than a properly functioning organ to worship God. As God redeems humans, the human heart begins to find delight in that which delights God.

Faith is the theological category that depicts this orientation of delight in the God who redeems. It is not a faith once and done, but rather an ongoing faith which looks to the grace of God in Christ as its only hope. It is sometimes weak, sometimes strong, but in its inner direction, its hope lies outside of itself in the God who redeems. By the presence of the Holy Spirit, the doxological nerve endings have been brought back to life, by means of which they begin to find satisfaction in the covenantal relation to God, and in whom they begin to sense the delight of that which is genuinely good.

Conclusion

In sanctification, it is not a believer's moral progress in view but rather the (relative) restoration of their worship organs. In the Christian life, the moral imperatives of Scripture guide the understanding of worship and many of its attendant consequences.[44] Obedience is motivated not by reward but by delight. Obedience motivated by reward is more nearly a sign of corrupted worship, and so no biblical doctrine of sanctification ought to affirm the "rewards of obedience." This promotes the very "boasting" the New Testament authors reject and the enslavement to self-interest at the heart of most idolatry. By contrast, faith as the enduring orientation, which shuns any "boast" before God, resists rewards as its motivation. It continues to cling to the God who redeems, because that alone satisfies hearts. Grace is sufficient for all of life because *God* is the One who sovereignly extends that grace.[45]

10

SOLA GRATIA AND ITS DILEMMA FOR SOCIAL ETHICS: REFORMATIONAL RESPONSES

Dennis P. Hollinger

Upon hearing the term *sola gratia* we most frequently think of salvation and justification. The common understanding is that human works are of no avail, for only by God's grace can a person be made right with God and receive the gift of salvation. *Sola gratia*, therefore, belongs to the realm of soteriology or the doctrine of salvation.

But for the Protestant Reformers, grace alone pertains not only to salvation but also to ethics. Virtuous character and actions were viewed not as human works achieved by people who had been justified, but rather were themselves a result of *sola gratia*. Because the Reformers by and large saw sanctification as the outworking of salvation in the life of a human, it is only natural that sanctified actions and character were also accomplished by God's grace alone.

Martin Luther, for example, developed his Christian ethics over against Scholasticism with its explicit dependence on philosophy, specifically Aristotle's philosophy as mediated through Thomas Aquinas. Rather than grounding ethics in natural law known by human reason, Luther believed that God's written word formed the guidance and that justification formed the source and motivation for all Christian ethics. Luther said, "Justification of necessity precedes love. One does not love until he has become godly and righteous. Love does not make us godly, but when one has become godly love is the result."[1] Ethical actions and character, then, are an overflow of divine grace made possible through Christ's atoning death on the cross and resurrection.

Early on, Luther and Melanchthon had hesitancy about affirming the third use of the law as guidance for the believer. They affirmed two uses of the law—namely, the civil use to keep sin in check within society, and the pedagogical use to show humans their sin and drive them to Christ. Though the third use eventually made its way into their writings and into the Formula of Concord and the catechisms, their early reluctance and adamant distinction of law from gospel demonstrates their belief that human actions do not flow from any native human capacity.[2] In society, the law did not evoke good actions but merely acted as a restraint on sinful behavior. They feared that even Christian ethical actions too closely linked to the law would throw one back upon oneself and a works righteousness in the Christian life. As Luther put it, "Good works do not make a good man, but a good man does good works."[3] And as Luther wrote in the Heidelberg Disputation, "The law says, 'do this,' and it is never done. Grace says, 'believe in this,' and everything is already done."[4] Thus ethical actions and virtues are an overflow of justifying faith through grace, producing in the believer works that are commensurate with the law of God. Christian ethics is impossible without enabling grace.

For John Calvin, the third use of the law as a guide for believers' lives was explicit and the principal purpose of God's law. But the expression of the law in humans "has respect to believers in whose hearts the Spirit of God already flourishes and reigns."[5] That is, true fulfillment of God's law in human actions depends on something outside of ourselves—namely, God's divine grace enabling justifying faith. In his discussion of regeneration, Calvin writes, "In the conversion of the life to God, we require a transformation not only in external works, but in the soul itself."[6] It is from the divine transformation by grace that new habits form and the sanctifying work of God takes place.

While grace alone produces these works of righteousness, Calvin does recognize that the unregenerate are able to do some good things in the world such as justice, moderation, and kindness. Later Reformed writers would come to call this common grace, meaning divine gifts that God imparts to all people, whether or not they are justified by faith through Christ. Yet, Calvin notes, "They execute these good works of God in the worst manner . . . not by a sincere love of goodness, but merely by ambitions or self-love or some other sinister affection."[7] None of these actions of common grace are sufficient for salvation, and none are true acts of justice, mercy, and love. Those are dependent upon grace alone.

Other Reformers could be added to the list, but it is clear that *sola gratia* for the Protestant Reformers is the source of virtuous actions and character. Ethics is the work of divine grace through Christ.

The Dilemma for Social Ethics

But all of this raises a dilemma for social ethics. If virtuous character and actions are a result of divine grace, then what can we expect in the larger society with those who have not experienced regeneration through Christ? Can human beings without the supernatural effects of redemption and without the regenerative work of the Holy Spirit live ethical lives in society and its varying institutions? If they cannot be ethical without grace, then it raises the question of what standards we can expect for government, economy, and the various professions such as medicine, law, business, and education. How does a society operate without ethics, if indeed ethical actions and character are dependent on God's work of grace in the lives of humans?

These are at the heart of what H. Richard Niebuhr called the Christ-culture questions, or "the enduring problem" of faith and culture.[8] How does Christian ethics relate to the broader culture and society? What are our expectations for society relative to Christian commitments, and how do Christians and the church position themselves within the society and its varied institutions?

These are complex questions encompassing not just theological assumptions but historical and sociological ones as well. Thus it should come as no surprise that the Reformation did not yield a singular answer to the dilemma; that if Christian ethics comes by grace alone, then the expectations for a society are not immediately clear. Essentially, there were four main responses to this dilemma at the Reformation. We will explore each of these responses, suggesting that each has some merits as well as challenges. At the end of this chapter, I will make some modest suggestions on how to proceed in light of our Reformation heritage and in light of the current secular, pluralistic context in which we find ourselves today.

Responses to the *Sola Gratia* Dilemma for Social Ethics

Luther: Two-Kingdom Approach

Martin Luther's response to the dilemma was to posit a framework of two kingdoms, in which there were differing ethical expectations for each kingdom. On the one hand are the kingdoms of this world based on natural orders that God has put in place for all humanity. The natural orders, constituting the earthly kingdoms, are domains of life created by God for the temporal world: government, family, economics, vocation, and at times Luther even puts the visible or institutional church in this sphere. On the other hand, the redeemed order is the kingdom of God, composed of all true believers in Christ, who is king of this kingdom. This kingdom results solely from divine grace and justification by faith.

Luther contended that the gospel or kingdom ethic cannot be applied to the kingdoms of this world. That is, we cannot expect the state or secular businesses to be established on an ethic of Christ's kingdom. The kingdoms of this world are under God's control but are ruled through divinely appointed offices through the natural orders: political leaders, judges, soldiers, business owners, and even parents. This is not Satan's realm, although he is at work in both kingdoms. But the expectations for the offices in these earthly kingdoms, whether the official is a believer or nonbeliever, are different from the expectations for life in Christ's kingdom.

As Luther sometimes quipped, God rules the kingdoms of the world with his left hand and the kingdom of God with his right hand.[9] In the natural realms, even a regenerate Christian may at times need to employ modes of action that would not be found in Christ's kingdom. In one work Luther wrote,

> God's Kingdom is a Kingdom of grace and mercy, not of wrath and punishment. In it there is only forgiveness, consideration for one another, love . . . the doing of good, peace etc. But the kingdom of the world is a kingdom of wrath and severity. In it there is only punishment, repression, judgment and condemnation for the suppressing of the wicked and the protection of the good.[10]

When a Christian through one of the offices of the natural orders carries out earthly kingdom responsibilities, they engage in actions that are different from the ethical guidelines within the kingdom of God. Nonetheless, they are operating under a God-ordained plan and divine expectations. The distinction hinges on a difference between a private person in God's kingdom and a *welt* (world) person in the earthly kingdoms. Luther emphasized that it was imperative that we not confuse these two kingdoms, for we can never turn the kingdoms of this world into the kingdom of God. That awaits the eschaton. In his frequently colorful language, Luther once stated, "Now he who would confuse these two kingdoms—as our false fanatics do—

would put wrath into God's Kingdom and mercy into the world's kingdom; and that is the same as putting the devil in heaven and God in hell."[11]

For Luther, then, we live with a paradox of living in two different spheres with two different sets of expectations. True Christian ethics and righteousness are only through God's grace. But through the orders and offices of the earthly kingdom, we operate with a different but noncontradictory ethic, yet under God's rule. As one contemporary Lutheran theologian summarizing Luther's approach put it, "God is at work in this broken world in two distinct ways, advancing his final purposes through both the temporal realm and the spiritual realm. Each realm has a peculiar sphere of responsibility and concern."[12]

How should we assess Luther's response to the dilemmas raised by *sola gratia* for social ethics? Certainly, Luther is right to recognize two kingdoms and an inherent tension between the two. Historically, attempts to mandate a Christian ethic for the kingdoms of this world have led to a watered-down Christian ethic and frequently a distortion of the faith. The danger of course comes in separating these kingdoms so far that the kingdoms of the world and people operating therein are given carte blanche on their actions. Some historians and critics have attempted to see a link between Luther's two kingdoms and the rise of Hitler's Nazism in Germany. While that accusation has been rejected by many Luther scholars,[13] it does point to the potential danger of separating the kingdoms in such a way that life is dichotomized into secular and sacred realms where faith is separated out from daily and cultural life.

John Calvin: Transforming Culture Approach

Like Luther, Calvin affirmed a twofold government of humanity, but he formulated it in a different way. One kingdom, the divine, relates primarily to the inward person, and the other, the temporal, to the external regulations within society. But Calvin also believed that we can never separate these domains and their requirements too far. As a matter of fact, though true Christian ethics is dependent on grace, there are commonly shared virtues among all humanity that make possible a society with greater ethical achievements than Luther conceived.

The Fall and human depravity do not negate these shared virtues from creation. Such human virtues will not earn salvation, but they do allow for a just, humane society in which God's law is honored, even if only partially fulfilled and out of false motives. Calvin writes, "Since man is by nature a social animal, he is disposed, from natural instinct, to cherish and preserve society and accordingly we see that the minds of all men have impressions of civil order and honesty."[14] All humans apart from Christ can comprehend the laws essential for human society; and while there are wars, thefts, lawlessness, and injustice in society, there is still a natural perception of God's laws to which we can appeal for a well-ordered society.

Human government has been ordained by God not just to restrain evil but also to build the common good. It is clearly distinct from the internal kingdom of Christ, but they are not averse to each other. According to Calvin, the role of civil government is "to foster and maintain the external worship of God, to defend sound doctrine and the condition of the Church, to adapt our conduct to human society, to form our manners to civil justice, to conciliate us to each other, to cherish common peace and tranquility."[15] Calvin went on to argue that its object is "not merely . . . to enable men to breathe, eat, drink and be warmed (though it certainly includes all these, while it enables them to live together)." But earthly government must also ensure "that no idolatry, no blasphemy against the names of God, no calumnies against his truth . . . break out and be disseminated among the people . . . that men may carry on innocent commerce with each other, that honesty and modesty be cultivated; in short that a public form of religion may exist among Christians and humanity among men."[16]

In these assertions, Calvin is arguing that the role of civil government extends in design to both tables of the law. Hence, Geneva was frequently labeled a theocracy, not meaning a rule by the church but by the law of God through civil magistrates. In this framework, Calvin's church in Geneva spoke to political matters, economic life, and punitive justice. The church lifted the ban on usury, hence allowing interest on loans, and directed welfare programs. While the divine law written on human hearts and mediated through civil magistrates could never achieve in humans what God's grace in Christ achieved, nonetheless that law could make a society more civil, just, and humane. It could even facilitate the gospel itself to prosper through civil governments that enabled such flourishing.

How, then, do we assess Calvin's transforming culture approach? Certainly, he rightly takes seriously Jesus' mandate to live in this world as salt, light, and leaven (Matt. 5:13–16; 13:33). This approach affirms a common grace given to humanity for life in a fallen world, which negates some of the worst effects of the Fall. It affirms the goodness of God's creation and the call to care for and cultivate that creation.

But Calvin, in my estimation, is far too optimistic about what can be achieved by government and other institutions of society. He did not sufficiently extend his doctrine of the Fall and human depravity into the realms of the earthly kingdoms. Moreover, Calvin banks on a Christendom model of Christianity that seeks to grant civil preference to the church over other segments of society. Too close an alignment of Christian faith and the social order (politics, economics, etc.) in the long run comes back to haunt the church and historically has engendered mediocrity of faith. We might ask the question: Do we really want the president of the United States, or Congress, or the Supreme Court making theological decisions? Later Reformed documents such as the Belgic Confession were moderated to move away from the theocratic tone of Calvin's transformationist stance.[17]

Anabaptists: Radical Separation Approach

The Anabaptist movement thought the Reformation had not gone far enough in reforming the church. They differed most from the other strands of the Reformation in their ecclesiology, asserting a believers-only church, affirmed by adult believer's baptism, strong church discipline, and a separation of the church from any state sanction, support, or involvement. Their stance toward society reflected a move from what Ernst Troeltsch called a church-type Christianity to a sect-type Christianity. The church type was at home in the world and sought a place of power and influence within social institutions. As Troeltsch in a nonpejorative manner understood it, church-type Christianity dominates the world and as a result is dominated by the world.[18] Sect-type Christians, as exhibited by the Anabaptists, viewed themselves in small voluntary communities, set apart from the world, and frequently over against the world.

The Anabaptists generally assumed a conflict with the two kingdoms, between the demands of Christ and the demands of the state. There is a legitimate role for the kingdoms of the world and their use of the sword and coercion, but the church is called to a different way. The church's ethic, stemming from God's grace and Christ's commands, is an ethic of discipleship, not an ethic of compromise with the world. The conflicts between the Christian ethic and the patterns of the world are real, and the dilemma is found in noncompliance or separation from the world's patterns, including those of government.

The first official statement of the Anabaptist movement was the Schleitheim Confession in 1527 from the Swiss Brethren in Zurich, Switzerland. The separation from society with a distinctive ethic for the church is clear:

> A separation shall be made from the evil and from the wickedness which the devil planted in the world; in this manner, simply that we shall not have fellowship with them. . . . For there is nothing else in the world and creation than good or evil . . . darkness and light, the world and those who have come out of the world.[19]

At the heart of this separation is the rejection of violence, warfare, and even the role of being a magistrate. While God ordained the sword outside the perfection of Christ to curb evil in a sinful world, it has no place in the believer's life. Speaking of governments and their magistrates, Schleitheim states:

> Their citizenship is in this world, that of the Christian is in heaven. The weapons of their battle and warfare are carnal and only against the flesh, but the weapons of Christians are spiritual, against the fortification of the devil. . . . The worldly are armed with steel and iron, but Christians are armed with the armor of God, with truth, righteousness, peace, faith, salvation, and with the Word of God.[20]

The dilemma over *sola gratia* is resolved through a separatist model from the world and most of its institutions. It is an ethic of faithfulness over effectiveness. While later Anabaptists would seek to modify the radical separatism from the world and even seek to be a force for peace within the world, the model retained a strong sense of distinctiveness in terms of the interface of Christian ethics and the institutions of society.[21] Because Christian ethics emanates from grace in Christ, the moral expectations for society and its institutions are quite low.

How do we assess the Anabaptist separationist model? On the positive side, it clearly understands the tension that can and frequently does exist between Christians and the world. The basic Christian assumptions about life and moral responsibility are frequently at odds with the patterns of social institutions and cultures. Moreover, there is no cheap grace in this model, and that is to be lauded. It takes seriously the notion that God's grace is essential for a true Christian ethic.

But the separationist model faces some genuine critiques in light of the whole of biblical teaching and theological reflections. It allows little room for creation gifts and common grace, in which humanity is granted some understanding of God's designs and some enablement to live accordingly. The goodness of creation is minimized, and it fails to take seriously the role of being salt, light, and leaven within the world. Moreover, there is a tendency toward a theological Marcionism, with its appeal primarily to Jesus and the Gospels and the functional minimization of the Old Testament and many of the Epistles.

The Roman Catholic Counter-Reformation: Natural Law Approach

It may seem odd to include the Counter-Reformation in an essay on the dilemma of *sola gratia*, as the Roman Catholic Church did not affirm this doctrine, which was one of the major reasons the Protestant Reformation emerged. Nonetheless, it is helpful to include their approach to culture, as it reflects another way in which even Protestants might respond to the social ethics dilemma. In fact, in recent times various Protestants have been drawn to this ethical tradition.[22]

The Counter-Reformation was the Roman Catholic Church's attempt to counter what was happening in Protestantism, but also to renew the church while reaffirming certain traditional Roman Catholic distinctives. The heart of the Counter-Reformation was established through the Council of Trent, which took place between 1545 and 1563. At this council, they issued condemnations of perceived Protestant heresies, reaffirmed the role of tradition and the theology of the Mass, and codified liturgies to be used throughout the church. From the Counter-Reformation also emerged new movements such as the Jesuits and renewed emphases on spirituality.

In the field of ethics the church reaffirmed and expanded the natural law approach over against the "Protestant erosion" with its emphasis on a strictly biblical ethics. There was recognition that the natural law tradition, formulated primarily through Thomas Aquinas, had at times been wrongly used to accept the societal status quo with injustices, such as slavery and colonial domination. Nonetheless, there was a determination in the Counter-Reformation to defend and build on the Thomistic natural law formulation in engaging the ethical issues of society. It provided a mechanism whereby the church could not only speak to but also maintain significant influence in society, particularly in the political sphere.

Aquinas taught that there are four kinds of law: eternal, natural, civil, and divine. The eternal law of God is the transcendent blueprint in the mind and nature of God. The natural law is the portion of eternal law that all humans can comprehend and follow.

> All things partake somewhat of the eternal law, in so far as, namely, from its being imprinted on them, they derive their respective inclinations to their proper acts and ends. . . . This participation of the eternal law in the rational creature is called the natural law.[23]

The civil law is the enacted law in societies. Because all humans can know natural law, it is possible to build governmental laws consistent with the laws known by reason and intuition. All natural laws pertaining to the common good of a society can be formulated into civil laws. Finally there is divine law, which is the portion of God's eternal law not known by reason or natural processes. The divine law is essentially the revelation given in Holy Scripture, encompassing salvation and the higher virtues of faith, hope, and charity. The cardinal virtues—such as wisdom, courage, temperance, and justice—were known and actuated through the natural law in all human beings.

The natural law approach does not perceive a tension between divine grace and Christian ethics, because Christian ethics is rooted in nature and nature is not antithetical to grace. While *sola gratia* meant for the Reformers that virtuous character and ethics cannot arise from nature or within the person, the Counter-Reformation and natural law tradition argued the opposite, because human nature itself has been "graced by God." As a contemporary Catholic theologian put it, "The Catholic tradition has always been insistent that the grace of God is given to us, not to make up for something lacking to us as human persons, but as a free gift that elevates us to a new and unmerited level of existence."[24] Thus social ethics is not dependent on adherence to a direct biblical standard, though it is not contrary to the biblical standards. Because all humans can know God's natural law, the expectations for government and other social institutions can be consistent with Christian ethics.

How, then, do we assess the natural law response to the *sola gratia* dilemma? We should of course affirm that Scripture supports both a natural revelation and some form of natural law. Writing about the unrighteous, Paul says,

> What may be known about God is plain to them, because God has made it plain to them. For since the creation of the world God's invisible qualities—his eternal power and divine nature—have been clearly seen, being understood from what has been made, so that people are without excuse. (Rom. 1:19–20 NIV)

Additionally, natural law has the advantage that it can articulate a Christian ethic to nonbelievers without their acceptance of biblical authority and the normativity of divine revelation.

The primary Protestant critique of the natural law tradition was its elevated estimation of human capacities. The Counter-Reformation's formulation of natural law saw grace as coming alongside natural human capacity to enable it in achieving its telos. The Reformers accepted a form of natural law that enabled some good in society, but the natural person's motive and achievement of that law was always far from the actual designs of God. Not only was human nature incapable of cooperation with divine grace for salvation, but also of achieving Christian virtues and patterns in life. This semi-Pelagian anthropology is why we needed the corrective of the Protestant Reformation.

We should also note that while many Protestants today find great value in using natural law arguments to defend biblical ethics, these natural law formulations have fallen on hard times in the same way as biblical or theological ethics. The temper of our times has questioned the very notion of givens within the world and the idea that there is an essence to realities such as marriage, sex, or human nature. Hence, both natural law and biblical/theological appeals frequently find opposition to a Christian ethic that affirms givens and essence in the created designs of God.

Conclusion

Given that the Reformation had no unified response to the dilemma of *sola gratia* and social ethics, how are we to proceed today in a complex, pluralistic, secular world? I would suggest that even with strong biblically and theologically informed positions, Christians may not always land in the same place in resolving this dilemma. Our societal contexts will play a significant role in our expectations for the social order and how we position ourselves relative to it. For example, Christians and churches in Islamic societies or in China will face very different options than those in Western democracies or in many countries of Africa. Thus we need a contextualized approach in our strategies that are theologically rooted, but with great wisdom in how to apply the Christian ethic in a given societal context.

It is a biblical given that the church should always be distinct from the culture around it. No fallen culture begins to approximate the full designs of God. The very fact that the church is called to be salt, light, and leaven within the world assumes that the world is frequently at odds with the patterns of Christ and his church. Because of this reality, we are called to live within the world and seek, at a minimum, to embody the Christian ethic in our personal lives and in the Christian community. Escapism from society is not an option for the Christian. But neither is a Constantinian theocracy with its expectations that a society can be Christian with the church at its center of power. Such expectations are contrary to the nature of human fallenness and the call of the church to be salt, light, and leaven. After all, these metaphors do not connote domination but influence from within.

Exactly how we seek to carry out the role of being salt, light, and leaven will likely change from context to context. The temptation to a politicized approach in which we equate Christianity with a particular political ideology or party is a dangerous one. It erodes the unique nature of the Christian ethic, the church, and the gospel. Moreover, we must recognize a difference between our ethical norms and the strategies with which we seek to implement those norms or bear witness to them within the institutions of society. We live in a time in which we have relativized the norms and absolutized the strategies, especially political ones. It ought to be the other way around: our norms from God's word, made possible by divine grace, are absolute. It should be our strategies for implementing those norms within the world that are relative.

All of this stems from the Protestant Reformation's affirmation of *sola gratia*. Salvation is only by grace through faith in Christ. And so is our Christian ethic, even when we sometimes find common ground through common grace with the fallen world around us.

11

God's Common Grace and the Theological Praxis of Counseling

Karen Mason

For many inevitable reasons, like getting licensed, many Christian counselors will deliver mental health services to unbelievers. Someone asked my colleague, "Are you just making people happy on the way to hell?" His question makes Christian counselors ask themselves the question: "Is counseling unbelievers a moral dilemma for Christian counselors or a front-row seat to God's common grace?" To respond to this question, I propose to discuss: (1) The Reformers' definition of common grace; (2) the biblical basis for God's compassion for all his creation; (3) Reformed perspectives on viable occupations for Christians; and (4) the theological praxis of counseling.

How Did the Reformers Define Common Grace?

As Louis Berkhof notes, Luther believed that "fallen man is by nature capable of doing much that is good and praiseworthy in the lower or earthly sphere, though he is utterly incapable of doing any spiritual good."[1]

Calvin, however, differed from Luther in this. According to Berkhof, Calvin "firmly maintained that the natural man can of himself do no good work whatsoever and developed alongside of the doctrine of particular grace the doctrine of common grace."[2] So what is common grace? Berkhof clarifies: common grace "does not pardon nor purify human nature. . . . [I]t curbs the destructive power of sin, maintains in a measure the moral order of the universe, thus making an orderly life possible, distributes in varying degrees gifts and talents among men, promotes the development of science and art, and showers untold blessings upon the children of men."[3]

In the *Institutes of the Christian Religion*, Calvin writes, "In reading profane authors, the admirable light of truth displayed in them should remind us, that the human mind, however much fallen and perverted from its original integrity, is still adorned and invested with admirable gifts from its Creator."[4] He adds, "God, by his providence, curbs the perverseness of nature, preventing it from breaking forth into action, yet without rendering it inwardly pure."[5]

The Synod of Dordrecht in 1618 makes clear that while this common grace allows humans to retain "some knowledge of God, or natural things, and of the difference between good and evil, and shows some regard for virtue and for good outward behavior," it is not saving grace.[6] As Richard Mouw writes:

> In 1924, the [Christian Reformed Church]'s synod issued an official declaration on the subject [of common grace], insisting that there is indeed a kind of non-salvific attitude of divine favor toward all human beings, manifested in three ways: (1) the bestowal of natural gifts, such as rain and sunshine, upon creatures in general, (2) the restraining of sin in human affairs, so that the unredeemed do not produce all of the evil that their depraved natures might otherwise bring about, and (3) the ability of unbelievers to perform acts of civic good.[7]

Louis Berkhof clarifies the difference between common grace and saving special grace:

- Special grace is limited to the elect, while common grace is granted to all people indiscriminately.

- Special grace removes the guilt and penalty of sin, changes the inner life, and gradually cleanses an elect person from the pollution of sin. Common grace never does this, but has only a restraining effect on the corrupting influence of sin and mitigates its results.

- Special grace is irresistible, making an elect person perfectly willing to accept Jesus Christ. Common grace is resistible.

- Special grace works in a spiritual and re-creative way, renewing the whole nature of an elect person. Common grace operates only in a rational and moral way by making people in a general way receptive for the truth, by presenting motives to the will, and by appealing to the natural desires of people.[8]

So, from a Reformed perspective, both the doctrine of total depravity *and* common grace coexist.[9] Richard Mouw cautions that common grace is not "an across-the-board upgrading of our original fallen state"[10] but instead restrains the ruin that would naturally come from humanity's sinfulness.[11]

One last important aspect of common grace is that it is the work of the Holy Spirit.[12] When speaking of common grace, Berkhof has in mind "those general operations of the Holy Spirit whereby He, without renewing the heart, exercises such a moral influence on man through His general or special revelation, that sin is restrained, order is maintained in social life, and civil righteousness is promoted."[13]

This fits with the work of my colleague, Dr. John Jefferson Davis,[14] who notes that the Holy Spirit is active at several levels (and I will illustrate these levels in a counseling context):

- Extraordinary Supernatural (the Spirit's extraordinary, miraculous cure of addiction);

- Ordinary Supernatural (the Spirit's healing over time of behavioral patterns); and

- Natural (the God-created natural healing process of talking through problems).

My working definition of common grace, borrowing largely from Berkhof, is as follows:

Common grace is the work of God the Holy Spirit in curbing the destructive power of sin, maintaining the moral order of the universe, making an orderly life possible, distributing gifts and talents to people, promoting the development of science and art, and showering untold blessings upon all people indiscriminately, and it is not saving grace.

The Biblical Basis for God's Compassion for All His Creation

While common grace encompasses the notion that unbelieving people, gifted by God, speak truth and justice and make orderly life, science, and art possible, it also encompasses the notion of indiscriminate untold blessings.[15] It is not surprising that the Reformers included this notion in their understanding of common grace, because this aspect of common grace flows from God's essential character of goodness and compassion as he relates to all of his creation, not just the covenant community. This is made clear in Psalm 145:9.

> The LORD is good to all;
>   he has compassion on all he has made.[16]

Blessing All His creatures

What will strike careful readers of Scripture is that God in fact is the One who makes people happy on the way to hell. He apparently bestows common grace gifts to people who are under the sentence of death.[17] Berkhof writes,

> Cannot God have compassion even on the condemned sinner, and bestow favors upon him? The answer need not be uncertain, since the Bible clearly teaches that He showers untold blessings upon all men and also clearly indicates that these are the expression of a favorable disposition in God which falls short, however, of the positive volition to pardon their sin, to lift their sentence, and to grant them salvation.[18]

This is clear throughout the Bible:

> He makes grass grow for the cattle,
>   and plants for people to cultivate—
>   bringing forth food from the earth:
> wine that gladdens human hearts,
>   oil to make their faces shine,
>   and bread that sustains their hearts.
>   (Ps. 104:14–15)

> The eyes of all look to you,
>   and you give them their food at the proper time.
> You open your hand
>   and satisfy the desires of every living thing.
>   (Ps. 145:15–16; see also Acts 14:16–17)

"And should I not have concern for the great city of Nineveh, in which there are more than a hundred and twenty thousand people who cannot tell their right hand from their left—and also many animals?"
(Jon. 4:11)

Do I take any pleasure in the death of the wicked? declares the Sovereign LORD. Rather, am I not pleased when they turn from their ways and live? . . . For I take no pleasure in the death of anyone, declares the Sovereign LORD. Repent and live!
(Ezek. 18:23, 32)

He causes his sun to rise on the evil and the good, and sends rain on the righteous and the unrighteous.
(Matt. 5:45)

"Jerusalem, Jerusalem, you who kill the prophets and stone those sent to you, how often I have longed to gather your children together, as a hen gathers her chicks under her wings, and you were not willing."
(Matt. 23:37)

"But love your enemies, do good to them, and lend to them without expecting to get anything back. Then your reward will be great, and you will be children of the Most High, because he is kind to the ungrateful and wicked."
(Luke 6:35)

As we have opportunity, let us do good to all people, especially to those who belong to the family of believers.
(Gal. 6:10)

God Has Other Goals in Addition to the Salvation of the Elect

Richard Mouw argues that the reason God does good to all people and asks us to do good to all people is that God is not only interested in doing good so that people will ultimately come to him,[19] or because he can't help blessing the nonelect as he blesses the elect, but because he cares for more than people's eternal destinies. He writes,

The underlying view I am endorsing here posits multiple divine purposes in the world. To state it plainly: I am insisting that as God unfolds his plan for his creation, he is interested in more than one thing. Alongside of God's clear concern about the eternal destiny of individuals are his designs for the larger creation.[20]

Part of Mouw's statement is based on his infralapsarian perspective where "first God decided to create the world; then God decided to permit the fall; only after these decrees did the divine decision occur with regard to election and reprobation. Thus God's electing and reprobating purposes were subordinate to, or 'infra,' the decision to create a world that would come to be plagued by sin."[21] He goes on to argue that "it is quite fitting for us to feature a similar multiplicity in our own theologies."[22]

God Is Well-Disposed toward the Well-Being and the Relief of Suffering of His Creatures

Our theology must feature God's goodness and compassion, which result in untold indiscriminate blessings and which spotlight his positive disposition toward the well-being of his creatures and the relief of their suffering. Mouw states, "We ought actively to *promote* 'the joy and hope' and to *diminish* 'the grief and anguish' of our fellow human beings, regardless of their election or reprobation."[23] One of the ways believers do this is by seeking the *shalom* or well-being of the people around us.

SHALOM

In Jeremiah 29:7, the exiles are told to "seek the *shalom* of the city to which I have carried you into exile. Pray to the Lord for it, because if it has *shalom*, you too will have *shalom*." *Shalom* is translated "peace and prosperity" or "welfare."[24] We are to seek the *shalom* of the whole city, even the *shalom* of unbelievers, because *shalom* curbs the destructive power of sin and makes an orderly life possible.

Where God gives *shalom* and where people seek *shalom*, there is peace and prosperity (Ps. 72:1–7), safety (Ps. 4:8), healing (Isa. 57:19), and good relationships between people (Gen. 26:29; 1 Chron. 12:17–18).

KINGDOM OF GOD

God is also positively disposed to relieving the suffering of his creatures. For example, in Luke 17:11–19, Jesus heals ten lepers. As Richard Mouw points out, we must face up to "a few stubborn and massive facts":[25] only one of ten lepers came to faith, even though Jesus healed all of them.[26]

Relief of the suffering of his creatures was a sign of the in-breaking of the kingdom of God. Jonathan Pennington explains that in the New Testament the kingdom of God is not only *from heaven* but is also *heavenly*;[27] that is, it is radically different from all earthly kingdoms and will replace them on the earth.[28] Jesus proclaimed this kingdom of God by *feeding and healing* people, and he sent out his disciples to do the same. Mouw adds, "If God's deep love for humanity persists even despite the effects of sin, then the theology of common grace is an important resource for our efforts as Christians to respect and reflect that love."[29] We see this clearly in the Gospel accounts:

> "Heal the sick, raise the dead, cleanse those who have leprosy, drive out demons. Freely you have received; freely give." (Matt. 10:8)

> He sent them out to proclaim the kingdom of God and to heal the sick. (Luke 9:2)

> So they set out and went from village to village, proclaiming the good news and healing people everywhere. (Luke 9:6)

I am not suggesting that Christians are ushering in God's kingdom to earth by helping people heal from their disorders. Our citizenship will always be in heaven (Phil. 3:19–20; Col. 3:1–4). But alleviating human suffering is part of the proclamation of the kingdom of God.

The early church apparently understood this, because it was focused on alleviating human suffering: Christians stayed in the cities to care for the sick in the Antonine Plague (the Plague of Galen AD 165–180) and in the Plague of Cyprian (AD 250–266). On Easter Sunday in AD 260, Bishop Dionysius of Corinth said:

> Most of our brother Christians showed unbounded love and loyalty, never sparing themselves, and thinking only of one another. Heedless of danger, they took charge of the sick, attending to their every need and ministering to them in Christ, and with them departed this life serenely happy; for they were infected by others with the disease, drawing on themselves the sickness of their neighbors and cheerfully accepting their pains.[30]

This focus on alleviating human suffering was not limited to caring for the sick. Tertullian wrote:

> Every one puts a little to the public stock, . . . and all these collections are deposited in a common bank for charitable uses, . . . for feeding the poor and burying the dead, and providing for girls and boys who have neither parents nor provisions left to support them, for relieving old people worn out in the service of the saints, or those who have suffered by shipwreck, or are condemned to the mines, or islands, or prisons, only for the faith of Christ.[31]

While we could give countless examples of Christians working to alleviate suffering throughout the centuries, more recent powerful examples are the missionaries in the nineteenth and twentieth centuries who brought medical care, education, and orphanages to the world.[32] Their aim was "not only to restore the wholeness violated by sin or disease, but to preserve it, ensuring that, so far as human science can assist the action of the grace of God, preventable ills shall be prevented."[33]

Medical missionaries were motivated by the belief that all people had "a sacred right to life temporal and life eternal, and to conditions of life, if not a little lower than those of angels, at least a little higher than those of beasts of the field."[34]

> In many of the missionaries' minds there grew up the conviction that physical effects could not be isolated from mental and spiritual causes, but that cause and effect, ignorance and suffering, sin and pain, were so closely knotted [sic] together that no single approach would ever be sufficient.[35]

In summary, within the Reformed notion of common grace, God indiscriminately blesses all his creatures. In the Old Testament, we read that the exiles sought the *shalom* or well-being of their city, and in the New Testament, we read that Jesus healed and fed the people as evidence of the in-breaking of God's kingdom. The church throughout the ages has understood this common grace to include alleviating human suffering. But there is one more aspect to the Reformers' notion of common grace: perspectives on viable occupations for Christians.

Reformed Perspectives on Viable
Occupations for Christians

My brother worked at L'Arche at Cuise la Motte/Trosly-Breuil, founded by Jean Vanier, which is dedicated to living in community with people with intellectual disabilities. He lived in community with folks who could not understand or accept the gospel. Was my brother's ministry of common grace a viable occupation for a Christian, given that it was not focused on the salvation of the severely disabled?

Luther was key in breaking down the distinctions between clergy and laity and laying the foundation for what would become known as the Protestant Work Ethic, the belief that lawful vocations were means to serve God.[36] But would counseling unbelievers be a viable occupation? Richard Mouw gives this example:

> Take the case of a Christian therapist counseling a nonbeliever couple whose marriage has been seriously wounded by the husband's adulterous affair. The therapist helps them to be honest about the hurts and fears and angers that have surrounded the infidelity. Finally, a moment comes when the husband tearfully acknowledges the pain he has caused and asks his wife to forgive him. She reaches out with a newfound tenderness toward him. They embrace, both of them sobbing. It is clear that they intend to build a new life together. They have not been "saved" in the process, but the therapist is convinced that she has witnessed—and has been privileged to be a human instrument in—a powerful display of healing grace. She senses that she has reinforced the kinds of behaviors and attitudes that God wants for human beings.[37]

From my vantage point, the Christian counselor was administering God's common grace to this couple: helping to curb the destructive power of the sin of adultery and a broken relationship, helping to maintain the moral order of a marriage covenant, making an orderly life possible because stable marriages are the cornerstone of a stable society, and administering the precious blessing of God's *shalom* on this couple and participating with the healing work of the Holy Spirit.

But there is more. Going back to our definition of common grace, the Reformers also noted that God distributes gifts and talents to people, promoting the development of science and art. This Christian counselor was not just salt and light (Matt. 5:13–16) with this couple, but she was also salt and light within the occupation of counseling. As Dr. Christopher Cook has said, there is a vital need for counselors who are informed with sound theology to shape the counseling profession and, in turn, society. Christians are needed to preserve what is good about counseling, the science that God in his common grace has allowed to develop, and society as a result. Within the Reformed perspective, we find this emphasis in neo-Calvinists such as Abraham Kuyper and classical Calvinists such as David VanDrunen.

Abraham Kuyper

Dutch theologian Abraham Kuyper (1837–1920) emphasized the work of God's common grace in superintending nonbelievers' discovery of God's truths through science.

> God himself developed his own divine plan for this construction, created the geniuses and talents for implementing that plan, and directed the labor of everyone and made them fruitful so that what he wanted and still wants would indeed become reality.[38]

We need to realize "on the one hand, the darkening of our understanding by sin, and on the other hand, God's common grace that has placed a limitation on this darkening."[39] Kuyper suggests that the darkening is because unbelievers do not apprehend the deep meaning of science. "Sin's darkening lies in this, that we lost the gift of grasping the true context, the proper coherence, the systematic integration of all things."[40] This reminds me of Elizabeth Barrett Browning's poem:

> Earth's crammed with heaven,
> And every common bush afire with God;
> But only he who sees, takes off his shoes;
> The rest sit round it and pluck blackberries.[41]

It takes Christians to see that blackberries are evidence of God's magnificent work of creation and that counseling is an evidence of God's intentional blessing of all his creatures, and his superintending of the discovery and development of the science of counseling as one means of alleviating human suffering.

David VanDrunen

David VanDrunen, the Robert B. Strimple Professor of Systematic Theology and Christian Ethics at Westminster Seminary California, argues from the vantage point of Christians living in two kingdoms:

> [Christians] rejoice to be citizens of heaven through membership in the church, but also recognize that for the time being they are *living in Babylon*, striving for justice and excellence in their cultural labors, out of love for Christ and their neighbor, as sojourners and exiles in a land that is not their lasting home.[42]

He is adamant that believers can be in any lawful occupation as part of this Babylonian kingdom:

> This two-kingdom doctrine strongly affirms that God has made all things, that sin corrupts all aspects of life, that Christians should be active in human culture, that all lawful cultural vocations are honorable, that all people are accountable to God in every activity, and that Christians should seek to live out the implications of their faith in their daily vocations.[43]

VanDrunen also emphasizes that our work in the common kingdom will necessarily be done with unbelievers. "Christians are not summoned to withdraw into their own cultural ghettos, but their cultural activities are intertwined with those of the world at large."[44] He gives the example of Daniel and his friends who became Babylonian political officials.[45] He also emphasizes Paul's message to the Corinthians:

> I wrote to you in my letter not to associate with sexually immoral people—not at all meaning the people of this world who are immoral, or the greedy and swindlers, or idolaters. In that case you would have to leave this world. (1 Cor. 5:9–10)

VanDrunen rejects the notion that working with unbelievers is just to evangelize them.[46] He also specifies that though our work is not eternal, it is important work:

> Many recent books on Christianity and culture target sayings such as "you don't polish the brass on a sinking ship," which some people use

to denigrate cultural work based upon the idea that it's all about to be destroyed anyway. Such sayings are indeed unhelpful and misleading, . . . our cultural products themselves are not meant to endure into the world-to-come. They belong to the stuff of the present world. Contrary to what some people suggest, we are to spend time on things that do not last. We are like the Israelite exiles, who built homes and planted gardens in Babylon, though they knew they would leave there after seventy years.[47]

In summary, all lawful work is a means to serve God, and cultural endeavors, such as science, are evidences of God's common grace. Laboring in the realm of counseling is honorable and will likely be done with unbelievers. And in this work, Christian counselors are accountable to God as they critically engage with the cultural endeavor of counseling.[48]

The Theological Praxis of Counseling

The theological basis for praxis as a Christian counselor working with an unbeliever is common grace. When I counsel a depressed unbeliever, I am participating in God's intentional pouring out of his grace on all of his creatures indiscriminately. I am working to alleviate human suffering. I am seeking the *shalom* of my city. I am demonstrating what the kingdom of God looks like. I am participating with God to curb the effects of sin, because depression results in broken relationships, occupational difficulties, and sometimes the devastation of suicide. I am helping to maintain the moral order by preventing depression from developing into substance abuse that may result in crimes such as selling drugs. I am making an orderly life possible when the depressed person returns to work and reconnects with family. I am using God's gifts to me and promoting the development of science as I do research.

Counseling Is a Front-Row Seat to God's Common Grace

Of course, as Mouw points out, the "vulnerability of infralapsarians"[49] (those who assert that God showers his grace on his whole creation) is that we can end up with a "'limp-wristed theology' that appropriates psychological themes in order to cater to the needs of a generation of self-actualizers."[50]

In order for the concept of common grace to not devolve into a twenty-first-century psychological lovefest, we need boundaries. Going back to our definition, common grace is not about self-actualization. It's other-focused, not self-focused. It is also not about me. It is God's common grace with which I participate to help others experience the indiscriminate untold blessings of God. I am dependent on God's grace and accountable to him, and I need to engage my culture critically.

Conclusion

In the theology of common grace, the Reformers gave us a basis for explaining what we all see—that the world is not as evil as it could be—a basis for the practice of counseling, and a basis for praising God for his great and unexplainable[51] love, compassion, and goodness that he graciously showers on all his creation.

The Superiority of Grace in Missions: A Comparison of Grace and Works in Christianity and Islam

Paul T. Martindale

Communicating the gospel in other cultures and among people of other world religions often leads to dialogues in which both sides are enriched. People of other cultures ask different questions from different worldview perspectives. Many times in the process of listening to their questions, we see for the first time new aspects of a theological issue enlarging our understanding and giving us a perspective beyond the limits of our culturally bound understanding. In its engagement with the world, mission often creates theology, new insights can sometimes confirm the hard work of biblical scholarship, and new areas are identified that must be examined from new angles of inquiry. This has been true in dialogues with Muslims over the years. What I intend to discuss here is a comparison of grace and works within the two theological systems of Islam and Christianity. The theological view of redemption in Islam is often characterized as a form of salvation by works in need of a reformation.

Missiology should demonstrate the articulation of biblical scholarship into specific cultural and religious contexts in such a way that it becomes understandable without distortion. It is my hope that this case study will show how the fruit of Reformation theology has been applied in the case of works and grace in a modern Muslim context.

Role of Works

One principle of effective witness with Muslims is listening and allowing them to identify the issues they find important in the discussion.[1] It is

then up to us to formulate our biblical understanding for them in response
to their questions. At a dialogue meeting between Muslims and Christians
on the topic of salvation, the role of works became central in the discussion.[2] The two main objections expressed by the Muslims present centered
on the apparent lack of works necessary for salvation in Christianity and the
carte blanche Christians seem to have for sin in their lives after conversion.
The easy grace of God in Christianity for the believer appeared to these
Muslims as a license or an excuse for sinning, since sin can be so easily
forgiven without believers working for it. This was a principle that they did
not find congruent with Islam and could not accept as an expression of authentic biblical Christianity. After listening to their objection, we were able
to formulate the following description to clearly portray the role of works
in salvation and show them that grace was not an automatic excuse for the
Christian to sin without regard to the consequences. Both the Muslims and
the Christians present were in agreement on the following formulation for
the role of works:

ISLAM

Faith + Works + Allah's Mercy = Salvation

CHRISTIANITY

Faith + Grace = Justification + Works

In Islam, the combination of three factors results in salvation: the faith
of the believer (the public declaration of the *shahada*), the works or deeds
of the believer, and Allah's mercy at the point of judgment. Islam teaches
Muslims that they will stand on their own on judgment day and that their
good deeds must outweigh their bad deeds. In Christianity, the role of
works is on the other side of the equation. For the Muslim, works are an
instrumental part leading to salvation. For the Christian, works grow out of
justification as a response to the grace one has received from God. Quoting
from Romans 3:28, we explained that we are justified by faith "apart from
observing the law." Citing verses from the book of James, we contended that
works are demonstrated in the life of the believer as a normal consequence
of regeneration.[3] James even stated that someone who claims to be saved but
does not demonstrate a changed life has a dead faith (2:22, 24). Thus works
are the evidence of authentic conversion and accompany conversion, even

though works play no instrumental role in earning our justification. Justification plus works must appear together in the believer's life as an authentic sign that the faith plus grace on the other side of the equation are genuine.

As a result of this formulation, the Muslims present were able to see that the role of works is taken seriously in Christianity, since works is the fruit and the evidence of justification and submission to God. Our Muslim friends were also able to see that the Christian does not have blanket permission for sinning at will, as this would call into question the veracity of the person's salvation as well as his or her submission to God. For the Christian, works, as the sign of an authentic conversion, also lead to assurance of salvation that is absent in Islam except for martyrs who die in a *jihad* defending Islam. Therefore, a biblical theology of works as the evidence and assurance of salvation in the believer's life may be very attractive to a Muslim who seeks to understand and compare his or her faith to our own. On the flip side, it was obvious that the Muslims present at the dialogue meeting did not respect a Christianity where works have no role or importance in salvation. Since works are so important in the Muslim's life, they needed to compare this to Christianity as a primary criterion; they were not able to take seriously a Christianity where the view of grace overwhelms and obscures the necessity of works.

Much of the Muslim's misunderstanding on this point may be the result of contact with nominal Christianity and our informal Western practice of "lifestyle" faith. A more formal and ritualized practice of Christianity would be more attractive to many Muslim seekers than what they see as the loose and careless informal Christian practice of most Westerners. Viewing us through their Islamic framework, they often equate this with a lack of commitment and dedication, calling into question the authenticity of the Christian faith and reinforcing their view that Islam was given to replace and update a corrupted Christianity.

Our dialogue with Muslims forced us to clarify our theology of works. The biblical emphasis we place on faith and grace in salvation is certainly appropriate. However, this is not true when it is taken to the extent that the role of works in the life of the believer is ignored or becomes extinguished in our theology or praxis. For Muslims, this appears to be a central issue, and they need to see how the role of works is affirmed in Christianity. Therefore, it is essential that we understand the role of works clearly and are able to articulate it well with Muslims in a way that helps them take Christianity seriously.

Islam's Concept of Salvation

In order to discuss the concept of grace in Islam, we must first understand Islam's concept of salvation and search for equivalent words for grace. In Islam, the idea of salvation is expressed in the Arabic word *falāḥ*, which means "well-being," "welfare," or "prosperity." The meaning of *falāḥ* is that salvation is accomplished within history in the Islamic nation or *umma* (community). Salvation was accomplished by Allah's "sending down" his revelation and establishing his true religious community. It is granted to a person when he joins that community and lives according to the "religious law." Religious, political, and social action are seen as Allah's saving work. Salvation is consummated only when, at the judgment, Allah forgives people their sins on the basis of deeds they performed according to the law and their reliance on God.

The Islamic view of salvation differs radically from that of the Bible. The choice of the word *falāḥ*, meaning "well-being," rather than the Arabic word *khalāṣ* is significant. *Khalāṣ* would be the word closest to the biblical idea of salvation meaning "payment," "deliverance," "liberation," or *fidā*, which signifies "redemption." Islam denies that humanity needs to be saved in the biblical sense of salvation from sin's guilt or power. Hence, the key elements of the biblical doctrine of salvation are excluded.

Concepts in Arabic similar to biblical salvation would be:

1. *Khalāṣ:* liberation, deliverance, rescue, salvation, redemption from a captor, payment, settlement

2. *Fidā:* redemption, ransoming, sacrifice (*Mufādāh*), price, redeemer (*Fādin*)

3. *Naja:* to save, be rescued, be delivered, to bring to safety, deliverance or release (*najan*); escape, flight, rescue, salvation, redemption, safety. The word *Naja* occurs more than sixty times in the Qur'an in its verb form; thus it is the activity of redemption and salvation described as dynamic and action oriented.

Despite the presence of these equivalent words in Arabic for salvation, the formula representing Islam uses the word *rahma*, or "mercy." This is the primary way that Muslims think in terms of the salvation of the individual. After declaring the *shahada* and cultivating good deeds, the Muslim believer then hopes that Allah will decide to be gracious or merciful to them at the time of judgment. The choice of the word *raḥma* is directly related to the Islamic doctrines of humanity and sin, which we will examine next.

Doctrines of Humanity and Sin

The problem of sin, and the corollary concept of grace, is rooted in the doctrines of humanity and sin in Islam. According to Islam, humanity was created basically good but a little weak and forgetful. Adam's sin in the garden is therefore considered a *lagish* (slip or mistake) and without *irāda* (intention). For a sin to be serious, it must have been done deliberately. Even then good works can outweigh intentional sin. The mercy of Allah is therefore a matter of whether the sin is counted against the person or not. Compared with the doctrine of sin in Christianity, the sinfulness of human nature is not a problem that requires divine help in Islam. Humanity is basically good and we can save ourselves by our own works if we attempt to live in submission to Allah's revealed law (*shariah*).

Islam teaches that human nature is intrinsically good; indeed, we are born Muslim (Surah 30:30 calls Islam "the endowment of God [*fitrat Allah*] with which He endowed mankind"). Muslims vehemently reject the Christian teaching that humanity is sinful by nature. They believe that human nature is perfectible, and this is where Islam comes in. Its absolute monotheism is said to "purify the individual's moral character."[4]

According to Abd-al-Rahman Azzam:

> Of greatest effect has been the belief in the one supreme God. . . . This belief perfects the human spirit, liberates it, and directs it toward the common welfare and the all-powerful God Who controls the destiny of all things and judges acts by the intention that motivates them, of which He is aware. With this belief Muhammad pointed out the path to virtue.[5]

If sin is not serious and humanity is not sinful, then a costly grace that satisfies divine justice is not required. What then really is *raḥma* or mercy in Islam? It is the decision or whim of Allah at the point of judgment either to accept or not accept the believer's works or hold the Muslim believer accountable for their evil deeds. The concept of mercy in this context is reduced to Allah looking the other way for the sins of some and not for others. Allah is free to do as he wills in each particular case without being held to a standard or reference of justice or righteousness because his ways are inscrutable.

This doctrine is closely associated with two other Islamic teachings concerning human nature that can be subsumed under the belief in humanity's perfectibility. The first is Islam's belief in the essential goodness of humanity, and its concomitant rejection of the biblical doctrine of a moral fall. According to Hammudah Abdalati, author of a manual widely used to promote Islam in the United States,

> The idea of Original Sin or hereditary criminality [sic] has no room in the teachings of Islam. Man, according to the Qur'an (30:30) and to the Prophet, is born in a natural state of purity or fiṭra, that is, Islam or submission to the will and law of God. Whatever becomes of man after birth is a result of external influence and intruding factors.[6]

To achieve perfect "submission" to Allah, it is believed that we only need divine "guidance" (*hidayah*) to enable us to know the will of Allah and to live in obedience to it. Muslims reject the Christian teaching that humanity needs salvation from sin.

The Christian Doctrine of Humanity

In evangelical Christianity, humanity is created in God's image but separated from the life of God and intrinsically sinful. God created man in his own image and, like him, without sin. However, by his decision to disobey, man submitted himself to Satan rather than to God, was separated from the life of God, and his nature became marred by sinfulness. Consequently, he is subject to the wrath of God and to death. He is in no way able to merit his salvation by his own efforts.

Three important conclusions follow from our belief in "original sin." Contrary to what Islam teaches, humanity is not born Muslim, human nature is not perfectible in this life, and divine "guidance" is not sufficient to make a person submissive to God's will. No one will reach perfection until the resurrection of the body at the second coming of Jesus Christ.[7]

The doctrine of original sin does not mean that people are totally evil, or "hereditary criminals" as Muslims often describe it. Far from it! From a human perspective, we might be basically good, but from God's perspective we are still sinful by nature. Even the best of us find ourselves "not able not to sin" (*non posse non peccare*), as the famous saying of Saint Augustine puts it.[8]

The predicament of humanity is much more serious than Islam imagines. By denying the "witness of their conscience" to the law written on their hearts (Rom. 2:15), Muslims are repressing the knowledge they have by nature. This serves to obscure the biblical understanding of salvation, grace, and works. Islam in general and the Qur'an in particular are good examples of a theological system that suppresses the knowledge of the necessity of an atonement. Muslims believe that people are born Muslim (submitted), essentially good, and perfectible, and that all they need is divine guidance to become submissive to God.

The Doctrine of God

Several aspects of the doctrine of Allah in Islam bear directly upon the Muslim's understanding of salvation. Allah is absolutely free and unrestricted, even in the realm of truth and morality. He is free to "abrogate" the truth or obligations of earlier revelations by subsequently revealed truths and obligations. He is free to judge the same act to be "good" in one circumstance and "evil" in another according to the situation, although in principle acts are "good" or "evil" according to whether they are commanded or forbidden in the Qur'an. The criteria by which Allah judges and assigns man his destiny are unknowable to man. He is free to forgive the sinner or to condemn him. He is free to do the opposite "as he pleases."

Allah is not holy or righteous in the sense of loathing and separating himself from sin. In Islam, the moral attributes of holiness and righteousness are not applicable to Allah; this would imply likeness to humanity and would compromise Allah's transcendence. For Islam, Allah is separated from us because he is totally different from us (a metaphysical separation), not because he is holy and we are sinful (a moral separation). Hence, humanity's separation from God—which, according to the Bible, is abnormal and intended to be temporary—is considered by Islam to be normal, absolute, and eternal.

Allah is not thought of as binding himself by covenant to do certain things for humanity. This apparently would contradict his freedom to do "as he wills." The Bible, in contrast, declares God to be a covenant-making and covenant-keeping God. He can be counted on to keep his covenant.

Allah is unknown and unknowable to man, both in this life and in the next.[9] Apart from *tanzīl* (Allah sending down revelation to us), we can know nothing about Allah or his requirements of us. For Islam, transcendence means it is impossible to know anything positive about Allah. There is an uncrossable gulf between man and Allah, which makes a personal knowledge of Allah a metaphysical impossibility. This conflicts with the biblical teaching that we have an intuitive knowledge of Allah and his law, and of our own guilt (Rom. 1–2), because we are made in God's image. The Bible teaches a creator-creature distinction that will never be erased, but it does not carry this to the extent of complete dissimilarity and unknowability. Islam makes this distinction to mean essentially that Allah is unknowable to man.

The word the Qur'an uses to describe the action of Allah in the salvation of the individual is *rahma*, which can be translated as "mercy," "kindness," and "compassion." Allah is described as the *Ar-Rahman*, the merciful, the kind, and the forgiving. Another of the ninety-nine names of Allah is *Ar-Ra'uf*, the gracious, the one who bestows boundless clemency, tenderness, and affection. *Ra'uf* is described as the ultimate limit of *rahma*.[10] In light of the doctrine of Allah, however, this mercy is limited in its application to some and not to others, as Allah wills. This mercy is not applied consistently with regard to any standard of justice, righteousness, or holiness.

The theological differences with Islam that come into play for our discussion are as follows:

1. The Fall of humanity included a moral separation from God.

2. Humanity's nature became corrupted as a result of the Fall.

3. Humanity is unable to save itself by its own works.

4. The seriousness of sin is rooted in the nature of God. God cannot excuse or overlook evil.

5. All sin in the Bible is against God.

6. Submission in Islam and Christianity are different. In Islam, submission is the path to salvation. In Christianity, however, submission happens after union with Christ and justification, and it is evidenced through good works done in response to God's grace rather than done to earn it.

The Role of Grace

In the simplified formula we diagrammed earlier for the Muslims present at our meeting, we stated that in Christianity faith plus grace equals justification plus works. This was sufficient for the initial presentation of this concept to the Muslims. I would now like to expand on this formula and present the following equation:

Faith + Grace > Justification + Works > Salvation[11]

To be a little more descriptive of the process of redemption, we should specify that faith plus grace leads to the state of justification plus the presence of works as the evidence of a genuine conversion and justification. Salvation will be determined on the basis of whether our works are genuine, reflecting the true state of justification from the grace we have received in Christ. John Piper says it this way, "I believe in the necessity of a transformed life of obedience to Jesus by the power of the Spirit through faith as a public evidence and confirmation of faith at the Last Day for all who will be finally be saved."[12] Or we might simply say that the state of our post-justification works is the basis for our final judgment. "Justifying faith is not merely alongside good works, but is also the agency employed by the grace of God to give rise to good works."[13] In Ephesians 2:10, we are told that we are created in Christ Jesus to do good works and that God has prepared these works for us in advance.[14] As Craig Keener says, "Good works flow from what God does in us, rather than God's work in us flowing from our works."[15] We can wholeheartedly affirm *sola gratia*—that salvation comes only by grace. The fact that faith is the vehicle through which grace is applied to us, and that post-justification works are the basis of judgment, does not in any way undermine that the sole foundation of salvation is the unmerited grace of God through the atoning work of Christ.

The differences between Islam and Christianity in the understanding of grace and works can be traced to the different views in the doctrine of God, the doctrine of humanity, and the doctrine of sin. These doctrines in the Islamic theological system serve to obscure and undermine the need for salvation by grace through the atonement. Since humanity is thought to be basically good, without original sin, and perfectible, the need for redemptive atonement is denied.

Conclusion

In Islam, Allah's mercy is applied unevenly to some and not to others "as Allah wills." It is also applied quite apart from the satisfaction of divine justice and righteousness, since "Allah can do whatever he wills." One person's faith and works can be accepted and another's not. Since no one knows the standard by which Allah's decisions are made, the basis of his judgments are not knowable to us and he cannot therefore be accused of being unfair or unjust.

In the Christian understanding, we will all be judged by the same standard according to our works, and at the same time none of us will ultimately be saved on the basis of our works. God's mercy is that we do not receive the penalty and judgment that our sins deserve, and that a way has been provided for the redemption of everyone. This mercy comes to us as a result of the costly and perfect sacrifice through the unlimited atonement of Christ. God's mercy does not come at the expense of justice or independently from it. Justice and mercy are both completely satisfied. At the root of Christianity, justification is a costly grace perfectly meeting all the requirements of divine justice. In Islam, mercy is applied unevenly without any reference to Allah's righteousness, holiness, or justice—which are deemed unknowable. It is also applied by a weakening of the seriousness of sin, a denial of universal (original) sin from Adam and Eve, and an unrealistically high view of humanity, who is thought to be created basically good and perfectible. The theological system of Islam denies our depravity and our rebellion against God, the seriousness of sin, and the justice and righteousness of a Holy God.

Five hundred years ago, Christianity in Europe was captive to a rigidly controlled state church where indulgences were sold and forgiveness for sins was by works of penance and obedience to the church. A renewed understanding of costly divine grace broke the European church out of this model and gave birth to the stream of reformation. Islam is still waiting for its reformation. A new understanding of divine grace would need to displace the concept of a salvation without justification by faith and grace alone and a mercy without justice. As we have seen, however, these are firmly rooted in the Islamic views of Allah, humanity, and sin—which would all have to be reformed.

The superiority of grace in missions is that our works come in grateful response to the wonderful and undeserved justification imputed to us that we were not capable of attaining ourselves. The superiority of grace in missions is that our works done in obedience are empowered by the Holy Spirit living within us, and therefore they are able to give God glory since they originate in the work of the Spirit in us. The superiority of grace in missions is that our post-justification works are worship to God, thanking him for his grace to us. The superiority of grace in missions is that our works serve to make God's grace visible in the world around us. The superiority of grace in missions is that this mercy has perfectly satisfied all the requirements of divine justice and righteousness and has therefore made our salvation sure. This is much more than human constructs of mercy; this is a divinely wrought grace that has come down to us, which lives in us, which produces works of righteousness, and which points others to a loving, just, righteous, and merciful God. *Sola gratia.*

Sola Fide:
By Faith Alone

13

"By Faith"? Ongoing Translation Issues (Five Hundred Years after the Reformation)

Roy E. Ciampa

The meaning of "faith" (Greek: *pistis*) has been of critical importance since the beginning of Christianity. It was stressed by Jesus himself (Matt. 8:10; 9:2, 22, 29; 15:28; 17:20; 21:21; Mark 2:5; 5:34; 10:52; 11:22; Luke 5:20; 7:9, 50; 8:25, 48; 17:6, 19; 18:8, 42; 22:32), and then became a central theme in much of the writings of the apostle Paul and other apostolic and post-apostolic writers. Its importance was reiterated in a forceful manner by the Protestant Reformers, and its meaning has been part of academic and inter-confessional debate ever since. In light of the importance of *sola fide* (faith alone) for the heritage of the Reformation, continuing debates about the meaning of *pistis* (the Greek word corresponding to the Latin *fides*) certainly merit our attention as we celebrate the anniversary of the start of the Reformation.

Luther himself instigated a translation debate relating to Paul's teaching about faith/*pistis* when his extraordinarily influential translation of the New Testament in 1545 rendered Romans 3:28 as "So halten wir es nun, daß der Mensch gerecht werde ... *allein* durch den Glauben" ("Thus we hold that a man is justified ... by faith alone"). Luther justified the inclusion of the word *allein* (alone) on the basis that it was required to properly communicate Paul's intent in German. Still, I'm not aware of any other German translation (or translation in a modern language) that does something similar. Remarkably, the one place in the New Testament where the expression "faith alone" does appear is James 2:24, which asserts that a person is not justified by faith alone (*ouk ek pisteōs monon*).[1]

The translation of Paul's texts about faith has continued to raise interpretive and translation issues through the centuries, and perhaps never more so than in the past several years. Here I intend to provide a brief overview and reflection on recent debates and some questions they raise for translators.

Faith or Faithfulness?

As far as English translation is concerned, the most enduring debate has been about whether the Greek word *pistis* (translated "faith" or "faithfulness"), when modified by a reference to Christ in the Greek genitive case (thus "*pistis Christou*"), should be translated "faith in Christ" or "the faithfulness [or faith] of Christ." The same question may be asked about many places where *pistis* appears separately from references to Christ.

As far back as 1650, Edward Leigh suggested the Latin translations *Fides* (faith) and *Fidelitie* (fidelity) as the first two options for the word.[2] Greek-English lexicons have historically indicated that "faith" and "faithfulness" (or "loyalty") are two possible (and seemingly exclusive) meanings for the Greek word *pistis*.[3]

Translation issues are also raised in light of the fact that a key text for Paul's discussion of faith is Habakkuk 2:4, where the word *pistis* was used by the ancient Greek translation for a Hebrew word (*'ĕmûnâ*), which entailed ambiguities of its own but which most likely referred to God's faithfulness.[4]

Richard Hays's published doctoral dissertation has served as the most impactful argument supporting the view that *pistis Christou* should be understood as a reference to Christ's faithfulness.[5] Hays's study argued (among other things) that understanding the narrative framework Paul used to understand the gospel makes it clear that Christ's own faithfulness is what is referred to in the *pistis Christou* passages, with believers' *pistis*/faith a response modeled on and elicited by Christ's own faithfulness. Hays's influential study took a rarely suggested minority viewpoint and turned it into a major contender with an ever-growing number of supporters within the academic community.

N. T. Wright—like Hays, one of the most influential New Testament scholars of this generation—is one of many convinced by Hays's argument.[6] The New English Translation Bible (NET, 2006) translates the *pistis Christou* texts as "the faithfulness of Christ," as does the more recent Common English Bible (CEB, 2011) and the recent translation of the New Testament by David Bentley Hart.[7] Examples from various translations will be given after the following section.

Of course, many scholars remain unconvinced. The book edited by Michael Bird and Preston Sprinkle, *The Faith of Jesus Christ: Exegetical, Biblical, and Theological Studies*, contains important essays by scholars taking various positions on the subject, and is the best place for someone to enter into the discussion for the first time.[8]

Allegiance (or Loyalty)?

Theologian Matthew W. Bates has recently made his own recommendation for a change in the translation of *pistis* as it relates to salvation or justification. Writing at a more semi-popular level than the other publications addressed in this essay, Bates's proposal is reflected in the main title of his book *Salvation by Allegiance Alone*. He argues in light of recent scholarship on *pistis* (and building on that scholarship) that the English word "allegiance" would be a better translation for the word normally translated "faith," at least in contexts where salvation or justification by *pistis* is being discussed. That is his way of getting to the element of loyalty associated with the Greek word in interpersonal relationships: "The Greek word *pistis* and its rough Latin equivalent, *fides*, had sociopolitical overtones of loyalty to the emperor (or other patrons) as well as reciprocity in receiving benefits in exchange for demonstrated loyalty."[9] He argues that "although *pistis* does have dimensions of interiority (emotion, cognition, and virtue) in the NT, it does not denote an interior movement of the will in the NT era. . . . Rather it is primarily an outward manifestation of trust or loyalty."[10]

Bates is reacting to the fact that in contemporary Christianity, "faith" is often taken to amount to nothing or little more than mental assent that the gospel is true, or that Christ saves, or just to a passive trust. In his view, "If we synthesize the biblical data, we discover that saving allegiance [his interpretation of *pistis*, traditionally translated "faith"] includes three basic dimensions: *mental affirmation* that the gospel is true, *professed fealty* to Jesus alone as the cosmic Lord, and *enacted loyalty* through obedience to Jesus as the king."[11]

Not all reviewers have been convinced. While generally receptive to many of Bates's points, New Testament scholar Tom Schreiner's review argues that "'allegiance' puts the emphasis squarely on the human subject—on what we do, on our commitment. 'Allegiance' captures the importance of subsequent good works, but it leaves something out as well, for faith is fundamentally *receptive*."[12] So "the term 'allegiance,' . . . though helpful in some respects, puts the accent at the wrong place." Kelly Kapic suggests that Bates's recommendation to translate *pistis* as "allegiance" "raises potential misunderstandings," possibly failing to distinguish "between faith and what is entailed by faith."[13] Kapic suggests that Bates's "solution to one problem gives rise to others," including the question: "When . . . have I shown enough allegiance?" Unfortunately, he fails to mention that Bates has a section of his book addressing that concern.[14]

The point about potential misunderstandings deserves some further attention. In fact, the nature of human language and of translation between languages and cultures is that there is always the potential for misunderstandings. There have clearly been differing understandings of what "faith" means or entails, with many contemporary Christians having a reductionistic understanding of what faith is. And, yes, translating *pistis* as "allegiance" (or "faithfulness") will have the potential for new and different misunderstandings, as all alternative translations do. And some will prefer the potential misunderstandings of one option over the potential misunderstandings of an (or any) alternative. From a translation theory perspective, there may be various reasons why one may or may not want to produce an alternative translation for a key term or expression. Among other grounds, in a situation where readers have a false sense of familiarity—an inappropriate perception that they understand a term or concept better than they actually do, where domesticating translations have allowed them to assume that the concept familiar to them is the one to which the text refers—a foreignizing translation[15] that makes them wonder if they have missed something may be considered desirable. A translation that causes the reader to think twice and wonder what is going on in the text, rather than assuming their pre-understanding should remain unchallenged, may be called for. This is not an argument for "allegiance" or "faithfulness" versus "faith," but a reminder that different situations may call for different translation strategies. We will return to questions raised by translation theory again further below.

Faith, Faithfulness, or Allegiance? Translations Compared

In the following sets of translations, the New International Version (NIV) is included as an example of a traditional translation of *pistis Christou* (though the 2011 edition now includes alternatives in footnotes). Other translations noted below include the New English Translation (NET), the Common English Bible (CEB), David Bentley Hart (DBH), and Matthew Bates (MWB). The key expressions have been placed in italics.

Galatians 2:16

- **NIV:** "A person is not justified by the works of the law, but by *faith in Jesus Christ* . . . that we may be justified by *faith in Christ*." [Footnote: Or, *But through the faithfulness of the justified on the basis of the faithfulness of*.]

- **NET:** "No one is justified by the works of the law but by *the faithfulness of Jesus Christ* . . . that we may be justified by *the faithfulness of Christ*."

- **CEB:** "A person isn't made righteous by the works of the Law but rather through *the faithfulness of Jesus Christ* . . . that we could be made righteous by *the faithfulness of Christ*."

- **DBH:** "A human being is vindicated not by observances of Law but by *the faithfulness of the Anointed One Jesus* . . . we might be vindicated from *the faithfulness of the Anointed*."

- **MWB:** "A person is not justified by works of the law but through *the allegiance of Jesus the Christ* . . . in order to be justified by *the allegiance of the Christ*." [Footnote: Or, through *allegiance to Jesus the Christ*; by *allegiance to the Christ*.]

Galatians 2:20

- **NIV:** "I live by *faith in the Son of God*."

- **NET:** "I live because of *the faithfulness of the Son of God*."

- **CEB:** "I live by faith, indeed, by *the faithfulness of God's Son*."

- **DBH:** "I live by *the faithfulness that is of God's Son*."

- **MWB** "I live by *the allegiance of the Son of God*." [Footnote: Or, by *allegiance to the Son of God*.]

Romans 3:22

- **NIV:** "This righteousness is given through *faith in Jesus Christ* to all who believe." [Footnote: Or, *through the faithfulness of.*]

- **NET:** "Namely, the righteousness of God through *the faithfulness of Jesus Christ* for all who believe." [Footnote: Or, *faith in Christ.*]

- **CEB:** "God's righteousness comes through *the faithfulness of Jesus Christ* for all who have faith in him."

- **DBH:** "And, by *the faithfulness of [Jesus] the Anointed*, God's justice is for everyone [as well as upon everyone] keeping faith."

- **MWB:** "The righteousness of God through *the allegiance of Jesus the Christ* for all who give allegiance."

The differing translations, and the footnotes that accompany some of them, remind us of multiple ongoing issues. First, translations that stay with "faith" or "faithfulness" consistently render the term "faith" when it is understood to refer to something manifested by believers and "faithfulness" when it is understood to refer to something manifested by Christ himself. Second, while fine scholars are divided over whether *pistis Christou* should be translated one way or the other (e.g., "faith in" or "faithfulness of"), they reflect a growing awareness that their preferred translation is not necessarily the best translation and certainly not the only reasonable translation. We also note that in Bates's translations, he consistently suggests rendering *pistis* as "allegiance," whether it is understood to refer to Christ's own allegiance or to the believers' own allegiance to Christ (and that interpretive question appears to be unresolved for him).

What could potentially be lost in weighing all these exegetical and translation options is that many readers and scholars will work from the unquestioned assumption that one of these proposed options is undoubtedly *the right* interpretive option that actually communicates the same thing(s) that would have been communicated by Paul's Greek texts. But given the natural differences between various languages and cultures, it is just as likely that there is no exact English (or other) equivalent to what the Greek would have communicated, even if scholars could agree on exactly what that was.

Faith and Faithfulness?

Several scholars have suggested (especially recently) that our understanding of *pistis* is probably best not reduced to either "faith" or "faithfulness" (or, one might add, "loyalty," "trust," or "allegiance"). In the past it was sometimes suggested that both faith and faithfulness were in play in a few occurrences of *pistis*, based on the somewhat questionable idea of a "plenary genitive"[16] intended to evoke both of the (normally exclusive) options (believers' faith in Christ and Christ's own faithfulness). Recently, however, several scholars have suggested that the word *pistis* itself, in perhaps a majority of its occurrences, points to a Greek cultural concept entailing a combination of trust, trustworthiness, faith, faithfulness, and loyalty when referring to persons and the relationships between them.

While, as indicated earlier, N. T. Wright is a strong supporter of translating *pistis Christou* as "the faithfulness of Christ," he has also sought to distinguish more generally between what modern readers typically mean by "faith" and what he thinks *pistis* meant to Paul. He distinguishes between "the modern sense of 'faith' as 'religious belief'" and faith for Paul, which was "much closer to 'the Messiah's "faithfulness" to the divine Israel-purpose' than the split between 'faith' and 'faithfulness' in western theology (and modern English usage) would indicate."[17] Elsewhere, he argues that believers in Christ "are to be the people marked out by *pistis*, 'faith' or 'faithfulness' or, better, both."[18]

The fullest argument supporting the idea that *pistis* tended to entail elements of both what we would call "faith" and what we call "faithfulness," "trustworthiness," or "loyalty" is that of Teresa Morgan's important, sweeping, and detailed study *Roman Faith and Christian Faith*.[19] In this book, Morgan notes that "trust and trustworthiness, trustworthiness and faithfulness, are all always implicit in [*pistis*]."[20] That is, "Greek speakers understand the operation of *pistis* (and Latin speakers that of *fides*) in general as always double-ended, and as incorporating both trust and trustworthiness, faithfulness and good faith, and so on."[21] She argues that, linguistically, *pistis* "is an action nominal, encompassing both active and passive meanings of its cognate verb (such that, for instance, both 'trust' and 'trustworthiness,' 'credit' and 'credibility' are always implicated in it)."[22] Morgan points out:

Pistis and *fides* have been found operating at every socioeconomic level, between individuals and groups. In some sense they always involve reciprocity, because they always involve relationships, but it has also been pointed out that their reciprocity is commonly asymmetrical.[23]

Furthermore,

The inescapable reciprocity of *pistis/fides* means that within relationships of *pistis/fides*, power (encompassing all kinds of status and authority) never runs all one way. . . . That being so, it is worth noting that Greek and Latin texts tend to avoid referring to the *pistis/fides* of both parties to a relationship in the same text or passage.[24]

This linguistic and cultural phenomenon of a reciprocity that tends to be only assumed or implied rather than made explicit is a reminder to translators that source and receptor languages and cultures will often have such nonequivalent dynamics. In translating the language of *pistis*, a translator should pay attention to what aspects of relational commitments tend to be assumed rather than made explicit in the receptor language.

The observation that *pistis* is always reciprocal in some way but that "texts tend to avoid referring to the *pistis/fides* of both parties to a relationship in the same text or passage" raises a question about her suggestion that we should understand *pistis Christou* "as simultaneously Christ's faithfulness to God and human faith in Christ."[25] In fact, she suggests Paul's use of *pistis Christou* in Galatians 2:16 may "capture his sense of the doubly reciprocal relationship of Christ with God and humanity, his sense of the place of Christ in the overarching relationship between God and humanity and his sense of the quality of Christ, his faithfulness, trustworthiness and trustedness by God and human beings, which makes his saving activity possible."[26]

But if both sides of the *pistis* relationship are not normally referenced in the same text, then would it be more likely for an ancient Greek reader to understand Paul to be referencing one part of the *pistis* relationship, with the other part remaining merely implied and understood but not actually explicitly evoked?

In light of Morgan's observations and arguments, it is interesting to note that a quick survey within the biblical Greek reminds us how often love and faith(fulness) are mentioned together in ways that may point to their being overlapping ways of referring to interpersonal commitments (between God and his people or within the people of God).[27] A subset of those texts suggests that the nature of the reciprocal relationship is frequently marked by the use of the language of faith/faithfulness on one side (usually the subordinate side) and the language of love on the other, with a common enough pattern being to describe a person as "faithful and beloved."

In these expressions, the person's own faithfulness is expressed alongside an expression of the love to which that faithfulness seems to reciprocate. These seem like good examples where reciprocal relationships are not expressed in terms of *pistis* on both sides (although, as Morgan argues, it is probably understood), but in terms of love coming from the superior to the subordinate and faith or faithfulness from the subordinate to the superior.[28] Similar, perhaps, is the expression "faithful friend" where, as Louw and Nida put it, a *philos*/friend is a "person with whom one associates and for whom there is affection or personal regard"[29] (so they are beloved, as suggested in the term *philos*, and faithful). In John 3:16, the relationship between God's love for people and their act of putting their faith in him fits with this broader pattern. Coming back to the question of *pistis Christou* in Paul, we may see this pattern in Galatians 2:20, where Paul says he now lives by faith in the Son of God or by the faithfulness of the Son of God, who loved him and gave himself up for him.[30] Does the *pistis* mentioned in Galatians 2:20 suggest the faithfulness of the Son of God, with the added mention of his loving and giving himself for us reinforcing the point, or is it more likely that Paul is referring to his own faith in and faithfulness to the Son of God as a reciprocation of the Son's faithfulness that is not explicitly spoken of in those terms but rather in terms of his love and self-sacrifice?

Here are my interim and provisional conclusions from my own weighing of Morgan's study. First, I understand that references to *pistis* between people (human and/or divine) suppose a reciprocal relationship of trust and trustworthiness. As Morgan puts it,

> The Janus-faced quality of *pistis* enables Paul to capture the qualities and practices of both partners in each simple relationship, and of both ends of each relationship in more complicated configurations with more partners. Trust and trustworthiness, trustworthiness and faithfulness, are all always implicit in it.[31]

So I do not need to find explicit references to Christ's faithfulness to understand that it is assumed as part of the conceptual background.

Second, in light of Morgan's study, I understand that Paul *may* be (somewhat) countercultural when he refers to the faith and faithfulness found on both sides of a relationship (although this was not usually done in Greek and Latin literature), or he *may* be avoiding such explicit references to faith/faithfulness on the part of the superior (Christ) and leaving it to be understood or, in some cases, referring to it as love or other terms (as in the final clause of Gal. 2:20). By all (or most) accounts, Paul is ambiguous in the *pistis Christou* passages, which makes it more difficult (for me at least) to decide whether an ambiguous reference to Christ's reference would count as conforming to or pushing beyond the normal linguistic practice in Greek and Latin literature.

With all that being said, I still tend to think that the combined evidence suggests that, while he is sometimes somewhat ambiguous, Paul understands the relationship to be one of mutual faith/faithfulness (as the use of *pistis* language tended to suggest in any case), but he puts somewhat heavier (and certainly less ambiguous) emphasis on the faith/loyalty that believers have toward Christ,[32] since that is repeatedly emphasized in the unambiguous statements that indicate who is exhibiting *pistis*. Neither we nor the ancient readers can/could be sure whether the ambiguous statements should be read similarly or differently from the unambiguous ones.

Hermeneutical and Translation Issues

Of course, when it comes to translating the text of the New Testament, one scholar's conclusion of what they deem most probable is not a solid foundation on which to build. Nor, I would suggest, is the consensus of any particular translation team. In this final section, we will pivot from discussing earlier translation debates and recent exegetical issues to focus on how translators might engage with all of the issues raised so far.

What Does "Faith" Mean?

Meaning leaks. Meanings of words, expressions, and associated concepts evolve over time, and translations and the terms they use are not anchored to ancient mind-sets and cultural cognitive frameworks. The translation issue addressed here is not confined to the translation of *pistis*, or to translation into English (as opposed to other languages), but it reflects the fact that terms in receptor languages of translations rarely have precisely the same meanings to begin with as the biblical terms they are used to translate. And over time, the words used in those translations take on new and different meanings and associations. So, "faith" (or *fé, fe, foi, Glaube,* or whatever the traditional translation may be in innumerable other languages) may or may not have had similar associations and a similar range of meanings as *pistis* when the term was originally chosen as the preferred "equivalent." Over time, the understanding of the translated term evolves in light of cultural developments and dominant traditional teachings where the term is used. An obvious case is the word "baptism," which appears in virtually all English Bibles but is understood quite differently by readers depending on their religious tradition (it could be the immersion of adults or the sprinkling or pouring of water on infants).

Biblical scholar John Barclay has helpfully shown how Jews and Christians have interpreted the word(s) for "grace" (or "gift") in a wide variety of ways, with certain emphases becoming dominant in particular periods or theological traditions.[33] Similarly, the word "faith" has come to mean different things to different people. What Christians think "faith" is and means will differ according to what they hear or read about faith, depending on the most influential teachers and preachers in their tradition. For many people today, it has come to mean merely "cognitive agreement" divorced from any volitional or behavioral commitment or manifestation.[34] This may especially be the case in some Protestant/evangelical contexts where "faith" has been understood to stand in direct antithetical opposition to "works" or "doing" (and the latter have been associated with Roman Catholic or any non-Protestant theology), rather than in opposition to a particular understanding of covenantal requirements of the Mosaic Law in some forms of Jewish theology in Paul's day.

The key issue may not be whether (in English) one translates *pistis* as "faith," "faithfulness," or "allegiance," but recognizing that any of those words (or another choice) has the potential to be filled with different meanings as interpretive traditions evolve over time. Those who criticize Bates's argument for "allegiance" sometimes do so because they fill the word with a meaning other than the one Bates himself has in mind, revealing again that the solution is not necessarily to find the one "right" word for the translation, but to recognize the extent to which interpretive tendencies or traditions govern the reading of whatever word is chosen.

One of the possible dangers of having settled on one way of translating a biblical term and staying with it for centuries is that, like a frog in a kettle, the meaning of the translation term can slowly develop and readers assume their current understanding (however it has evolved) remains precisely the same

as that of ancient readers/hearers. It may well be that there is no better translation for *pistis* in many New Testament passages than "faith" (or, in some
contexts, "faithfulness"). But one possible advantage of people being exposed
to translations that do things a bit differently (e.g., translating *pistis* as "allegiance" rather than "faith," or *pistis Christou* as "Christ's faithfulness" rather
than "faith in Christ") is that it can alert pastors and other readers that there
may be something going on with the word beyond what they had tended
to assume. And depending on how they preach and teach about "faith," the
word may come to have greater nuances associated with faithfulness, loyalty,
or allegiance, or readers may read "faith in Christ" or "the faithfulness of
Christ" and think that the expression has something to do with both.

In later interviews about his argument for "allegiance" as a translation
of *pistis* in his book *Salvation by Allegiance Alone*, Bates acknowledges that
influencing people's understanding of "faith" may be a more important (and
realistic) goal than actually changing the word typically chosen to translate
pistis in most translations:

> I wish I had been clearer that my argument really hinges on the pres-
> ence of the "embodied loyalty" nuance with regard to the *pistis* word
> group (not in all passages, just in certain ones). That is, it does not
> ultimately turn on whether or not "allegiance" (or the like) is the single
> best translation of *pistis* or *pisteuō* in any given passage. . . . My point
> is that loyalty or allegiance is part of the semantic range of the word
> *pistis*, so when we are speaking about Jesus the Christ, it is problematic
> to evacuate allegiance entirely—which is not quite the same thing as
> saying allegiance is the best translational choice.[35]

In another interview, he rightly points out that influencing the understanding of *pistis* for future Bible readers is an endeavor that "can only start
small and grow—one disciple telling other disciples. Hopefully Bible translators will begin to consider how to better convey the allegiance nuance that is
embedded in the *pistis* word-group too."[36] Whether or not he is right about
the nuance of allegiance (and to the extent that his argument overlaps with the
insights of Teresa Morgan, I think he is right that there is such a nuance), he
is right that the understanding of *pistis* in the future—whether translated as
"faith," "faithfulness," "fealty," "allegiance," or some other term—will depend
not just on the term selected but on the meaning given by influential preachers, teachers, scholars, and other leaders over an extended period of time.

How to Translate a Term for Reciprocal (although Asymmetrical) Interpersonal Commitments

Established "key terms" in translation (such as "faith") will of necessity push interpretations in particular directions (which by now may well be considered the only appropriate and acceptable directions by the community), especially as interpretive traditions take hold in the vernacular. But those directions would not be the only directions allowed or suggested by the biblical texts, and they will almost certainly not reflect the same network of cognitive assumptions, associations, and cultural expectations.

Morgan's study strongly reinforces earlier suggestions that New Testament uses of *pistis* relate to the term's background in reciprocal (though asymmetrical) interpersonal relationships and the commitments they entail. Ceslas Spicq, among others, pointed in the direction of interpersonal relationships, writing, "*Pistis* . . . always implies confidence, which is expressed in human relationships as fidelity, trust, assurance, oath, proof, guarantee."[37] More recently, Moisés Silva has pointed out that "already in its earliest uses the word group appears in contexts having to do with an agreement or bond. The terms have a social orientation."[38]

Especially in the case of Bible translation for languages where there is not already a standard translation for *pistis* that is unlikely to be overturned, translators should keep in mind the relationship of *pistis* with such a social orientation and association with interpersonal relationships. They would do well to consider terms related to (mutual) interpersonal commitments, confidence, integrity, reliability, loyalty, allegiance, and trustworthiness. Due consideration should be given to the translation possibilities and the hermeneutical potential of various translation options in diverse contexts and hermeneutical traditions.

Translators should consider the viability of terms and expressions from a wider range of semantic domains, especially semantic domains related to interpersonal commitments entailing trust, and not begin with or limit themselves to semantic domains related to intellectual convictions, trust related to inanimate objects, or religious beliefs. It will often be the case that no term or domain will be a perfect match for the Koine Greek terms and expressions. A term may need to be not only adopted but also adapted, and filled over time with content and associations that approximate those of the Greek term *pistis*.

In cases where a traditional translation for *pistis* is well established but may have lost important nuances that attached to *pistis*, translators may have opportunities to introduce more information into glossaries, footnotes, or other paratextual materials so as to enrich the traditional term with more of the nuances of interpersonal commitments associated with *pistis*.

Conclusion

Faith (or *pistis*) has been a crucial theme for biblical (and especially Pauline) teaching for almost two thousand years. It has been even more central to Christian (and especially Protestant) theology since the time of Martin Luther and the Reformation. And yet, five hundred years after the start of the Reformation, we continue to grow in and debate over our understanding of the term and how best to translate it and the expressions in which it is used. Discussions of faith have served both to unite and to divide communities of faith over many centuries. At times, our translation choices may either unnecessarily reinforce traditional divisions or deflect from helping readers understand some associations that would have been intuitive in the original/ancient context. Any translation will tend to close off some interpretive possibilities and open others up. Translations of *pistis* (and teaching on those translations) that reflect the semantic domains of embodied interpersonal commitments will open up different understandings than those that relate simply to the domain of an interior religious affirmation.

Given the importance of *sola fide* for the Protestant and evangelical traditions, any potential advancements in our understanding of *fides/pistis* are always relevant and worthy of our attention. If there is any tradition that should recognize the importance of the careful translation of language associated with interpersonal relationships, it might be the evangelical tradition with its emphasis on the importance of a personal relationship with Christ. Perhaps it is part of the genius of the evangelical tradition that its emphasis on faith is so closely tied to its emphasis on the importance of having a personal relationship with Christ. The growing recognition that the language of *pistis* is fundamentally the language of reciprocal interpersonal commitments should find a particularly welcome home in the evangelical strain of the Reformation tradition and in its thinking about the continuing debates about translating "faith" in the twenty-first century.

$$14$$

FIDES QUAE CREDITUR? THE NICENE BACKGROUND TO THE REFORMATION

Donald Fairbairn

I often tell my students that our natural tendency in dealing with historical materials is to read backward rather than forward. By this I mean that we tend unwittingly to read a given historical concept in light of what has been done with that concept subsequently, rather than understanding it in light of its own background. This tendency, I suggest, is manifest in the way contemporary Protestants treat the ancient creeds, and our way of reading the creeds in turn leads us to miss part of their significance. I would like to argue that reading the creeds in light of the distinction between *fides quae creditur* ("the faith which is believed") and *fides qua creditur* ("the faith by which it is believed") masks the major function of the creeds (especially the Nicene Creed), a function that was crucial as background to the Reformation.

Fides Quae, Fides Qua, and the Creeds

As articulated by Protestant theologians, the distinction between *fides quae creditur* and *fides qua creditur* highlights the "what" and the "how" of faith. *Fides quae* refers to what one believes, to the content of one's faith. This focus on content derives from Jude 4, in which Jude uses the arthrous noun *he pistis*, "the faith," to refer to the Christian faith as a body of beliefs. In contrast, *fides qua* focuses on the trust by which one believes the body of doctrine. This way of thinking about faith is based on Galatians 2:16 and similar passages, and Protestants highlight the contrast between this faith/trust and works of the law.

From this starting point, Protestants tend to view the creeds as focusing on the "what," the body of doctrine. Because we believe that the creeds—in

particular, the Nicene Creed—emerged in the midst of theological controversy, we see their place as the articulation of the central doctrines of
the faith. This way of conceptualizing the creeds is shown by the way we
commonly frame them. Protestant traditions that recite a creed in public
worship typically introduce that recitation with the question, "Christians,
what do you believe?"

When we conceptualize the creeds as short statements of the content of
our faith, they may make us more than a little uncomfortable. The creeds
bother us, first of all, for what they seem to omit. Where is *sola scriptura* in
the creeds? Where is *sola fide*? Where is justification? If the ancient creeds
were supposed to lay out for us the content of our faith, then they seem
to have done a rather incomplete job of it. But in the second place, and
maybe even more significant, the creeds disturb us for what they include.
Regarding the affirmation of "the holy catholic church" in the Apostles'
Creed, Haddon Robinson once wryly commented that as a boy, he couldn't
understand why we were giving the Catholics so much free press every
Sunday. And even after we get our minds around a proper understanding
of the word *catholic*, the Nicene Creed's affirmation of "one baptism for the
remission of sins" surely gets us upset. In addition, I have encountered one
Protestant blogger who even objects to the seeming uncertainty of starting
with "I believe" or "we believe," rather than asserting hard facts with no
room for argument.

As a result, we Protestants may be embarrassed by the creeds' prominence in the church's historic worship patterns. We may not recite them at
all, or if we do, likely only the Apostles' Creed. Our congregations may know
the Nicene Creed only by name and the Athanasian Creed not at all. Most
important, we may see the recitation of the creeds as being at odds with
the Reformation's recovery of genuine Christianity, as a vestige of Roman
Catholicism that didn't sufficiently disappear. We may wish the creeds were
more like the Reformation confessions that we know and cherish: more
comprehensive, more detailed on key Protestant distinctives, more obviously shaped by Scripture, and less "Catholic."

Behind the *Fides Quae*/*Fides Qua* Distinction

I suggest, however, that our discomfort with the creeds does not derive
from any problems with the actual documents. (This is not to say that they

are all of equal worth. I believe the Nicene Creed is superior to the Apostles', and I would place the Athanasian Creed in a distant third position after those two.) Rather, the creeds bother us because we are unconsciously reading them "backward," in light of the later distinction between *fides quae* and *fides qua* that would have been foreign not only to the framers of the creeds in the patristic era, but to the early reformers as well. To state this plainly, I do not believe that the creeds' troubling omission of key doctrinal concepts is actually a problem, because I don't think the creeds were meant to be about the "what" of the Christian faith, at least not directly. Please let me explain.

The distinction between *fides quae creditur* and *fides qua creditur* is sometimes traced back to Augustine in the fifth century, although he did not use either of those phrases in the sense in which we take them today. Aquinas (thirteenth century) is also cited as a proponent of this distinction, although the former phrase never occurs in his writings and the latter phrase only once. Indeed, Luther and the sixteenth-century reformers were also unaware of such a distinction, and the contrast between *fides quae* and *fides qua* was absent from Catholic or Protestant literature until the early seventeenth century.[1] Olivier Riaudel, to whom I am indebted for the history of this distinction, summarizes aptly: "One does not speak of *fides quae creditur* until one begins to represent the object of faith in terms of 'content,' of 'doctrine' in the modern sense."[2]

So for the sake of argument, let's set aside the schema of "what we believe" and "the trust by which we believe it," and take a closer look at "faith" and Christian identity.[3] At the very heart of the Christian faith lies not an ethical system (as important as that is), nor a set of commandments (although there are many of those), nor even a set of doctrines (although they too are important), but a *name*. Peter tells the Jewish leaders, "There is no other name under heaven given among men by which we must be saved" (Acts 4:12).[4] Following Jesus' command, new Christians are baptized "in the name of the Father and of the Son and of the Holy Spirit" (Matt. 28:19). Indeed, by calling ourselves "Christians," we are *naming* ourselves after Christ, our Lord. The most important thing about us is not what we do, or even *what* we believe per se, but *to whom we belong* as shown by the one *whose name we bear*.

Furthermore, the one to whom we belong is also the one *in whom we believe*. Paul writes to the Romans, "If you confess with your mouth that Jesus is Lord and believe in your heart that God raised him from the dead, you will be saved" (Rom. 10:9). This simple statement includes a fact that we believe—that God raised Jesus from the dead—but even more fundamental is its confession of who it was that God raised from the dead. He was and is the Lord. Therefore, at the most basic level, being Christian involves *confessing who Jesus Christ is* in relation to God, affirming that we belong to him because we *bear his name*, and *believing the fundamental truths* of his history—his incarnation, life, death, and resurrection. What we do grows out of what we confess, which grows out of the one to whom we belong and in whom we believe, the one by whose name we are called. If we think about Christian identity in this way, then we may be able to see that the ancient creeds were not meant as comprehensive declarations of what we believe. They were and are more like pledges of allegiance to the one in whom we believe, the one to whom we belong and by whose name we are called.

The Origin and Purposes of Creeds

Thinking about creeds in terms of "in whom we believe" rather than "what we believe" per se, let's look behind the Arian controversy (the Nicene Creed's immediate background) to the deeper background of that creed and others. Let's consider the origins and original purposes of the creeds.

The Primal Creed-like Affirmation

It is persuasively argued that the initial source of all Christian creeds was a statement from well over a millennium prior to the time of Christ and the apostles. In Deuteronomy 6:4, the Lord says through Moses, "Hear, O Israel: The LORD our God, the LORD is one." Of course, this is not actually a creed, since a creed is a statement *by the people* about the God in whom they believe, whereas this is a statement from God *to the people*. Nevertheless, one can argue that this statement functioned as a creed, focusing Israel's attention on the one, undivided God in whom they believed.

As the nations around Israel conceived of the world, it was controlled by a host of gods and goddesses, none all-powerful, who competed with one another for power over the cosmos and the people in it. Human life was thus perceived to be a bewildering task of guessing which god to appease at which time, so as to gain the smoothest passage through the chaos of the world. To make matters even worse, people were never sure whether the gods wanted them to be here at all—many origins accounts saw this world as an accidental byproduct of a primordial clash between gods. In vivid contrast to these jumbled accounts of the world and of humanity's place within it, the first words of the Bible proclaim, "In the beginning, God created the heavens and the earth" (Gen. 1:1). There was, in fact, no jumble of gods fighting one another, no guesswork for humanity about which gods to try to placate. There was only one God, present in the beginning, who made absolutely everything that exists outside of himself. The Shema of Deuteronomy 6 is the explicit affirmation of what is implicit in Genesis 1:1—there is the one true God, and everything else is below him. The Bible is in effect drawing a hard line between God on one hand and all else that exists on the other.

This metaphysical line is ineradicable and unbridgeable, and its presence shapes everything about the Jewish (and later Christian) faith. We are in a *dependent* position with respect to God the Lord. We do not try to bend him to our will; we exist to serve his will. We do not manipulate him; he directs us. But we are also in a *confident* position with respect to the Lord. He is the only one out there, and he has no division of will within himself, so we need have no divisions in our loyalty to him. We never need to wonder whether there is another god waiting in the wings whom we need to buy off or appease. We are free to serve the one, undivided God with our own undivided loyalty. This was the lesson Israel had to learn in the midst of the pagan, polytheistic world of the ancient Near East, and above all else, the Shema encapsulated this lesson. It rightly stood at the very center of Israel's faith, as a declaration of allegiance to the one true God.

Then the Christian church moved out of the Jewish world—a world that by the first century had thoroughly imbibed the absolute monotheism of the Old Testament—into the pagan world of Africa, Europe, and Asia, and the mainly Gentile church had to learn the same lesson in a different kind of pagan world, filled with a different but equally complex array of perceived gods and goddesses. Into this new but basically similar world, the church now had to affirm again that there is a hard line between God and everything else. The Lord is the only, undivided God of the universe, who made everything and to whom everything is subservient. As Paul eloquently puts it in 1 Corinthians 8:5–6, "For although there may be so-called gods in heaven or on earth—as indeed there are many 'gods' and many 'lords'—yet for us there is one God, the Father, from whom are all things and for whom we exist . . ." The most basic affirmation of ancient Israel has become—in a context at once very different and yet fundamentally similar—the most basic affirmation of the church as well. We pledge allegiance to the one true God.

A Glorious Complication—Creedal Language in the New Testament

Of course, in the first century the Christian church did not simply need to relearn the central lesson of Israel's faith in a new context. There was also another stunning truth—seemingly in conflict with the first—with which they had to wrestle. In fact, you may have noticed that in the biblical quotation above, I stopped in the middle of a sentence. The rest of 1 Corinthians 8:6 reads, " . . . and one Lord, Jesus Christ, through whom are all things and through whom we exist." Here we must notice the striking parallels between the way the one God, the Father, is described and the way the Lord Jesus Christ is depicted. The Father is the one *from whom* everything exists and *for whom* we exist; Jesus Christ is the one *through whom* we and all other things exist. The question of *how* Jesus Christ can be both distinct from God and identified with God was indeed an urgent one, and it complicated the creedal affirmation of one God considerably. But such complexity did not lead the New Testament writers to retreat from the affirmation that Jesus Christ is the Lord.

Along with confessing the identity of Jesus with God, the New Testament writers also affirm creed-like summaries of the saving events of Christ's life. Paul describes the gospel in 1 Corinthians 15:3–4 as follows: "For I delivered to you as of first importance what I also received: that Christ died for our sins in accordance with the Scriptures, that he was buried, that he was raised on the third day in accordance with the Scriptures." Similarly, in Philippians 2:6–11 Paul affirms in creed-like fashion that Christ

> did not count equality with God a thing to be grasped, but emptied himself, by taking the form of a servant, being born in the likeness of men. And being found in human form, he humbled himself by becoming obedient to the point of death, even death on a cross. Therefore God has highly exalted him and bestowed on him the name that is above every name, so that at the name of Jesus every knee should bow, in heaven and on earth and under the earth, and every tongue confess that Jesus Christ is Lord, to the glory of God the Father.

So we see that the New Testament writers complicate the creedal affirmation of faith in one God by affirming with equally creedal force that Jesus Christ is to be identified with that one God, and by attaching particular creed-like significance to the events of Christ's life, death, and resurrection. The line between God and everything else is no less hard than it was before, but

Christians affirm that Jesus belongs *above* that line and yet lived an earthly life as one *below* it.

There is yet another complication in the nascent creedal affirmations of the New Testament. Some of them confess not only God/Father and Jesus/ Lord, but also a Third Person. Paul concludes 2 Corinthians with the famous benediction (13:14), "The grace of the Lord Jesus Christ and the love of God and the fellowship of the Holy Spirit be with you all." And of course, we have already seen that in Matthew 28:19, Jesus commands Christians to baptize "in the name of the Father and of the Son and of the Holy Spirit." While the Holy Spirit receives far less attention in the New Testament than Jesus does, the creed-like affirmations in these and other passages indicate that he too belongs above the hard line that divides God from all created things.

One could adduce many more biblical passages, but the ones we have considered should be sufficient to demonstrate that the New Testament writers make affirmations that have a creedal flavor to them, and that these affirmations tend to include at least two of the following four elements:

1. A confession of the one God, the Father

2. A confession of Jesus Christ, linked to the Father by calling him "Lord" or "Son"

3. A summary of the events of Christ's earthly life, death, and resurrection

4. An affirmation that the Holy Spirit is linked to the Father and Son

From the New Testament's reflection on and additions to the Shema, then, we find the beginnings of the creedal impulse among Christians. Just as the biblical writers professed their allegiance to the one true God, his Son, and his Spirit, so would the writers of the early church.

Creed Writing in the Second and Third Centuries

The creedal impulse latent in the New Testament documents continued into the second and third centuries, and the creeds produced then were of two major types: (1) creeds beginning with Christ, focusing on summaries of his earthly life; and (2) creeds that were explicitly threefold in structure and dealt at least in a rudimentary way with the Spirit as well as the Father and Son. The first type followed the pattern of the Synoptic Gospels, while the second followed the pattern of John 1 more closely—beginning with the Trinity in eternity and then moving to the incarnation. Thus both kinds of creedal statements had biblical precedent. Over time, though, the threefold pattern came to predominate. The main reason was that creedal statements were used not merely for proclamation/preaching but also especially in connection with baptism. Matthew 28:19 provided the pattern for Trinitarian baptism, and Jesus' specific mention of all three persons under the one "name" in that passage provided the rationale for the development of baptismal symbols in which one would confess each person sequentially and be immersed after each confession. At first, the confession of each person would be made in response to a question, "Do you believe in God the Father? . . . Do you believe in Jesus Christ his only Son our Lord? . . . Do you believe in the Holy Spirit?" Over time, these interrogatory creeds were rewritten as declarative creeds, with a sentence or paragraph for each of the persons. Thus the baptismal use of creeds—growing out of the Lord's command—came to dictate the pattern that future creeds would follow.

From this sketch, it should be clear that creeds grew out of biblical precedents and were used in proclamation of the story of Christ and, especially, in baptism. As a result, the purpose of creeds was never to give a comprehensive outline of the "what" of salvation, and thus the omissions that disturb us should not do so. Instead, they served as pledges of allegiance by which new converts and worshipers affirmed their loyalty to God, to his Son, and to his Spirit. The content of creeds was primarily designed to indicate the persons to whom the worshipers were pledging their allegiance. Thus the three articles of the Apostles' Creed begin: "We believe in God, the Father almighty . . . and in Jesus Christ his only Son our Lord . . . and in the Holy Spirit." The corresponding articles of the Nicene Creed begin: "We believe in one God, the Father . . . and in one Lord Jesus Christ, the only-begotten Son of God . . . and in the Holy Spirit, the Lordly and life-giving one."

The Arian Controversy and the Nicene Creed in Relation to the Reformation

With this general background in mind, we need to turn our attention specifically to the fourth-century Arian controversy that led to the production of the Nicene Creed in AD 381. In this book, which is specifically honoring the five-hundredth anniversary of the Reformation, an appropriate entry point into that specific background is to note again that the Nicene Creed does *not* mention faith alone or justification by faith directly, and to ask how I can claim that the creed should be seen as background to the Reformation when it omits those two great Reformation emphases.

To address this question, we need to recognize that part of the point of justification by faith—in Paul's letters and in Reformation teaching—is to remind us that we are not the objects of our own faith. We depend for salvation not on what we have done or can do, but on what Another has done and is doing. This is why we Protestants so insistently contrast faith (directed toward Another) with works (a way of saying that we would trust in our own ability and performance). Here we should recognize that this is what the Nicene Creed does, but in a different way. By telling the story of Jesus and by naming the Father, Son, and Spirit as the actors in that story, the creed is specifically *not* describing our own action or performance. The omission of what we do from the creed is just as significant as the inclusion of what Jesus did. By that very omission and inclusion, the creed calls us to look elsewhere besides ourselves—to the Father, Son, and Spirit—for our salvation. One could say that the very act of telling the story of Jesus (as the Gospels do, as the New Testament preachers do in the book of Acts, and as the preachers and creed writers of the early church do) is just as much an affirmation of justification by faith as we make when we—following Paul in Romans and Galatians—actually expound upon that phrase itself. If Protestant readers can remain attuned to what the creeds *don't* say, as much as to what they do say, then we may find some of our suspicions allayed. Indeed, we may find that talking about the God in whom we are to trust is just as compelling a way to foster trust in him alone as talking about justification by faith directly!

But I believe that the Nicene Creed covers what we mean by justification by faith, not merely through its omission of human action but also positively through a phrase that comes at the very center of the creed. The second paragraph, on the Son, begins with a description of who the Son is eternally in relation to the Father: He is "light from light, true God from true God, begotten not made, *homoousios* with the Father." Then the paragraph transitions to what the Son has done by giving a short account of his life, death, and resurrection. The transition between who he is and what he has done marks the center of the creed, and the language used there is striking: "For us humans and for our salvation *he came down* from heaven."

Let's consider the significance of this assertion by contrasting it with ancient thought about salvation.

In Greco-Roman society, as in many pagan societies, there was great variety in how one described God (or the gods, or the divine realm, or ultimate reality), and also great variety about what a person had to do in order to attain to the realm of God or the gods (or to gain salvation, if one wants to say it that way). But what the many different gods and paths to God had in common was that whatever had to be done, human beings had to do it themselves. Varying religions offered competing versions of self-salvation. In the many popular religions of the Roman world, salvation was accomplished through rituals that allegedly united practitioners to one or another of the Roman gods. The great thinkers of the Greco-Roman philosophical scene, however, prescribed varied approaches to ethical behavior, while usually insisting that the path to union with the gods was a matter of ethics and morality, not just ritual observance. In both low and high forms, pagan religions started from the premise that we can and must rise up to the divine realm ourselves.

In sharp contrast, Christianity affirms that what is necessary for people to be united to the true God is *not* something that fallen human beings can do themselves. It follows, therefore, that if we are to be saved, then God has to come to us. Scripture describes God's descent to us in many ways—God's calling of Abraham, his leading Israel out of Egypt, the establishment of Israel as a nation, and so on. But all of these events are precursors to two main descents: the incarnation and the descent of the Holy Spirit to indwell believers. In short, our salvation is accomplished because the Son of God has come down to live *among* us, and the Holy Spirit has come down to live *within* each of us.

If we can agree with this biblical-theological logic that God had to come down to save us and that this "coming down" was accomplished primarily through the incarnation of the Son and the indwelling of the Spirit, then two things follow readily:

1. The Son and the Spirit have to be *just as fully and equally God* as the Father. Otherwise, it wouldn't be *God* who came down to save us, and we would be left with the impossible task of saving ourselves.

2. The Son really had to *come down* through the incarnation. Otherwise, we would again be left with the impossible task of rising up to God on our own.

These two assertions summarize the main emphases of the church through-out virtually the entire Arian controversy, as well as most of what the Nicene Creed affirms. Arius saw salvation as an upward movement of humanity to God, and accordingly, he saw the Son as a created being, less than God but better than us, who first rose up to God and then enabled us to follow. In contrast to Arius and others like him, the church insisted that the Son and the Spirit had to be fully God, and that the Son had to come down to become fully human. These are the main assertions of the Nicene Creed, and at the very center of the creed is the statement that the Son came down for our salvation.

At this point, it should be clear that what I am calling "rising up to God" is what Protestants call "salvation by works." It is the belief that whatever it takes to be saved, human beings can and must do that themselves. The church was rejecting this in the fourth-century Arian controversy just as much as the Reformers were rejecting this in the sixteenth-century Refor-mation. On the other hand, what the Nicene Creed calls "God coming down" can be seen as perfectly consistent with the Pauline and later Protestant emphasis on justification by grace through faith. In rejecting Arius, the church was *implicitly* rejecting the same approach to salvation—that people could rise up to God through our own actions—which the Reformers later rejected *explicitly*. And in insisting that God the Son had to come down to save us, the church and the Nicene Creed were *explicitly* affirming some-thing akin to Protestant "justification by faith," albeit with different words.

Conclusion: Not What but Whom

I have argued in this chapter that the ancient creeds were never meant primarily as explications of *what* we believe. Instead, they were meant as affirmations of our allegiance to the three persons in whom we believe, to whom we belong—the Father, Son, and Spirit. The content about each person of the Trinity serves to identify the person whom we trust, without pretending to be an exhaustive treatment of what we believe about that person, let alone what we believe about the Christian faith as a whole. I have argued furthermore that in the case of the greatest and most widely accepted ancient creed, the Nicene, the truth that we could not rise up to God and instead God had to come down to us is enshrined at the very center of the paragraph about the Son. Thus the creeds in general and the Nicene

Creed in particular can be seen as affirming something like justification by faith alone, albeit in a rather different way than we do. God had to come to us to save us, and we affirm that we trust him, not ourselves or our works, for our salvation, when we say, "We believe in God, the Father almighty . . . and in Jesus Christ his only Son our Lord . . . and in the Holy Spirit." The ancient creeds are consistent with the later Reformation emphasis on faith alone.

But I would like to suggest more than this. In addition, I suggest that the creeds, and especially the Nicene Creed, are not merely consistent with later Reformation emphases; they are also crucial as background to and context for those emphases. You see, if you *start* with justification by faith, with faith alone, and spend all of your time and effort contrasting faith with works, then it is easy for you to turn faith itself into a kind of pseudo-work: I am saved because of *my* faith. Only if this focus on faith and justification is *preceded* by an unequivocal affirmation that faith is directed toward God, his Son, and his Spirit can a focus on faith itself avoid turning faith into a work. What we all assume—perhaps without ever articulating it—is that faith is efficacious only when it is directed the right way. The point is not whether we have faith (after all, everyone does) or whether we have enough of it (no one does). The point is that our faith is directed toward God, Christ, and the Spirit, and these three *alone*. The ancient creeds served—and still can serve—as an eloquent way for us as God's people to declare our allegiance to God, to direct our faith anew toward him (them!) alone. Such a declaration of trust and allegiance to the true God is the indispensable background and context for the Reformation, without which discussions of justification by grace through faith could be prone to misunderstanding or distortion.

At the end of the day, I ask that as we celebrate the great rediscovery of "faith alone" in the Reformation, we also recognize and appreciate the place of the ancient creeds, written more than a millennium prior to any Reformation documents. A simple way we can do this is by reciting the creeds publicly, with a more appropriate introduction. I suggest to you (as I have suggested to my pastor and others) that we not ask, "Christians, *what* do you believe?" Instead, ask, "Christians, *in whom* do you believe?"

> We believe in one God, the Father . . . and in one Lord Jesus Christ, the only-begotten Son of God . . . and in the Holy Spirit, the Lordly and life-giving one.

> Amen.

15

Faith: The Foundation of Preaching

Scott M. Gibson

"The complete statement is that we are justified
Meritoriously, by Christ,
Instrumentally, by Faith
Evidentially, by Works."
A. J. Gordon[1]

Introduction

In the 1880s and 1890s, a debate erupted in evangelical circles over the doctrine of faith. Popular Scottish Free Church evangelist, biologist, and lecturer, Henry Drummond, wrote a book titled *The Greatest Thing in the World*. In its pages, Drummond claimed that love was the *summum bonum*, the supreme good, building off Paul's words in 1 Corinthians 13.[2] Among those who rebutted Drummond was Boston Baptist A. J. Gordon. His published response, *The First Thing in the World: or, The Primacy of Faith*, does not name Drummond, but it takes Drummond's ideas to task. Gordon wrote:

> Love comes with full hands bringing something to God; Hope comes with outstretched hands expecting something yet to be given from God; Faith comes with empty hands to receive something which he has already been given by God. Therefore, since it is necessary that we receive before we give, Faith must come first, however welcome her sister graces may be afterwards. For let it be distinctly recognized that Faith originates nothing; she only recognizes what is, and receives it on the soul's behalf. The opening eye did not create the lovely landscape which it pictured to the mind; it simply apprehended what was there

already, and received the impress of it upon its sensitive retina, and so made an inward reality of what before was an outward fact. So Faith appropriates and rests in the accomplished work of Christ.[3]

Both Drummond and Gordon were associates of the eminent American evangelist Dwight L. Moody. Drummond delivered the "Greatest Thing" lecture at Moody's Northfield summer student retreat center.[4] Gordon was also a longtime advocate and at times co-laborer with Moody, having spent numerous weeks teaching and preaching over several summers at Northfield.[5]

Both Drummond and Gordon wanted to establish a firm biblical and theological foundation for ministry, but their foundations differed and they were not able to agree. In their debate, one is able to see how the great doctrines of the Reformation are played out on the pavement of life, in the everyday lives of Christians as they wade through the challenges and pleasures of life. In addition, the debate between Drummond and Gordon framed the ongoing considerations for the theological foundations for practical theology. For Henry Drummond, love was the driving force for ministry. For A. J. Gordon, faith was primary. The Reformation teaching of *sola fide* is the foundation of ministry for Gordon. He argued:

> Therefore, let there be no rivalry or strife for preeminence among these three. Yet we can but observe that Faith stands in her old place at the head of the line. And why this persistent priority? Only because we are justified by Faith; and justification is the first and initial transaction of the Christian life.[6]

This chapter explores the foundation for ministry—more specifically, the foundation for the ministry of preaching. First, focus will be placed in the act of preaching itself. Second, the role of faith in preaching will be explored. This chapter argues that *sola fide*, faith alone, is the foundation and the driving force of the ministry of preaching.

The Act of Preaching

The apostle Paul reminds all preachers, "Faith comes from hearing the message, and the message is heard through the word about Christ" (Rom. 10:17 NIV). Preaching plays a crucial role in the cultivation of faith in the lives of one's listeners. As Greg Scharf, chair of the Pastoral Theology Department and professor of homiletics at Trinity Evangelical Divinity School, reminds those who preach, "God himself speaks through us when we speak in Christ's name."[7] Scarf continues,

> I can and should expect my listeners to hear God's authoritative, powerful voice creating faith and doing its sanctifying work whenever I preach, to the extent that I am faithfully respeaking God's written Word in ways that reflect its truths, ethics, tone, and aim.[8]

James Muilenburg, a pioneer in the field of rhetorical criticism of the Old Testament, notes that in preaching "the Word is alive in speaking. Therefore we speak. Therefore we proclaim." He continues, "Let it never be forgotten that the most immediate and authentic response to the Word of God is preaching, announcing, telling, proclaiming, publishing. Faith comes from hearing and hearing comes by preaching the Word of Christ, by speaking it."[9] Charles Cameron agrees, "Through his Word, God is able to lift us out of our unbelief and bring us into the assurance of faith."[10]

The act of preaching provides the platform, the foundation for a clear word from God. Louis Berkhof highlights the place of the preached word in the implanting of faith:

> The ultimate ground on which faith rests lies in the veracity and faithfulness of God, in connection with the promises of the gospel. But because we have no knowledge of this apart from the Word of God, this can also be, and frequently is, called the ultimate ground of faith.[11]

God uses preachers to communicate the word to listeners, to show them the evidence of God's grace toward them, to demonstrate that faith is not faith in faith for faith's sake, but that there is hope for life in the God who gives justifying faith. William E. Hordern articulates:

> Faith does not mean believing without evidence; rather, faith means being persuaded of the decisive significance of certain evidence. As Willem Zuurdeeg, professor of philosophy of religion at McCormick Theological Seminary, asserts in *An Analytical Philosophy of Religion*, faith is "convictional language." A man's perspective is formed by the fact that he has been convicted by a "convictor." The convictor is that which has the power to persuade a man that "this is significant, this is

decisive evidence." It is only in life as lived, not in rational argument, that we meet convictors.[12]

These convictors are preachers, used by God to communicate his word to men, women, boys, and girls. Harold J. Koelpin reminds us that in the "Preface to the Epistle of St. Paul to the Romans," Martin Luther "spells out how the church lives by the preaching of justification."[13] Faith alone is the foundation for preaching that provides preachers with solid footing for a ministry of the word.

The Role of Faith in Preaching

The role of faith in preaching is foundational. The faith of the preacher marks the absolute beginning for the preacher in his or her relationship with Christ. Without justifying faith, preachers lose the capacity to connect with people. "What is of greater interest to us in this context is whether God's Word retains that power *when meditated through people*," notes Greg Scharf.[14] Faith makes that connection. Faith is foundational for the preacher and for preaching. In this section, we will explore the foundation stones forming the role of faith in preaching: (1) the preacher has faith; (2) the preacher's life matches his or her foundation of faith; (3) the preacher has faith in the Bible; and (4) the preacher is faithful.

The Preacher Has Faith

The opposite of faith is unbelief. There is outright unbelief—an unbelief that goes through the motions of ministry but denies or fails to acknowledge the power thereof. There is another kind of unbelief. Greg Scharf helpfully notes,

> Preachers who fail to trust God or believe what he has said will not consistently speak for him. When it comes to speaking for him, faith is foundational. If we either do not trust God or do not have a solid theology of preaching or belief in the truths revealed in his Word, we simply will not preach as God intends.[15]

This kind of unbelief can be observed in the preacher when "alternatives to faithful preaching will appeal to you more than true biblical preaching," notes Scharf.[16] Preachers must come to terms with the essence of biblical, justifying faith. To understand the Reformers' perspective, Franz Arnold observes, "But what did Luther and the Council of Trent understand by *faith*? Not primarily the purely intellectual acceptance of certain truth, but rather the biblical *pisteuein*, confidence in the pardon of Christ and in the mercy of God."[17] Likewise, Millard Erickson underscores, "The type of faith necessary for salvation involves both believing that and believing in, or assenting to facts and trusting in a person. It is vital to keep these two together."[18] Louis Berkhof reminds us,

> The Reformers . . . were unanimous and explicit in teaching that justifying faith does not justify by any meritorious or inherent efficacy of its own, but only as the instrument for receiving or laying hold on what God has provided in the merits of Christ. They regarded this faith primarily as a gift of God and only secondarily as an activity of man in dependence on God.[19]

What is a preacher to do when plagued by this second kind of unbelief as described by Scharf? Lawrence A. Castagnola suggests some self-examining questions:

> One commissioned to communicate the Gospel should submit himself to a kind of self-examination which might include the following questions: (1) What do I really believe? (2) Do I express these beliefs in my preaching? (3) Do my beliefs represent the Gospel brought up-to-date? (4) Do my words correspond to my actions? (5) Am I adapting the message? (6) Is dialog integral to my faith? In short, what is the relationship of my preaching to my faith?[20]

Perhaps the most powerful weapon for preachers who battle unbelief is, as Jerry Bridges suggests, to "preach the gospel to yourself."

> To preach the gospel to yourself, then, means that you continually face up to your own sinfulness and then flee to Jesus through faith in His shed blood and righteous life. It means that you appropriate, again by faith, the fact that Jesus fully satisfied the law of God, that He is your propitiation, and that God's holy wrath is no longer directed toward you.[21]

Franz Arnold reminds all preachers who wrestle with unbelief:

> The fundamental fact to be fully realized is that faith as a personal com-
> mitment is the one way to salvation for the faithful, and is that super-
> natural reality which unites man to Christ, Who is our Salvation. "The
> just man lives by faith" (Rom. I, 17).[22]

Admittedly, some preachers are troubled with unbelief. Those who preach
the gospel, the stumbling block to those who are confronted by its truth
and power, recognize that the word they study will convict them in the process of preaching preparation. This is to be expected. As Haddon Robinson
notes in his definition of preaching, the preacher is to be confronted with
the truth of the passage before he or she preaches it to the congregation.[23]
The preacher is not exempt from engaging personally with the truth of the
biblical text. Castagnola notes, "Preaching involves a struggle with personal
faith," which makes us into better persons and preachers.[24]

What does a preacher do when faced with unbelief? "A good starting
point in addressing unbelief is confession," suggests Scharf. "Confession is
crucial, but it is only a start. We need to supplement it with supplication—
asking God for help."[25] Confession and faith in the God who helps, who
justifies, enables the preacher to stand on the solid ground of faith.

When the preacher has a firm foundation of faith, what they preach will
be used by God in the communication of his word. Emeric A. Lawrence
encourages us:

> So the first and most essential agent in bringing the faithful to an awak-
> ening in faith is the priest or catechist. If he believes, it will not take long
> till the faithful come to realize that the mystery of salvation is meant by
> God for them, too; that they are involved in it; that the history of salva-
> tion is still going on; and that God is intervening in their lives here and
> now every time they submit to His action in . . . hearing His Word.[26]

A foundation stone of faith in preaching is the faith of the preacher.
Another foundation stone of faith is that the preacher's life matches his or
her faith foundation.

The Preacher's Life Matches His or Her Faith Foundation

The foundation of personal, justifying faith provides the preacher with
the capacity to communicate with their listeners honestly, truthfully, con-

sistently. Scharf reminds preachers, "We must have faith in order to preach. We are in desperate straits without it."[27] This faith in the Faithful One is the preacher's and no one else's. As Kathryn A. Kleinhans writes, "Faith alone is deeply personal, however, because it trusts that God's promise is given specifically *to me*."[28]

In light of this, preachers are called to live lives that are consistent with what they say in the pulpit. All preachers—and Christians for that matter—face the same challenge of living a life without contradictions. And we often miss the mark. Castagnola admits honestly, "This inability to put our money where our mouth is may be called 'preacher's syndrome.' We all have it to a certain degree."[29]

What is a preacher to do? Martin J. Lohrmann suggests, "As St. Augustine put it, our words and actions as Christians can naturally grow from our spiritual center: to do this, the preacher must first become a person of 'prayer before becoming a person of words.'"[30] This is a similar reminder from Eugene Peterson: "Three pastoral acts are so basic, so critical, that they determine the shape of everything else. The acts are praying, reading Scripture, and giving spiritual direction."[31] These reminders return preachers to the faith-formed foundations for preaching and pastoral ministry.

Lohrmann points out Martin Luther's words about the preacher's life and foundation. Luther writes:

> The call [to preach] is this: watch, study, attend to reading. In truth you cannot read too much in Scripture; and what you read you cannot read too carefully, and what you read carefully you cannot understand too well, and what you understand well you cannot teach too well, and what you teach well you cannot live too well.[32]

The preacher's life is to match his or her faith foundation.

The Preacher Has Faith in the Bible

The next foundation stone on which a preacher stands is faith in the power of the infallible and inerrant word of God, the Bible. Scharf relates:

> *Faith is trust in God*, believing that he is who he claims to be and does what he claims to do, and therefore that he can be relied upon (Rom. 4:20–21; Heb. 11:6). There will be no faithful preaching—speaking in

God's name, on his behalf, for his glory, and for the good of his people—
if preachers do not trust God to speak through them and to open the
ears and hearts of their listeners. That kind of trust is rooted in their
other sort of faith of which the Bible speaks.[33]

John Stott notes, "It is certain that we cannot handle Scripture ade-
quately in the pulpit if our doctrine of Scripture is inadequate."[34] A solid
doctrine of Scripture enables a preacher to recognize that God still speaks
today through the Bible by way of preachers.

The preacher demonstrates faith in God's word by nonverbal communication (poise, gestures, and presence) and by verbal cues (tone, force,
and rate). As Emeric Lawrence observes, Faith, conviction and deep
reverence for God's Word will be evident in the very voice of the one
who proclaims it; and these virtues will also prompt sufficient practice
before the reader appears before the people. A dramatic reading without faith and love will fool no one.[35]

The preacher has faith in the Bible. The Scriptures are expounded, and the
preacher gets out of the way and lets the word do its work.

The Preacher Is Faithful

The faithful preacher is used by God in the lives of his or her listeners.
Scharf urges:

Faithfulness is multifaceted; there is much more to it than simply cap-
turing the dominant thrust of the passage we are expounding, essential
as that is. Faithful servants of God's Word prove themselves to be faithful stewards of it when they:

1. Trust God.
2. Speak as those assigned, equipped, and empowered to do so.
3. Speak from the Bible in ways that reflect the Bible's composition.
4. Listen to God before they attempt to speak for God, discerning what
   he is saying.
5. Understand those to whom God has called them to speak.
6. Respect and reflect the clarity and orderliness of Scripture while discerning the way people hear.

7. Respect and reflect the ways that Scripture communicates in stories, propositions, and images.

8. Take seriously their role as messengers who also embody the message they proclaim.[36]

Millard J. Erickson makes this interesting observation about faith:

In a very real sense, Old Testament Hebrew does not have a noun for faith, except perhaps אֱמוּנָה (*'emunah*) in Habakkuk 2:4, but that word is usually rendered "faithfulness." Instead, Hebrew conveys the idea of faith with verb forms. Perhaps that is because the Hebrews regarded faith as something that one does rather than as something one has. It is an activity rather than a possession.[37]

Faithful preachers are justified by faith, and this reality moves them into not only a state of being but also a way of living. There are hindrances to living faithfully—pride, the cult of personality, one-upmanship, ambition, self-centeredness, and many other plagues of the pulpit. As William E. Hill Jr. frankly observes, "The man who is desperately concerned to be accepted, to be praised by men, to be considered great or good, or even godly, seldom becomes a man of great faith."[38] A preacher who is justified by faith is to be faithful.

Conclusion

Gary M. Simpson makes the following observation:

It is appropriate that justification by "faith alone" comes first as a kind of *primus inter pares* because, as Robert Bertram once put it, faith alone always has been the "most embattled *sola* of all." The Lutheran confessors focused on faith alone because they understood the gospel "based upon the nature of a promise," and faith alone is promise's correlate, is the Promisor's correlate.[39]

The role of preaching in the life of the church is primary. This faith-implanting task has been used by God for millennia, and even in our day when men and women continue to struggle with belief, preaching has its place. Franz Arnold writes, "The task of proclaiming the faith is therefore all the more urgent, but at the same time all the more difficult. Our teaching must prepare the way, rescue man from this nihilism, and root him in God by faith."[40]

Sola fide, faith alone, is the foundation and the driving force of the ministry of preaching.

16

FAITH: AMENING GOD

Jeffrey J. Niehaus

The great reformational doctrine of *sola fide*—justification *by faith alone*, apart from works—is something to which we hold and, truth be told, on which we depend; for, after all, who could do works sufficient to merit God's favor? We remember the powerful words of Paul:

> We who are Jews by birth and not sinful Gentiles know that a person is not justified by the works of the law, but by faith in Jesus Christ. So we, too, have put our faith in Christ Jesus that we may be justified by faith in Christ and not by the works of the law, because by the works of the law no one will be justified. (Gal. 2:15–16 NIV)

Paul made that affirmation in response to Judaizers in Galatia who wanted Gentile believers to be circumcised. As Paul pointed out, if one becomes circumcised, one thereby becomes obligated to obey "the whole law" (Gal. 5:3)—an impossible assignment! Paul wrote to prevent such a retrograde movement because, like him, believers in Christ have "died to the law" (Gal. 2:19; cf. Rom. 6:14). In passing, we note that Paul says "the whole law" and not just "the law," and with good reason. Circumcision was the sign of the Abrahamic covenant. It was *not* the sign of the Mosaic covenant. The sign of the Mosaic covenant was the Sabbath (Exod. 31:14–17), although the Mosaic covenant law did *require* circumcision (Lev. 12:3). That requirement was an indication that the Abrahamic covenant continued in force, *in tandem* with the Mosaic covenant, so that Jesus, who fulfilled both covenants, was both circumcised and "born under the law" (Gal. 4:4). Paul's point in Galatians 5:3 is therefore as follows: If one takes on circumcision—*one* requirement of the law—then one takes on "the whole law." And no one can be justified by doing that. We are, therefore, justified by faith.

At this point, it is important for us to understand biblical faith—not only because we are justified by it but also because faith plays an essential role in a dynamic of divine activity that deserves more discussion. That dynamic is the way the Holy Spirit works through the Son and through others to advance God's kingdom. The advance of God's kingdom with respect to any covenant takes the form first of that covenant's institution and then afterward the form of all human behavior that involves faith in the one true God, under any of the divine-human covenants. A diagram illustrates the dynamic as it plays out in the Adamic and new covenants:

Adamic Covenant	*New Covenant*	*Church Life*
Father	Father	Father and Son
⇩	⇩	⇩
Spirit	Spirit	Spirit
⇩	⇩	⇩
Pre-incarnate Word	Incarnate Word	Church
⇩	⇩	⇩
Kingdom Creation	Kingdom Creation	Kingdom Advance

We will consider the role of faith in this dynamic (which applies to every divine-human covenant, although not every covenant is illustrated above) as a major part of this study. Before that, it may be good to remember that every human being who ever lived (or will live) lives under at least two divine-human covenants: the common grace Adamic covenant and its common grace renewal, the Noahic covenant. Those common grace covenants apply to all people, whether they believe in any god or not. Christians live under those common grace covenants as well, e.g., as per the terms of the Adamic covenant they all *die*, but they also live—*we* also live—under the one special grace covenant that still functions, namely, the *new* covenant.

Faith, it will be argued, is essential to all this. It may be presumptuous to suppose that we can understand fully something as "unseen" as faith. But some improvement in our understanding may be possible. Such improvements are presumably one of the goals of theology!

One who would ask "What is biblical faith?" naturally turns for an answer to the Bible's one propositional statement on the matter. The writer of Hebrews tells us: "Faith is the substance of things hoped for, the assurance of things unseen" (Heb. 11:1; author's translation). A list of illustrations follows, from the days of our first parents to the writer's own day—and so implicitly to our day also—because those illustrations are not only examples, they also challenge us to understand and apply the propositional statement of 11:1, a statement that may not have its full impact (and possibly was not meant to) without some probing.

Ancillary to our probe, a prior way is open for us to understand biblical faith. Study of the Hebrew verb יִמְאָה ("to believe") offers a perspective that agrees with Hebrews 11:1 and with all biblical illustrations of faith. The root of the Hebrew (*Hiphil*) form is the verb מָא ("to confirm, support"), from which the adverb מָא ("*amen*," "verily, truly") derives.[1] The basic sense of the *Hiphil* (יִמְאָה, "to believe") is actually, to paraphrase, "to affirm, to agree that it is so."[2] That understanding renders the actual substance of biblical faith.

How can our affirmation or agreement that "it is so" be the same as the faith the Bible portrays? For the following reason: Biblical faith is in fact *agreement with what God is doing*, and this is why it is so close to righteousness, which is conformity to God's standard or nature. It is not mere intellectual assent. It is "ownership" of what God is doing. When I "believe in" or "put my faith in" Jesus Christ, I actually agree and "own" or "make my own" what God has done, is doing, and promises to do in Christ for me. I conform to God's way of seeing this truth, or to his standard of perception and affirmation. This agreement or "ownership," however, is an agreement with or ownership of something that is unseen. So, if I "amen" what God has done in Christ, I "amen" an invisible reality. That is, I can look at the life, death, and even the resurrection of Christ but not know from these events that they have one—and only one at that moment for me—core significance: God's atonement for sin, which I may in effect apply to myself by "amening" it. The facts of Jesus' life, ministry, death, and resurrection have a significance that one apprehends by faith, by "amening" that significance, or embracing it for oneself.

On such a definition of faith, one may contend that Jesus led a life of perfect faith—and of perfect righteousness. Jesus agreed constantly and totally with what the Father was doing, and so he was "Jesus Christ the righteous" (1 John 2:1) because he conformed entirely to his Father's character. He could say, "I tell you the truth, the Son can do nothing by himself; he can only do what he sees his Father doing, because whatever the Father does the Son also does" (John 5:19). As we noted, faith is an "amening" of what is unseen. And although Jesus "saw" in a way that we typically do not, what he saw was invisible to the outward senses, and he had to trust in the reality of that "unseen" that he saw. So Jesus is called "the faithful witness" (Rev. 1:5). That is, he was faithful to, or he "amened," what he saw his Father doing.

Faith and Agreement with God

We affirm, then, that faith is in its simplest form agreement with God. Although Hebrews 11:1 does not make this obvious, one event in the ministry of Jesus does bring clarity on this point. Jesus had an encounter with a Roman centurion that can teach us much about faith:

> When Jesus had entered Capernaum, a centurion came to him, asking for help. "Lord," he said, "my servant lies at home paralyzed and in terrible suffering." Jesus said to him, "I will go and heal him." The centurion replied, "Lord, I do not deserve to have you come under my roof. But just say the word, and my servant will be healed. For I myself am a man under authority, with soldiers under me. I tell this one, 'Go,' and he goes; and that one, 'Come,' and he comes. I say to my servant, 'Do this,' and he does it." When Jesus heard this, he was astonished and said to those following him, "I tell you the truth, I have not found anyone in Israel with such great faith." (Matt. 8:5–10)

The centurion says to Jesus, "Just say the word, and my servant will be healed," but how can the Roman know this? He reasons by analogy; that is, he compares Jesus with himself. The centurion has an understanding of his own authority: whatever he commands must come to pass. He *intuits* that the same is true of Jesus, and that intuiting is part of faith. The centurion understands that Jesus has authority, but he understands much more than that: he understands that Jesus is part of an authority *structure*. Just as the centurion is under authority, so Jesus is under authority. The centurion is under Caesar; Jesus is under God. Because he is under authority, the centurion can also be sure that his own orders carry authority and must come to pass; moreover, he intuits that the same is true of Jesus. The following diagram illustrates these points:

Caesar	God
⇩	⇩
Centurion	Jesus
⇩	⇩
soldier(s)	unnamed agent (angel? Holy Spirit?)
⇩	⇩
work to be done	work to be done (healing of servant)

Jesus stands in an authority structure comparable to the centurion's own. How does the Roman know this? We said that he reasons by analogy. But it is better to say that he *senses* an analogy that actually exists. Both authority structures *do exist* and they are analogous, and the centurion intuits the same. However, although his intuition is true and necessary, it is not, by itself, sufficient. More is required for the centurion's knowledge to become faith. The centurion must also affirm (or "amen") that his intuition is true. He does so in two ways. First, he declares it. Second, and more importantly, he trusts Jesus for the outcome. If the authority structure is true, then Jesus can heal the Roman's servant with a word. And Jesus does so.

Jesus' commentary on the centurion, and thus on the whole matter, is decisive: "I tell you the truth, I have not found anyone in Israel with such great faith." The centurion both affirms Jesus' own authority structure and trusts Jesus for the outcome, and Jesus calls that faith. So it is, and the Bible hardly offers a better example as this confirms the understanding of faith offered above. Faith, then, is an *"amening" of who God is and what he is doing*—whether one only intuits such matters when they are not in evidence (as in the centurion's case), or one has palpable evidence that invites such an *amen* (e.g., the testimony of the Bible).

What God is doing (or is about to do) is often unseen; so faith is also called "the substance of things hoped for, the assurance of things unseen" (Heb. 11:1). Faith is the "substance of things hoped for." What one hopes for in faith is indeed substantial. That is because faith intuits what God is doing, and nothing can be more substantial than God and his work. Faith is also the "assurance of things unseen." That is because, although God and his work may be unseen, faith—that *inner grasp of who God is and what he is doing*—assures us of the substantial reality and eventuality of all that.

Because faith is the assurance of things unseen, "We live by faith, not by sight" (2 Cor. 5:7). That is, we live by our sure knowledge of God and his work, which includes the ongoing work of the Holy Spirit in our lives. All who follow Christ are called to be like him (Matt. 10:25) and to walk as he walked (1 John 2:6)—that is, "by faith and not by sight." Such a life is also "in step" with God's Spirit (Gal. 5:25). One who lives in that way will more and more know what the Father is doing and do it, and know what the Father is saying and say it. As in the case of Jesus, the Spirit will produce his words and deeds.[3]

It follows that every act of God through his servants/children is made possible by faith—because those people own and then obediently give themselves to what God is doing. The owning (faith) comes first, then the act of obedience. That is the logical—and also the actual—order. Paul affirms the same, for he calls us "to . . . the obedience that comes from faith" (εἰς ὑπακοὴν πίστεως, Rom. 1:5).

The incarnate Word shows the purest form of faith for, as we said, Jesus led a life of perfect faith. But if the incarnate and now ascended Word, through whom God by his Spirit produces the kingdom among us, led a human life of faith, and if the advance of that kingdom is also by faith, then we may pose another question. Was the kingdom work of the pre-incarnate Word also by faith? For there, too, the Son agreed with what the Father was doing, so that through the Word the Spirit spoke the Father's words that created the kingdom that then was. Was that creation by faith?

The statement of Hebrews 11:1 may seem to provide an answer. It emphasizes that which is not seen: "Faith is . . . the assurance of things unseen." One could object, then, that faith was not operative at the Creation, because the Son surely saw and understood what the Father would do (in creating the world). The Father's plan was not "unseen." But this understanding is made impossible by the fact that Jesus also saw what his Father was doing as he walked this earth (John 5:19), and yet Jesus led a life of perfect faith. That is how he can be called "the faithful witness" (Rev. 1:5). Rather, our understanding of Hebrews 11:1 must take into account its audience of fallen human beings. The definition of faith in Hebrews is composed for our sake, who often do not see what the Father is doing—and perhaps rarely, if ever, as clearly as Jesus saw it (even though in John 14:12 Jesus said that those who believe in him would do the same works he did and greater works). When we operate in faith, we are in a state of agreement with what the Father is doing through Christ, even if we cannot "see" it (or prove it) at the time. That is, we agree with God, who is unseen, and so he works through us.[4] Finally, it must be added that faith does not preclude sight even in Hebrews 11, for we read of the saints of old that "all these people were still *living by faith* when they died. They did not receive the things promised; they only *saw* (ἰδόντες) them and welcomed them from a distance" (Heb. 11:13; emphases added). Now, the Epistle to the Hebrews, like the rest of the Bible, is not a logical treatise. It tells us things in parts. So then, it tells us that faith has to do with what is unseen, but it also tells us that the people of old who lived by faith *saw* things God had promised. It does not tell us their mode of seeing, or if the word *saw* is merely figurative in this context. However, we note that the author of Hebrews could make it clear (and in the passage at hand) when he was speaking figuratively; for example, "Abraham reasoned that God could even raise the dead, and so *in a manner of speaking* [lit., "in a figure," ἐν παραβολῇ] he did receive Isaac back from death" (Heb. 11:19; emphasis added). We conclude, then, that faith can sometimes entail sight, although only in rare cases for fallen human beings. At the Creation, the Son saw what the Father was doing, and he was in total agreement with the Father. So the Father by the Spirit created the world through the agreeable and faithful Son.

Our understanding of biblical faith (as agreement with who the Father is and what the Father is doing) leads us logically to affirm that by faith the world was created. The pre-incarnate Word was by faith the mediator of Creation—he *amened* what the Father was doing; and the incarnate Word was by faith the mediator of Recreation (salvation). And since we are told that "the Son is the radiance of God's glory . . . sustaining all things by his powerful word" (Heb. 1:3), we may also conclude that the Spirit works through the Word to produce that word of power that *sustains* the created order that that same Spirit, through the Word, created.[5] So the Father works by the Spirit through the agreeable Son to sustain (cf. Isa. 32:15) and also to save that which he created. By faith the Son has mediated Creation, does mediate the continuation of the created order, and mediates also God's great salvation (Recreation) until all those who shall be redeemed have been found. The Father's creation and maintaining of the created order may be shown by the following simple schema:

Father   Father

⇩   ⇩

Spirit   Spirit

⇩   ⇩

Pre-incarnate Word   Pre- and Post-incarnate Word

⇩   ⇩

Creation Work   Sustaining Work

The repeated pattern whereby the Father causes his Spirit to work through the Son/Word to do kingdom work demonstrates the divine consistency. Moreover, the Son has done—and does—all of this *in conformity with the Father's nature*, and so the Son has done—and does—all of this in *righteousness* (and also, *by faith*, by "amening" what the Father does).[6] We are patterned after that Son through whom the Father so works, so we also by faith can be channels of God's salvation—his new kingdom work in the world.

Faith and Sin

We should not end our discussion of faith without considering sin, because Paul tells us, "Whatsoever is not of faith is sin" (Rom. 14:23b KJV). Although longer discussion of this definition is in order, we do not have time here to do so. I have taken up the issue in my book *Biblical Theology*, and for now will share some of the thoughts expressed there. We take Paul's statement as definitive, and I believe more ample discussion shows it to be so.

Sin is *whatever* is not of faith. At its root, we have understood biblical faith to be an amening of who God is and what he does. Therefore, sin is *whatever does not amen* God's nature *in that nature's entirety*. It is absolutely important that one understand this. Once one understands it, one sees how utterly impossible it is for any person to be justified by mere works. It is not our works or lack of works that show us to be righteous or condemn us—for an unrighteous man may yet do a good work, and a righteous man may fail to do a good work God has prepared for him (cf. Eph. 2:10), or may even do a bad work. If one did every good work one could possibly do, it could not save one. The problem is not with our behavior, but with ourselves. A human is ineluctably a fallen creature who *cannot invariably amen God with every fiber of his or her being.* Only Jesus did that. Only he could say,

> "Very truly I tell you, the Son can do nothing by himself; he can do only what he sees his Father doing, because whatever the Father does the Son also does." (John 5:19)

> "These words you hear are not my own; they belong to the Father who sent me." (John 14:24b)

> "I and the Father are one." (John 10:30)

Jesus made those statements without qualification. He did not say, "I do what I see the Father doing *some of the time*" or even *"most of the time."*

Such a standard is impossible for us to meet. We are *constitutionally unable* to meet it. If we think otherwise, then we hold a diminished and un-biblical view of sin. The flaw is in ourselves and is unavoidable. Nonetheless, we are not without hope. One can enter into that condition Jesus requested for his followers from the Father in his "High Priestly Prayer" (as it is called):

> "Holy Father, protect them by the power of your name, the name you gave me, so that they may be one as we are one." (John 17:11b)

> "Father, just as you are in me and I am in you. May they also be in us so that the world may believe that you have sent me." (John 17:21b)

It ought to go without saying that the oneness Jesus portrays here is utterly without precedent in the old covenant or in the whole Old Testament. Such ideas are not even mentioned in the literature of the Old Testament.

The condition Jesus portrays in the prayer of John 17 comes about only through faith in that name he invokes with the Father—his own name, his own essential nature that the Father gave him. As Peter says, "Salvation is found in no one else, for there is no other name under heaven given to mankind by which we must be saved" (Acts 4:12); and again, as Paul and Silas say, "Believe in the Lord Jesus, and you will be saved" (Acts 16:31). His name is salvation—the Lord saves—and that is the aspect of God's nature in view (cf. Matt. 1:21). One can be saved by faith; that is, by amening who Jesus was and is and what God did and offered—and still offers—in and through him. One cannot amen God in everything that has to do with God, but if one amens him *in this one thing*, then he *credits* to one the righteousness that would be a flawless and unintermittent amening of God—to which in this life one cannot attain. That righteousness, again, is conformity to the nature of God and thus it is the same for God, by whom it is credited to us (for God conforms perfectly to his own nature), and for Israel and anyone who amens God in his or her being and behavior—and to whom a perfect righteousness (or conformity to God's nature) unattainable by works is *credited* by his or her amening what God has done in Christ—this amening is itself a righteous act (cf. Gen. 15:6; Gal. 3:6–9).

What we have said indicates a close connection between faith and righteousness; and although much more can be said about that connection than may be said here, we can say this much in conclusion:

1. By faith—by amening God's nature—we, like Abraham, are credited with righteousness; we are justified by God.

2. By faith we grow in righteousness—amening God's nature and growing in conformity to God's nature, in a life of ongoing amening of God's nature. That is a faithful life, a life growing in righteousness.

3. Our faith or our faithfulness—that is, our ability to amen God's nature at any time—is a gift from God; for as Paul tells us, faith is a gracious gift (Eph. 2:8), and as James tells us, "every good and perfect gift is from above" (James 1:17).

Solus Christus:
By Christ Alone

17

The Centrality of Jesus Christ in Paul's Exhortations

Eckhard J. Schnabel

Jesus Messiah—the Son of David, the Son of God, who is Lord (*Kyrios*)— is foundational for understanding God and for being granted salvation, and he is foundational for understanding how Christians behave as authentic followers of Jesus. Paul's first letter to the Christians in the city of Corinth provides insight into the relationship between the significance of Jesus Messiah for both theology and ethics. The apostle Paul begins, and ends, his letter with these words:

> Paul, called to be an apostle of Christ Jesus by the will of God, and our brother Sosthenes, To the church of God that is in Corinth, to those who are sanctified in Christ Jesus, called to be saints, together with all those who in every place call on the name of our Lord Jesus Christ, both their Lord and ours: Grace to you and peace from God our Father and the Lord Jesus Christ. . . . I, Paul, write this greeting with my own hand. Let anyone be accursed who has no love for the Lord. *Marana tha* (Our Lord, come!). The grace of the Lord Jesus be with you. My love be with all of you in Christ Jesus. (1 Cor. 1:1–3; 16:21–24)[1]

Introduction: The Significance of Jesus Messiah in 1 Corinthians

Following the Hebrew Scriptures and Jewish tradition, Paul describes in 1 Corinthians 8:6 the one true God as creator of the universe (*ta panta*), the creator of humankind (*kai hēmeis*), and the goal of history and the consummation of salvation (*eis auton*). In the same sentence, Paul describes Jesus

Messiah as the Lord (*Kyrios*) who is the creator of the universe (*ta panta*) and the creator of humankind (*kai hēmeis*), thus including Jesus Messiah in the unique identity of the one God of Israel.[2]

Because Jesus the Son is *Kyrios* as God the Father is *Kyrios*, Paul connects Jesus with divine functions and divine actions: Jesus makes holy and he is the object of prayer; Jesus grants grace and peace; the day of judgment is the day of the Lord Jesus Messiah; Jesus has divine glory; the Spirit of God is the Spirit of Jesus Messiah; the judgment of God takes place when Jesus comes, who will bring to light the things now hidden in darkness and who will convey God's commendation to Jesus' followers; Jesus died for our sins; Jesus died as our paschal lamb, inaugurating the new era of salvation of the new covenant; nobody is stronger than Jesus Messiah, who must not be provoked to jealousy since he, like Yahweh, will not acquiesce to his people behaving as if he were not the one and only true God; and Jesus will return (1 Cor. 1:2–3, 8; 2:8, 16; 4:4–5; 5:7; 8:11; 10:22; 11:25–26; 15:3). Paul repeatedly mentions Jesus' death by crucifixion (1:13, 17–18, 23; 2:2, 8; cf. 11:24), a message that is the foundation of the church (3:10–15), which is God's temple in which God's Spirit dwells (3:16–17).

For Paul, the problems in the church in Corinth are the result of bad theology.[3] A defective understanding of who God is and who Jesus Messiah is lead to a defective understanding of what the church is, all of which leads to behavior that is not always fully authentically Christian.

Jesus Messiah and the Foundation of Christian Behavior

The behavior of some Christians in the church in Corinth, which was informed by the values and behavioral patterns of Roman society, reflected the fact that these believers had not fully grasped the redemptive and transformative power of the gospel. This explains why Paul does not merely correct wrong behavior by admonishing them and reminding them of authentic Christian behavior or by issuing commands. Paul does indeed rebuke, admonish, reprimand, warn, correct, and encourage the believers in Corinth. The focus, however, is on the theological basis of authentic Christian thinking and acting, again and again focusing on Jesus Messiah and his death and resurrection. As Paul treats various ethical problems that characterize the behavior of some church members, he never begins with an imperative. Paul is convinced that the everyday life of Jewish and Gentile believers arises out of the reality of the gospel of Jesus Christ, who mediates the holiness of God who is present in the church through his Spirit.

The goal of Christian ethics is the glory of God: "So, whether you eat or drink, or whatever you do, do everything for the glory of God" (1 Cor. 10:31). The model of Christian ethics is the behavior of Jesus Christ and the example of the apostles: "Be imitators of me, as I am of Christ" (11:1). The principle of Christian ethics is love, which reflects both God's character and Jesus' behavior:

> Anyone who claims to know something does not yet have the necessary knowledge; but anyone who loves God is known by him. . . . If I speak in the tongues of mortals and of angels, but do not have love, I am a noisy gong or a clanging cymbal. And if I have prophetic powers, and understand all mysteries and all knowledge, and if I have all faith, so as to remove mountains, but do not have love, I am nothing. If I give away all my possessions, and if I hand over my body so that I may boast, but do not have love, I gain nothing. Love is patient; love is kind; love is not envious or boastful or arrogant or rude. It does not insist on its own way; it is not irritable or resentful; it does not rejoice in wrongdoing, but rejoices in the truth. It bears all things, believes all things, hopes all things, endures all things. (8:2–3; 13:1–7)

The power of Christian ethics is in the Holy Spirit of God, who mediates the saving and transformative work of Jesus Christ:

> You were washed, you were sanctified, you were justified in the name of the Lord Jesus Christ and in the Spirit of our God. . . . Your body is a temple of the Holy Spirit within you, which you have from God, and that you are not your own. (6:11, 19)

It is only in 1 Corinthians that Paul quotes the words of Jesus as arguments in his exhortation.[4] He bases his "command" to married believers "that the wife should not separate from her husband" as a command of the Lord (7:10), alluding to what Mark reports Jesus saying:

> "Whoever divorces his wife and marries another commits adultery against her; and if she divorces her husband and marries another, she commits adultery." (Mark 10:11–12; cf. Luke 10:7; Matt. 10:10)

He quotes the words of Jesus to his disciples during the Last Supper on the night in which he was betrayed:

> "This is my body that is for you. Do this in remembrance of me. . . . This cup is the new covenant in my blood. Do this, as often as you drink it, in remembrance of me." (1 Cor. 11:24–25; cf. Mark 14:22, 24; Matt 26:26–27; Luke 22:19–20)

Paul's assertion in 1 Corinthians 13:2—"If I have prophetic powers, and understand all mysteries and all knowledge, and if I have all faith, so as to remove mountains, but do not have love, I am nothing"—is perhaps an allusion to Mark 11:23:

> "Truly I tell you, if you say to this mountain, 'Be taken up and thrown into the sea,' and if you do not doubt in your heart, but believe that what you say will come to pass, it will be done for you." (cf. Matt 21:21)

The statement in 1 Corinthians 1:23 that he proclaims the crucified Messiah as "a stumbling block to Jews" is perhaps an allusion to Matthew 11:6 ("And blessed is anyone who takes no offense at me"; cf. Luke 7:23). Paul uses the noun *skandalon*, usually translated as "stumbling block," while the Gospels report Jesus' statement using the verb *skandalizein*, translated as "take offense" (NRSV) or "stumble" (NIV). Some take Paul's discussion of wisdom and foolishness in chapters 1–4, and his emphasis on the need for the power of God to convince Jews and Gentiles of the truth of the gospel, to be an echo of what Jesus says in Matthew 11:25–27:[5]

> "I thank you, Father, Lord of heaven and earth, because you have hidden these things from the wise and the intelligent and have revealed them to infants; yes, Father, for such was your gracious will. All things have been handed over to me by my Father; and no one knows the Son except the Father, and no one knows the Father except the Son and anyone to whom the Son chooses to reveal him."

Paul's point that those who are involved in building the church must build on a sure foundation—"According to the grace of God given to me, like a skilled master builder I laid a foundation, and someone else is building on it. Each builder must choose with care how to build on it" (3:10)—may be an allusion to Matthew 7:24–27:

"Everyone then who hears these words of mine and acts on them will be like a wise man who built his house on rock. The rain fell, the floods came, and the winds blew and beat on that house, but it did not fall, because it had been founded on rock. And everyone who hears these words of mine and does not act on them will be like a foolish man who built his house on sand. The rain fell, and the floods came, and the winds blew and beat against that house, and it fell—and great was its fall!" (cf. Luke 6:47–49)

Paul's statement in 4:1–2—"Think of us in this way, as servants of Christ and stewards of God's mysteries. Moreover, it is required of stewards that they be found trustworthy"—is perhaps an echo of Luke 12:42:

"Who then is the faithful and prudent manager whom his master will put in charge of his slaves, to give them their allowance of food at the proper time?"

And Paul's explanation of his missionary ministry in 9:1–14 is probably influenced by Jesus' missionary discourse in Matthew 10:1–10.[6]

For Paul, the words of Jesus have unquestionable authority. If and when Jesus has spoken on a particular matter, then his words are the end of the discussion.

Divisive Behavior Undermining the Unity of the Church

The unity of the church is not a mere idea, and not an unreachable ideal, but a tangible, experiential reality that results from the presence of God, of Jesus Messiah, and of the Holy Spirit in the church and in the lives of the followers of Jesus if and when they behave as authentic believers. Most imperatives in 1 Corinthians are concerned with the unity of the church.[7] Since the unity of the church is reflected in specific behavior, it is as much part of Christian ethics as it is a topic of Paul's theology.

The divisions in the Corinthian church were triggered by the attachment of some of the educated Corinthian believers to the contemporary secular competitiveness of teachers and orators, accompanied by declarations of loyalty of their students.[8] They promoted personal attachment to Paul, the missionary teacher and theologian who had founded the congregation, or, respectively, to Apollos, a subsequent teacher in the congregation, or to

Cephas, Simon Peter, who may have visited Corinth or whom they met in some other city of the eastern Mediterranean.[9] In his response, which aims to redirect the thinking of the Corinthian believers who have been causing the divisions and to reorient their behavior, Paul focuses fundamentally and extensively on Jesus Messiah.

Paul begins the first section of his discussion (1:10–17) by clarifying that he appeals to them "by the name of our Lord Jesus Christ" (1:10). He asks the rhetorical question whether the Messiah has been divided and whether Paul was crucified for them (1:13), arguing that there is only one Messiah in whom both the Jewish and the Gentile believers in the congregation have found their new identity as members of the messianic people of God; and there is only one death by crucifixion that brought about God's forgiveness of sins and that achieved their salvation. Since there is one Messiah, there is one messianic people of God. To divide the messianic people of God into factions of competing loyalty pledges to missionaries, teachers, and preachers is to divide the Messiah, which is a grotesque suggestion. To pledge loyalty to different Christian leaders is to negate the significance of Jesus' death on the cross: followers of Jesus who owe their salvation to Jesus' death owe loyalty exclusively to Jesus, the only Messiah and Lord.

In the second section of his treatment of the divisions in the church, Paul explains the gospel as the message about the cross on which Jesus Messiah died, a message that cannot be grasped by and thus must not be aligned with the wisdom of the world (1:18–2:5). The gospel, focused as it is on the crucified Messiah Jesus, is regarded as foolishness by Jews and Greeks who cannot understand God's revelation in the Messiah Jesus, despite their eagerness to understand signs given by God and, respectively, despite their claims to philosophical sophistication and rhetorical expertise. The gospel of the crucified Messiah Jesus is understood by Jews and Gentiles, not as the result of argumentative brilliance or miraculous signs, but as a result of the power of God, who leads Jews and Gentiles to a saving knowledge of the crucified Jesus Messiah.

> The message about the cross is foolishness to those who are perishing, but to us who are being saved it is the power of God. . . . For Jews demand signs and Greeks desire wisdom, but we proclaim Christ crucified, a stumbling block to Jews and foolishness to Gentiles, but to those who are the called, both Jews and Greeks, Christ the power of God and the wisdom of God. . . . He is the source of your life in Christ Jesus, who

became for us wisdom from God, and righteousness and sanctification and redemption. . . . My speech and my proclamation were not with plausible words of wisdom, but with a demonstration of the Spirit and of power, so that your faith might rest not on human wisdom but on the power of God. (1 Cor. 1:18, 22–24, 30; 2:4–5)

Since it is the power of God that convinces people of the truth of the gospel of Jesus Christ crucified, through the work of the Holy Spirit (2:6–16), boasting in the rhetorical capabilities of missionaries, preachers, and teachers is not only vain but an insult to God, since the presence of God Almighty annuls all human boasting. Paul asserts, "No one might boast in the presence of God," and he quotes Jeremiah 9:23, "Let the one who boasts, boast in the Lord" (1:29, 31). The foundation of the metaphorical temple—which is the congregation of Jesus' followers that Paul has laid as the pioneer missionary in the city of Corinth, a foundation that cannot be replaced or amended—"is Jesus Christ" (3:11) to whom all believers in the congregation belong (3:23).

Believers belong to Jesus, not to Paul or Apollos; they believe in the gospel of the crucified Jesus Christ, not because of Paul or because of Apollos, but because of the power of God mediated through his Spirit. The one foundation, the one gospel message, the one Messiah, the one death of Jesus on the cross render congregational factions illegitimate. Understanding the gospel of Jesus Christ crucified should prompt a rejection of secular values of competitive superiority and the abandonment of speech that praises this or that teacher over against another teacher. This is as much a theological necessity as it is an ethical choice.

Litigation among Believers

In his disquisition on litigation between members of the congregation in the courts of Corinth, Paul argues that followers of Jesus must not appeal to unbelievers to decide personal controversies, which is absurd (6:1, 6). They should solve legal problems about minor matters internally (6:5), which is both possible and natural since these are disputes among brothers and sisters (6:5–6, 8) who will inherit the kingdom of God (6:9–10) and who, because they are saints, will judge the world (6:2–3). Paul reminds the believers that they no longer live according the behavioral patterns of society in Roman Corinth where fornication, idolatry, adultery, prostitution, sodomy, theft, greed, and drunkenness are everyday realities. He tells them,

> You were washed, you were sanctified, you were justified in the name of
> the Lord Jesus Christ and in the Spirit of our God. (6:11)

The formula "in the name of" refers to the power and authority of the person mentioned; here he refers to the power and authority of Jesus who is
Lord and Messiah. God purified the members of the Corinthian congregation from the impurity of sinful behavior and declared them holy and
righteous on account of the authority of Jesus, who is the crucified and risen
Messiah and Lord who sits at the right hand of God, and who is the judge
of the living and the dead, in whose judgment over the world his followers
will participate.

The Holy Spirit makes God's actions become a reality, bringing the authority of Jesus Christ to bear on the lives they live as people who have been
washed, made holy, and declared righteous. The reality of the merciful and
gracious God became a reality in their lives as they came to faith in Jesus,
Messiah and Lord, and as they experienced the power of the Holy Spirit.
This reality is not just words but personal experience in everyday living. It is
a reality that makes followers of Jesus willing to be wronged and defrauded
rather than fight against fellow believers before unrighteous judges (6:7).

Sexual Ethics

Paul discusses two matters of sexual ethics. The first involved a church
member who lived in an incestuous relationship with his stepmother (5:1).[10]
The church had tolerated this behavior, presumably because they did not
want to lose this particular member of the church, who was probably a
member of the elite on account of whom they were proud (5:2 NIV).[11] Paul
points out that this type of immoral behavior is "not found even among
pagans" (5:1). Indeed, it was illegal to marry persons to whom one was
related by marriage, including an aunt, a mother-in-law, a sister-in-law, or
a stepmother.[12] In Roman law, sexual relations between a stepmother and
a stepson were regarded as incest,[13] which was also prohibited according
to Mosaic and Jewish law (Lev. 18:8; 20:11; m. Sanh. 7:4). The punishment
for incestuous relations was harsh: The two people involved were sent into
exile to live on an island, and they lost both their property and their honor.

Paul calls on the congregation to deal with this matter immediately and
decisively: remove the man from the congregation, evidently in the hope

that he would then repent and be saved on the day of judgment (5:3–5). The one argument Paul provides about why the behavior of the incestuous man is wrong is his brief reference to the criminal nature of such behavior (five words of Greek text in 5:1). He elaborates much more fully on the intolerable behavior of the congregation who had refused to take action against the man (5:6–13).

Paul argues for the purity of the church whose members constitute the messianic people of God in the new covenant (5:6–8). Paul uses three metaphors: the church is a house that needs to be kept pure, as old yeast is removed from Jewish houses before the Passover festival; the church is a new batch of (unleavened) dough that guarantees the saving presence of God; and the church is the place at which God's people celebrate God's salvation.

The central argument that links the three metaphors refers to Jesus' death on the cross and is found in 5:7: "For our paschal lamb, Christ, has been sacrificed." Paul presupposes that the Corinthian believers know the early Christian tradition of a typological understanding of Jesus' death as Passover lamb: God's liberation of the people of Israel from slavery in Egypt corresponds typologically to God's liberation of human beings from the slavery of sin. Jesus' death saves sinners from the divine death sentence on the day of judgment; it liberates sinners from the bondage of sin; and it constitutes a new phase in the history of the people of God. Since Jesus' death effected their liberation from sin, the Corinthian congregation cannot tolerate sinful behavior; since Jesus' death constitutes the messianic people of God who share in God's purity and holiness, the believers in Corinth must make sure that the church member—who is evidently unwilling to repent and change his behavior—is removed from the congregation, whose purity and holiness must be preserved.

Another matter of sexual ethics that Paul discusses is the practice of some believers in Corinth to continue their visits to prostitutes, which was acceptable behavior in Greco-Roman society. Pseudo-Demosthenes says in his speech against Neaira: "We have our courtesans for pleasure, concubines for looking after our daily physical needs, and wives for the procreation of legitimate children and to take good care of domestic matters."[14] Plutarch advises women not to become angry when their husbands have sex with other women, perhaps slaves; he suggests that they should recognize that when their husbands have extramarital sexual relations, they express their respect for their spouses, whom they do not want to humiliate with the sexual fantasies they live out with other women.[15] It was not a coincidence that the Latin language had about fifty synonyms for the word *prostitute*.[16] Although some moral philosophers criticized extramarital sexual activities,[17] their exhortations were ignored.[18]

Paul decisively rejects premarital and extramarital sex, providing four reasons: he explains the authentic understanding of Christian freedom, the authority of Jesus Messiah over one's personal body, the identity of the followers of Jesus, and their unity with Jesus Messiah, which is compromised by visits to prostitutes.

First, Paul emphasizes that Christian freedom does not mean that I make my own laws so that I can say, "All things are lawful for me" (6:12); it is limited by the question of what benefits others, which is a fundamental criterion of Christian ethics (cf. 10:23, 33). The sentence "Not all things are beneficial" (6:12) applies, among other things, to prostitution. The freedom of the gospel is the freedom to live in such a manner that others benefit from what I do.

Second, freedom is further limited by the avoidance of new dependencies. The freedom of a believer is not a freedom in seemingly splendid independence. A believer is committed to the conviction, "I will not be dominated by anything" (6:12). Paul argues that as food and the stomach have a mutual relationship that is clearly defined, so the human body fulfills its particular role only when it acts in its relatedness to the Lord, which means that as Jesus is Lord, so he is "the Lord for the body" (6:13). The body is the realm where Lord Jesus exercises his authority: believers do not belong to themselves but to the Lord; they do not freely decide what they can and cannot do since they are subject to the authority of the Lord. Paul goes on to state that food and stomachs will perish, but the body will be raised from the dead, as God raised Jesus from the dead by his power (6:14). This means that believers will not allow their bodies to engage in unholy acts: they live holy lives in anticipation of living in the presence of God who is holy.

Third, since the bodies of believers are members of the body of Jesus Messiah, they cannot be at the same time members of a prostitute, becoming one body with her (6:15–17).

Fourth, unity with the Messiah Jesus who bought them with a price— that is, who paid with his life to save them from God's judgment of their sins—constitutes their identity as temples of the Holy Spirit, which means that they can and must glorify God in their bodies (16:18–20) and that they cannot visit prostitutes.

Social Ambitions

In a brief, extraordinary passage about Christian slaves (7:21–24), Paul emphasizes that slaves who have been called by God to faith should "not be concerned about it" (7:21), meaning that they should not let their social status as slaves weigh on their mind.[19] Paul states that if they have the opportunity to gain their freedom, they should do so.[20] Then he says,

> For whoever was called in the Lord as a slave is a freed person belonging to the Lord, just as whoever was free when called is a slave of Christ. You were bought with a price; do not become slaves of human masters. (7:22–23)

The first statement substantiates the exhortation that Christian slaves should not be preoccupied with their social status as slaves. A Christian slave needs not be fixated on his fate because the Lord has called him to be a member of God's holy people and he is thus "a freed person" who belongs to Jesus Messiah who is his Lord. The identity of a Christian slave is not tied up with his or her social status as a slave but with his or her association with Jesus, a bond that constitutes freedom from any preoccupation with social status.

The second statement reminds believers who were born as free persons, or who had been manumitted, that they have no advantage over against their fellow believers who were slaves: they are "a slave of Christ"; they belong to Jesus Messiah just as the believing slaves belong to him. Paul, who was a citizen of Tarsus and also held Roman citizenship, repeatedly calls himself a "slave of Jesus Messiah" (Rom. 1:1; Phil. 1:1). Faith in God's salvific action in and through Jesus Messiah renders freeborn slaves of the Messiah and slaves. Christian slaves are assured that their social status as slaves is irrelevant in the messianic people of God: their bond with Jesus Messiah makes them free before God. Freeborn Christians are reminded that their privileged social status is irrelevant in the church: they are not their own masters since they have become slaves of the Messiah and are subject to Jesus' authority.

The third statement explains the bond that ties all believers to Jesus Messiah with a reminder that repeats 6:20: "You were bought with a price" (7:23). Jesus liberated both slaves and freeborn from the power of sin; the price of liberation was Jesus' life, given in his death on the cross, with the result that all who believe in him and who received forgiveness of sin, whether freeborn or slaves, belong to Jesus Messiah who is Lord.

A second example of social realities that are impacted by faith in Jesus Christ concerns Paul's discussion of whether Christians can participate in banquets held in pagan temples where they eat meat sacrificed to idols, a question he answers with a decisive "no" (10:23–11:1), repeatedly referring to Jesus Christ and his death. He asserts that believers who worship the one God the Father who is the creator of the world have one Lord, Jesus Messiah, who also is the creator of the world to whom they owe their salvation: Jesus the creator inaugurated the beginning of the new creation. Paul argues that when members of the church participate in banquets held in pagan temples, they endanger new converts whose faith is weak and who may be tempted to return to idol worship. Paul reminds the Corinthian believers that Jesus Messiah has died for all of them, including new and weak believers, and he argues that contributing to the destruction of the faith of a brother consti-tutes sin not only against the brother but also against Jesus Messiah:

> So by your knowledge those weak believers for whom Christ died are destroyed. But when you thus sin against members of your family, and wound their conscience when it is weak, you sin against Christ. (8:11–12)

Against the claim of Corinthian believers that they have a right to dine in pagan temples (8:9), Paul asserts that as an apostle he has the right to financial support but that he does not make use of this right, willing to "en-dure anything rather than put an obstacle in the way of the gospel of Christ" (9:12). When they participate in idolatrous practices, which they do when they dine in a pagan temple and which is tantamount to dining in the pres-ence of the god who is worshiped in that particular temple, they "put Christ to the test" (10:9), which means they are in danger of being destroyed, as many Israelites died in the desert when they put God to the test by indulg-ing in idolatry and sexual entertainment (10:7–8).[21] Paul then argues the impossibility of believers participating in meals held in pagan temples by explaining what happens when they celebrate the Lord's Supper (10:14–22):

> The cup of blessing that we bless, is it not a sharing in the blood of Christ? The bread that we break, is it not a sharing in the body of Christ? Because there is one bread, we who are many are one body, for we all partake of the one bread. . . . You cannot drink the cup of the Lord and

the cup of demons. You cannot partake of the table of the Lord and the table of demons. Or are we provoking the Lord to jealousy? Are we stronger than he? (10:16–17, 21–22)

Loyalty to Jesus Messiah, who is Lord, regularly and personally reconfirmed in the celebration of the Lord's Supper, excludes loyalty to idols, which is signaled by eating at the tables in their temples. Followers of Jesus who believe in the one true God and in the Lord Jesus Christ cannot at the same time dine in the pagan temples of the city of Corinth, which observers must understand if not as expressions of loyalty to the gods of Corinth then at least as a tacit acknowledgment of their existence. This is idolatry that the Lord will not tolerate.

The third example of social status concerns dress code. Some Corinthian believers were members of the elite. They flaunted their social superiority by praying and prophesying with their heads covered (11:4), as was the custom in contemporary society when elite citizens officiated in religious cults *capite velato*, with their heads covered by their toga. And the integrity of the church was threatened by women who prayed and prophesied without covering their head (11:5), contrary to the practice of married women who appeared in public with their heads covered with a veil (*palla*).[22] Paul frames his comments on the relationship between married men and their spouses by two statements about Jesus: Jesus Messiah is "the head of every man," and God is "the head of Christ" (11:3), highlighting the prominence of Jesus with regard to men and the prominence of God with regard to Jesus Messiah.[23] As Jesus acknowledges God's prominence and authority, so spouses should acknowledge the prominence and authority of their husbands by appearing in public with the traditional veil of married women. In his Letter to the Ephesians, Paul calls on husbands to love their wives "just as Christ loved the church and gave himself up for her," and he calls on wives to respect their husbands (Eph. 5:25, 33), which is also Paul's concern here in 1 Corinthians 11:2–16. In both passages, Paul argues with the example of Jesus Messiah, who submitted to God's authority by sacrificing himself for others. In Ephesians 5, Paul urges husbands to love their wives sacrificially as Jesus loved sacrificially; and in 1 Corinthians 11, he exhorts wives not to bring shame on their husbands but to honor them as Jesus honored God by obediently fulfilling the mission with which God had charged him.

A fourth area where social status came into play was the treatment of poor believers in the Corinthian congregation by the socially superior, well-to-do members of the church (11:17–34). It appears that when the members of the congregation met in the house of one of the believers, everyone brought and ate their own food, which resulted in a situation where the well-to-do Christians who had more and better food shamed the poorer Christians who had little and inferior food.[24] In order to correct the problematic effect of the behavior of the wealthy believers, Paul recites the tradition of the Lord's Supper in order to make the point that followers of Jesus must not allow the communal meals of the congregation to highlight the social differences between poor and rich Christians:

> For I received from the Lord what I also handed on to you, that the Lord Jesus on the night when he was betrayed took a loaf of bread, and when he had given thanks, he broke it and said, "This is my body that is for you. Do this in remembrance of me." In the same way he took the cup also, after supper, saying, "This cup is the new covenant in my blood. Do this, as often as you drink it, in remembrance of me." For as often as you eat this bread and drink the cup, you proclaim the Lord's death until he comes. (11:23–26)

Paul's interest here is not the liturgically correct celebration of the Lord's Supper or new teaching about the Lord's Supper, but the consequences that arise from the regular celebration of the Lord's Supper for the behavior of rich Christians during congregation meals, which starts with a reminder of Jesus' broken body and ends with a reminder of Jesus' shed blood. Christians who shame fellow believers in congregational meetings prove themselves unworthy of participating in the reality signified by the bread and the cup of the Lord's Supper: they commit a sin and thus are "guilty of sinning against the body and blood of the Lord" (11:27). A correct discernment of the body of Jesus who died at the cross for the forgiveness of sins, the body represented in the Lord's Supper by bread and wine, must go hand in hand with a proper discernment of the congregation as the body of Christ (11:29). Enjoying the benefits of Jesus' death on the cross excludes the possibility that believers shame fellow believers. Paul then admonishes believers that when they gather to eat, they "should all eat together" (NIV);[25] that is, they should organize their communal meals as potluck dinners in which everyone shares the same food. Understanding Jesus' death on the cross makes it possible, indeed necessary, that believers meet together without displays of social status and superior lifestyles.

Spiritual Gifts and Personal Behavior

The practice of speaking in tongues (glossolalia) and prophesying was a problem in the Corinthian congregation, as indicated by the specific directives Paul gives in 1 Corinthians 14:1–40. Paul begins his discussion of the gifts of the Holy Spirit with a brief introductory section, in which he demonstrates the fundamental connection between the Holy Spirit and the confession of Jesus as Lord:

> I want you to understand that no one speaking by the Spirit of God ever says "Let Jesus be cursed!" and no one can say "Jesus is Lord" except by the Holy Spirit. (1 Cor. 12:3)

Before Paul discusses details concerning the gifts the Holy Spirit has given to the members of the Corinthian congregation, he reminds them that their most fundamental and essential experience is the power of the Holy Spirit, who brings people to faith in God's redemptive revelation in Jesus Messiah and his atoning death on the cross. The basic Christian confession that the crucified Jesus is the risen Lord (*Kyrios*) can be spoken only as a result of the effective agency of the Spirit of God, who convinces Jews and Gentiles of the truth of the gospel. Paul implies again that the confessional assertion that the crucified Jesus is Messiah and Lord has practical consequences for the behavior of the individual believer. More important than any gift of the Spirit one might have is the effective work of the Spirit in all believers who confess Jesus as Lord.

Paul begins his description of the diversity of spiritual gifts by emphasizing that there are varieties of gifts, or allotments of gifts, all of which are given by the same Spirit; that there are allotments of services connected with these gifts, all of which are given by the same Lord Jesus; and that there are allotments of capabilities ("varieties of activities"), all of which are given by the same God "who activates all of them in everyone" (12:4–6). Paul clarifies that the sphere of power in which the Holy Spirit and his gifts are effective cannot be separated from the sphere of salvation in which Jesus' death on the cross is the effective reality.[26]

Paul illustrates the necessity of all spiritual gifts in their diversity with the metaphor of the human body (12:14–26): a body has many members, all of which have different functions, and all of which are necessary for the body to function. Paul applies the metaphor to the church by emphasizing the connection of the church and her individual members with Jesus Messiah: "Now you are the body of Christ and individually members of it" (12:27). The congregation is not simply "a body" but "the body of Christ," which means that individual believers are members of the body of Christ. The formulation of "body of Christ" means that the congregation as well as individual believers belong to Jesus Messiah. Since believers belong to Jesus Messiah, they have become members of the church. The irreversibility of this sequence is important: "Christ is there before the church, and he is not absorbed into that church. As creator and judge, he remains the counterpart of his members."[27]

Because Jesus Messiah is primary, because all gifts of the Spirit are important, and because the building up of the church is the central criterion for the activities in the assemblies of the congregation, only two or three members who have the gift of speaking in tongues must be allowed to speak, always with a translator.[28] Similarly, only two or three prophets should be allowed to speak, always accompanied by an evaluation of the theological authenticity of what is being said, so that believers who have a hymn or a lesson can address the congregation as well (14:26–36). Monopolizing the assemblies of the church by insisting on exercising a particular spiritual gift is an ethical problem that can be solved by focusing on Jesus Christ, who helps us to understand the nature of the church and the manner in which spiritual gifts are to be used.

Conclusion: The Relevance of the Body

In the long, extraordinary exposition of the argument for the future bodily resurrection (15:1–58), Paul begins by reciting the early Christian tradition of Jesus Messiah's death for our sins in accordance with the Scriptures, his burial, his resurrection on the third day, and his appearances to many witnesses (15:3–7). Paul asserts that if the Messiah Jesus has not been raised from the dead, then the apostolic proclamation of salvation is in vain, faith in Jesus is in vain, God's revelation is misrepresented, sins cannot be forgiven, and sinners will perish on the day of judgment (15:12–19). Paul reiterates the central message of the gospel: After sin had come into the world through the one man Adam, with the result that all his descendants die, so resurrection will come through Jesus Messiah (15:20–22). In the time between Jesus' resurrection and the future resurrection of the believers,

Jesus reigns, as God "has put all things in subjection under his feet" (15:27). Because there will certainly be a future bodily resurrection (15:35–57), our behavior—which is always attached to our bodies—matters:

> Do not be deceived: "Bad company ruins good morals." Come to a sober and right mind, and sin no more; for some people have no knowledge of God. I say this to your shame. . . . But thanks be to God, who gives us the victory through our Lord Jesus Christ. Therefore, my beloved, be steadfast, immovable, always excelling in the work of the Lord, because you know that in the Lord your labor is not in vain. (15:33–34, 57–58)

18

How Athanasius and Calvin Championed a High View of Christ with Implications for Today

William David Spencer

Athanasius against the Arians

Athanasius was stung!

As the young secretary of Bishop Alexander, overseer of the church of Alexandria, Egypt (which in its time was the seat of Christian erudition), Athanasius received his boot-camp training at the Council of Nicaea in AD 325. Now, later in life, weathering the siege of the unitarian Arians, he had emerged (after Alexander's death) as the most prominent of the defenders of the orthodox creed of Nicaea—the hard-fought, premier definition of the Christian faith. Given his own commitment as champion of the Nicaean Council's conclusion,[1] it galled Athanasius to find himself the target of a heresy charge that would eventually escalate and force him into exile, as he was progressively overwhelmed by the political maneuvering of the two heterodox parties who opposed Nicaea's conclusions: the outlawed Arians and the unsettled moderates.

These moderates—led by Eusebius of Caesarea, the famed church historian—held a position that Athanasius defined as semi-Arianism. The Arians are known to us today because their legacy continues in movements such as the Jehovah's Witnesses, who believe that Jesus is the first of God's created beings, but not a person of the Godhead or, in the words of the Jehovah's Witnesses themselves in their booklet *Reasoning from the Scriptures:* "Jesus referred not to himself but to his Father in heaven as 'the only true God.' "[2] For Arians, Jesus Christ is only a created being.

But who were these ancient semi-Arians, and why should I begin a discussion on Calvin's view of Jesus, or what we call his Christology, by reviewing a struggle between the semi-Arians and Athanasius some twelve hundred years prior to the Reformation? I begin with them and their opposition to Nicaean orthodoxy, because I find myself struck by a parallel between the plight of Athanasius in contending with the theological moderates of his time and a similar struggle Calvin faced as he articulated his own high view of Jesus in the Reformation. The attacks by the enemies of Athanasius and those by the opponents of Calvin brought to each a similar charge and based their arguments on a similar concern, as we will see below.

John Henry Cardinal Newman provides a helpful summary in his "Appendix of Illustrations" that sheds light on Athanasius's protests in the *Epistle of S. Athanasius, Archbishop of Alexandria, Concerning the Councils Held at Ariminum in Italy and at Seleucia in Isauria*[3] (which we will refer to as the *De Synodis*, or "of the councils," which is Athanasius's critique of the heterodox councils that opposed Nicaea's creed). Cardinal Newman describes the semi-Arians as having "an orthodox interpretation" but also a "heretical" one. He notes that these semi-Arians were contrasting two persons of the Trinity with one (the Father) as "a greater God" and the other (the Son) as "less," one as "a true God" and the other "a so-called God," one "a God of all" and the other only "a Divine Mediator and representative God." Cardinal Newman views these christological moderates as prevaricating: "Though our Lord was not in being from everlasting, and though He had been brought into being at the will of the Father, still a *gennesis* was a divine act in kind different from a creation; not indeed an emanation."

Cardinal Newman reminds us that the ad hoc leader of the semi-Arians, Eusebius of Caesarea, "calls our Lord a second substance, another God, a second God." Cardinal Newman was right.[4] Eusebius, the influential leader of the moderates, was proposing just that. In a letter to Bishop Euphration, Eusebius raised this question about the Father and Son: "If they coexist, how shall the Father be Father and the Son Son? or how the One first, the Other second? and the One ingenerate and the Other generate?"[5]

In response, Athanasius charged that "Eusebius of Caesarea in Palestine, in a letter to Euphration the Bishop, did not scruple to say plainly that Christ was not true God."[6] Athanasius's conclusion was confirmed when Eusebius was recorded at the Seventh General Council (Act 6) as declaring, "The Son Himself is God, but not Very God."[7]

Not content with letters and vocal public statements, Eusebius and his colleagues composed their anti-Nicaean protests in the form of a series of semi-Arian creeds, beginning with the Dedication Creed of AD 341, which then bombarded the post-Council of Nicaea world like mortar shells, each one wreaking progressive damage to adherence to Nicaea's creed. Their target was Athanasius's insistence that the relationship of the Son of God, Jesus Christ, to God the Father was that "He has equality with the Father by titles expressive of unity, and what is said of the Father, is said in Scripture of the Son also, all but His being called Father."[8]

Further, these semi-Arians were disturbed by Athanasius's proof of this point—as he launched into a careful paralleling of Bible verses that show the Son as being equal to the Father—by revealing from Scripture that both Father and Son are almighty, eternal, worshiped equally, honored equally, both are called "Lord God," and therefore, as Athanasius concluded, the Son has "equality with the Father."[9] As a result, Athanasius reported that the semi-Arians charged him with this accusation:

> They say then, as you have written, that it is not right to say that the Son is one in substance with the Father, because He who speaks of one in substance speaks of three, one substance preexisting, and that those who are generated from it are one in substance.[10]

In other words, his opponents accused him of a kind of tri-theism: that the Father preexists and the Son and Spirit come later of the same substance, so there are three gods, the latter two dependent on the Father for their existence.[11]

Athanasius, shocked at this conclusion, countered that the earlier church overseer Ignatius (AD 100s)—whom all respected including Eusebius himself, who honored Ignatius as "distinguished" and "a famed name as second after Peter to succeed to the bishopric of Antioch"[12]—had already pointed out that the Son is both ingenerate and generate: ingenerate in that the Son is eternal, and generate in that he was begotten at the incarnation. As Athanasius noted, "We are persuaded that the blessed Ignatius was orthodox in writing that Christ was generate on account of the flesh, (for he was made flesh,) [sic] yet ingenerate, because He is not in the number of things made and generated."[13] By this appeal to Ignatius, Athanasius affirmed that the Son did not come later, originally not existing, or not being distinguished in the Godhead, and then suddenly coming about as the Father emitted substance, producing a Son at some point in timelessness who takes on personhood somewhere in eternity.

But that defense did not stop the condemnation levied at Athanasius. His critics then charged him with proposing that "the One is not Father and the Other Son, but they are brothers together."[14] Athanasius replied that human fathers and sons can very well be equal in maturity, though he warned against pressing any human analogy too far. Athanasius's opponents, however, still had one more great accusation against him: they charged him with promoting a condemned heresy, and here we may have come to the crux of their concern.

What worried these moderates was that Nicaea's insistence that the Father and Son shared the same substance (*homoousios*) was reintroducing Sabellianism, a heresy condemned by all the faithful involved in this dispute. Sabellius, who taught in the early 200s, followed in the wake of what were called the Modalists, so-called for their belief that God was revealed to humanity in different modes: God being the Father in the Old Testament, then transforming to the Son in the New, and reappearing as the Holy Spirit at work in the church.

Noetus of Smyrna became prominent in the late AD 190s and was condemned around AD 200 for teaching this simple Modalism, also called Dynamic Monarchianism, which describes God as an actively changing Monarch, or Monad, taking on these three successive modes. Praxeus was another proponent of a similar view.[15] He was censured by Tertullian, the outspoken Christian lawyer, who charged him with having "crucified the Father,"[16] meaning that Praxeus presented God, formerly of the Father mode, now on the cross in the Son mode. Both of these teachers were understandably condemned for heresy, and the theological absurdity of their teaching is obvious. For one thing, if God moved from being the Father to being the Son, then who sustained the universe when God died on the cross? Why did it not implode or explode in chaos? If the Second Person of the Triune Godhead did not die, however, then what happened to Jesus's hell-defeating, humanity-rescuing substitutionary atonement? It would not have taken place, and all humanity would still be in sin. Another option, attributed to Pope Zephyrinus, was that the Father may have been conceived in and born from Mary and co-suffered on the cross (a variation called Adoptionism contended that the Spirit of God arrived on the human Jesus at his baptism, then cleared out and left the man Jesus hanging on the cross, baffled, asphyxiating, and abandoned); however, "the Father did not die, but the Son"[17] did. This would mean that the divine Father suffered on the cross for us, but only the human Jesus could and did die. Such a solution, however, would not solve the soteriological dilemma. Having all of God die in the crucifixion or nothing of God in a solely human Jesus die would not be enough to accomplish human salvation. Christ, the incarnated Son of God, had to be both fully God and fully human to defeat the spiritual forces of evil, while also substituting fully for fallen humanity in his sacrificial death. Both views, simple Modalism and Adoptionism, were therefore condemned as heresies.

Retooling the Heresy

Some one hundred years before the Arian controversy, Sabellius had appeared during the see of Pope Callistus (AD 217–222) with what J. N. D. Kelly terms "a more systematic, philosophical shape" to his Modalism.[18] Sabellius agreed that God was a Monad, but rather than successive modes, he posited the Monarch as emitting from himself manifestations of a Father, Son, or Holy Spirit who are "projected like a ray of the sun and then withdrawn" back into the Divine Monad.[19] In the incarnation, this refinement of Modalism envisioned the appearance of a temporary manifestation, not a distinctly eternal Second Person of the Godhead who was totally committed to being fully human, taking on limitations (as Phil. 2:5–8 explains), and becoming capable of dying—while at the same time remaining fully divine and also completely capable of defeating the powers of hell and death.

Instead, in Sabellius's view, what hung on the cross was merely a temporary manifestation of an emanation from the Monad, who only appeared as the Son of God. In this view, an eternal person of the Godhead did not die, though a human life was laid down. In this theology, there is no scandal of the cross in the crucifixion death of an incarnate eternal person of the Godhead.

Sadly, Modalists still exist today. Noetian and Sabellian views are very much alive in the teaching of the United Pentecostal Church International (UPCI) and in some of the churches calling themselves "Apostolic" (these are sometimes called "Oneness" or "Jesus Only" churches), who baptize in the name of Jesus alone since, as the General Superintendent of the UPCI explains,

> Our Creator became our Savior. The God against whom we sinned is the One who forgives us. God loved us so much that He came in flesh to save us. He gave of Himself; He did not send someone else. Moreover, our Creator-Savior is also the indwelling Spirit who is ever-present to help us. God told us how to live and then came to live among us. He

showed us how to live in the flesh and laid down His human life to purchase our salvation. Now He abides within us and enables us to live according to His will. Jesus Christ is the one God incarnate, and in Him we have everything we need: healing, deliverance, victory, and salvation (Colossians 2:9–10). By recognizing the almighty God in Jesus Christ, we restore correct biblical belief and experience apostolic power.[20]

Therefore, in this unitarian church's view:

There is one God, who has revealed Himself as our Father, in His Son Jesus Christ, and as the Holy Spirit. Jesus Christ is God manifested in flesh. He is both God and man. (See Deuteronomy 6:4; Ephesians 4:4–6; Colossians 2:9; I Timothy 3:16.)[21]

No wonder the trinitarian Athanasius—who insisted on the biblical view of Jesus Christ having equality with the Father (Phil. 2:6) in the eternal Triune Godhead while humbling himself to add on humanity in the incarnation—was stung by the semi-Arian charge that he was actively preaching unitarian modalistic heresy, therefore grouping him into the camp that claimed God the Father and God the Son were the exact same person in different guises.

Calvin Continues to Fight for the Faith

Now we see the point of all this background as one great link between Athanasius and John Calvin, especially as we note Calvin's similar reaction when he is accused of Sabellianism on account of his own high Christology.

Writing from Berne in May 1537, Calvin complained to Simon Grynée, a scholarly theologian, a friend of both Melanchthon and Erasmus, and the rector of the Academy of Basle. Eventually, Grynée would give Calvin refuge in his own home when the fiery young Reformer was kicked out of Geneva. In gratitude, Calvin would dedicate to Grynée his commentary on Romans.[22] Here was a trusted friend to whom Calvin could open his heart. Thus Calvin wrote to him about his initial dismissal of what became an increasingly hostile war against him, leading to his banishment. He gives this defense:

When first we heard, therefore, that the Arian heresy was imputed to us, and then a little afterwards the Sabellian, none of these things very much disturbed us, seeing that our ears had long since been well seasoned against such calumnies; and we entertained the assured hope that they would eventually pass away in a wreath of smoke.[23]

Calvin explained to Grynée that this attack had been instigated by the catechism Calvin had written:

> We embraced the Father, the Son, and the Spirit, under one essence of the Godhead: making, nevertheless, such a distinction between each from the other, that no room might be left for any crooked suspicion of ambiguity.[24]

That anyone could label him as an Arian naturally mystified Calvin, for he contends,

> We taught, certainly, that Christ is the true and natural Son of God, who had possessed the like essential deity with the Father from all eternity, who in the fullness of time had assumed our flesh, foreordained for our redemption.[25]

Likewise, Calvin protested that he had been labeled a Sabellian for what he called the "one capital offence" of which he was "guilty" in his catechism: His claim that "Christ was there affirmed to be that Jehovah, who of Himself alone was always self-existent, which charge I was quite ready to meet."[26] And meet it he does:

> Certainly, if the distinction between the Father and the Word be attentively considered, we shall say that the one is from the other. If, however, the essential quality of the Word be considered, in so far as He is one God with the Father, whatever can be said concerning God may also be applied to Him, the second person in the glorious Trinity.[27]

Here Calvin is echoing Athanasius's central contention, which is the very argument Athanasius used in his own defense of his Nicaean Christology— namely, that whatever can be said concerning the Father may also be said of the Son. Calvin adopts this approach, basing his proof of the equality of the Father and the Son on the titles shared between the Father and the Son in the Bible. One example is when Calvin writes:

Now, what is the meaning of the name Jehovah? What did that answer imply which was spoken to Moses? I Am That I Am. Paul makes Christ the author of this saying.[28]

One can read this same argument in Athanasius's *De Synodis* when he notes that sharing the same titles indicates that Father and Son share the same substance—both are distinctly, eternally God. In Athanasius's words, as already noted, the Son "has equality with the Father by titles expressive of unity, and what is said of the Father, is said in Scripture of the Son also."[29] The arguments of Calvin and Athanasius are basically the same on this key point, as Athanasius writes, "What is said of the Father, is said in Scripture of the Son also"; Calvin writes, "Whatever can be said concerning God may also be applied to Him, the second person in the glorious Trinity."

So Calvin and Athanasius both rest their defenses of the equality of the persons of the Trinity on this biblical argument. Furthermore, Athanasius appeals to it in his apology for the Council of Nicaea's high Christology:

And since the Scriptures precede you which say, that the Lord is Son of the Father, and the Father Himself precedes them, who says, *This is my beloved Son*, and a son is no other than the offspring from his father, is it not evident that the Fathers [of Nicaea] have suitably said that the Son is from the Father's substance?[30]

Calvin's problems, however, did not end here with his establishment of his adherence to the teaching of Scripture and the Nicaean theology of Athanasius. No, his opponents still assailed him for his controversial claim that not only the Father but the Son is also self-existent—that is to say, auto-theos.

But, again, this doctrine came straight to Calvin from Ignatius and what Athanasius understood about Ignatius's view, as we noted earlier, which was supported by the Athanasian Creed in which Athanasius's disciples summarize their mentor's teaching: "And in this Trinity none is before or after other; none is greater or less than another. But the whole three Persons are coeternal together, and coequal."[31] We can also read this Athanasian-style teaching in Calvin's *Institutes*: "The eternity of the Father is also the eternity of the Son and the Spirit, since God could never exist apart from his wisdom and power, and we must not seek in eternity a *before* or an *after*."[32]

Further, Calvin writes:

Nothing should be more intolerable to us than to fancy a beginning of that Word who both was always God and afterward was the artificer of the universe. But they think they are reasoning shrewdly when they aver that Moses, by narrating that God then spoke for the first time, hints thereby that there had been in him no Word before. Nothing is more trifling than this![33]

Again Calvin affirms that Christ is equated with the Old Testament Jehovah in the revelation to Moses in Exodus 34:6–7: "Here let us observe that his eternity and his self-existence are announced by that wonderful name twice repeated."[34] Calvin even quotes Moses quoting God:

"Jehovah," he says, "Jehovah a merciful and gracious God, patient and of much compassion, and true, who keepest mercy for thousands, who takest away iniquity and transgression, . . . in whose presence the innocent will not be innocent, who visitest the iniquity of the fathers upon the children and the children's children." [Ex. 34:6–7, cf. Vg.][35]

Theologian Charles Hodge summarized Calvin's argument very clearly:

If Christ be Jehovah, and if the name Jehovah implies self-existence, then Christ is self-existent. In other words, self-existence and necessary existence, as well as omnipotence and all other divine attributes, belong to the divine essence common to all the persons of the Trinity, and therefore it is the Triune God who is self-existent, and not one person in distinction from the other persons.[36]

So much for the charge of Sabellianism.[37]

Conclusion

Calvin groups Arius and Sabellius with what he calls "other ancient authors of errors,"[38] and he rails against Arius, whom he calls "this turncoat": "Arius says that Christ is God, but mutters that he was made and had a beginning." Against Sabellius, Calvin complains,

Sabellius says that Father, Son, and Spirit signify no distinctions in God. Say they are three, and he will scream that you are naming three Gods. Say that in the one essence of God there is a trinity of persons; you will say in one word what Scripture states, and cut short empty talkativeness.[39]

In summary, we see the words of Athanasius echoed in Calvin's language about Christ. Similar are the charges opponents laid against both of them. But similar also is the triumph of Athanasius and Calvin, each maintaining a high Christology in the face of mounting opposition. Therefore, Calvin is distinguished for his loyalty to Scripture and his respect for the great Creed of Nicaea, as is Athanasius before him. Both Athanasius and Calvin promote Christ being coequal and coeternal with the Father, and they establish the self-existent quality of all the persons of the Trinity by appealing to proof from the Bible.

This high Christology is a precious legacy handed down to us today from the New Testament revelation through champions of orthodoxy (that is, right Christian doctrine) such as Athanasius and John Calvin, which we who are Christ's defenders need to safeguard in our own generation. We still face persuasive arguments that reintroduce Noetianism, Sabellianism, and Arianism, and we find tri-theism in Mormon teaching and so much else in our pluralistic global culture—all of which threatens the spiritual and doctrinal well-being of the contemporary Christian church.

Recently, even in evangelicalism, proponents of a low Christology have arisen, making claims such as the following:

The Father is supreme in authority, the Son is under the Father, and the Spirit is under the Father and the Son.[40]

The Father gets top billing.[41]

To the Father, then, we owe our deepest thanks and highest allegiance.[42]

He has in the trinitarian order the place of highest authority, the place of highest honor.[43]

This kind of language echoes the ancient semi-Arian creeds such as the Dedication Creed (AD 341), which also distinguishes Father, Son, and Spirit by these "titles not being given in a vague or meaningless way but accurately denoting the particular existence [or personality] and rank and glory of each."[44] Such a hierarchical formulation of the Trinity is much closer to the language of Eusebius and the semi-Arians than it is to that of Nicaea's Council, Athanasius, or Calvin.

We also live in a time when religions are urged on bumper stickers to "coexist," instead of battling one another. For some, such a call for everyone to learn to get along does not necessarily mean that all religions are the same, or that they should become inclusive. Others in this postmodern age, however, urge all faiths, including Christianity, to relativize and become inclusive. While cooperation on issues—such as providing famine relief, stopping human trafficking, or interceding in natural disasters—involves common ground, the doctrines of exclusive faiths do not. Christianity is an inclusive faith in that its message of liberation in Jesus is extended to all, but it is an exclusive faith in that this message cannot be compromised with the dogmas of other faith stances.

If the Renaissance reached back into the past to retrieve learning that had been lost, then the Reformation reached back and retrieved doctrine that had become obscured. This is the gift the Reformation gave to us. It pared away accretions that had adhered over the years and sharpened expressions of the central doctrines under the banners of *sola scriptura, sola gratia, sola fide,* and *solus Christus.*

The legacy we have received in the divine revelation on which our Christian doctrine is built is our treasure. It is the basis of the "once-given-to-the-saints faith" (Jude 3).[45] It is important that we follow the examples of Athanasius and Calvin and preserve God's biblical revelation and its resulting doctrines within our churches, despite the opposition of our age. We should fight as these champions of orthodoxy did despite the opposition they faced, so that we may hand the Nicaean/Reformed faith on to our spiritual descendants, just as it was handed on to us.

19

JUSTIFICATION FIVE HUNDRED YEARS LATER: SHOULD IT STILL BE A CHURCH-DIVIDING ISSUE?

John Jefferson Davis

> Many members of our communities yearn to receive the Eucharist at one table, as the concrete expression of full unity. We experience the pain of those who share their whole lives, but cannot share God's redeeming presence at the Eucharistic table. . . . We long for this wound in the Body of Christ to be healed.[1]

In this joint declaration issued on October 31, 2016, after an ecumenical prayer service in Lund, Sweden, commemorating the five-hundredth anniversary of the start of the Reformation, Pope Francis and Martin Junge, the general secretary of the Lutheran World Federation, alluded to the pain felt by Swedish married couples in mixed Catholic-Lutheran marriages who could not come to the same Communion table together, and pledged to work together for changes in church policies that would allow for a shared Eucharist.[2]

The title of this chapter is "Justification Five Hundred Years Later: Should It Still Be a Church-Dividing Issue?" My purpose is to argue that the biblical doctrine of justification by faith—which divided the Western Church half a millennium ago—when rightly understood, actually provides a theological mandate for the visible unity of the churches and, in particular, removes barriers to intercommunion or "Eucharistic hospitality" between Roman Catholic and Protestant Christians.

The outline of this chapter is as follows: first, we will review recent Roman Catholic-Protestant ecumenical discussions on the doctrine of justification; second, we will examine biblical texts that speak to church unity in general and Eucharistic fellowship in particular; third, we will look at objections to intercommunion from Protestant perspectives; fourth, we will consider Roman Catholic objections to intercommunion; and fifth and finally, there will be a conclusion and practical recommendations.

Recent Ecumenical Discussions on Justification

The 1999 "Joint Declaration on the Doctrine of Justification"[3] from the Lutheran World Federation and the Roman Catholic Church marked a historic movement toward rapprochement between these two ecclesial bodies on the topic of justification. Noting that the doctrine of justification was a principal cause of the division of the Western Church in the sixteenth century, the declaration stated that, in light of new insights from recent biblical studies and the history of theology and dogma, a "notable convergence" between Protestant and Catholic understandings had occurred, such that the mutual doctrinal condemnations of the sixteenth century "do not apply to today's partner" (2.13).

The statement declared such a convergent understanding of the doctrine of justification as follows:

> Together we confess: By grace alone, in faith in Christ's saving work and not because of any merit on our part, we are accepted by God and receive the Holy Spirit, who renews our hearts while equipping and calling us to good works. . . . Through Christ alone are we justified. . . . Faith is itself God's gift through the Holy Spirit. . . . [O]ur new life is solely due to the forgiving and renewing mercy that God imparts as a gift and we receive in faith, and never can merit in any way. (3.15–17)

It is notable that the joint declaration uses the terminology of both *sola gratia* and *solus Christus*, and while not explicitly using the terminology of *sola fide*, they understand faith itself as "God's gift through the Holy Spirit" and not as a human work. The characteristic Catholic linkage of justification (acceptance by God) and sanctification (renewal of the heart) is retained.[4]

The declaration concludes that a "consensus in basic truths of the doctrine of justification exists between Lutherans and Catholics" (5.40), and that this consensus "must come to influence the life and teachings of our churches" (5.43).[5] The declaration is seen by both parties to be a "decisive step forward on the way to overcoming the division of the church" (5.44).

In May 1994, a group of evangelical and Roman Catholic leaders in the United States released the document "Evangelicals & Catholics Together: the Christian Mission in the Third Millennium."[6] The participants, including Charles Colson and J. I. Packer on the evangelical side, and Avery Dulles and George Weigel on the Catholic side, affirmed together that "we are justified by grace through faith because of Christ," and that "Evangelicals are brothers and sisters in Christ" (4). Given this mutual recognition of membership in the larger body of Christ (as authentically Christian), both sides agreed that it was not theologically legitimate for one Christian community to proselytize among "the active adherents of another Christian community" (17).

It was recognized that significant differences in theology and practice remained—for example, the Lord's Supper as Eucharistic sacrifice or memorial meal—but that nevertheless, in light of the substantial agreement on justification and the mutual recognition of one another as Christian, both sides were "called by God to a fuller realization of our unity in the body of Christ" (4, 8).

J. I. Packer, in responding to some critics who felt that this notable Reformed theologian had "gone soft" in signing the document, stated that he indeed recognized the substantive theological and ecclesiological differences that still separated Catholics and Protestants. However, the common affirmations of Jesus as Lord and Savior, of the Apostles' Creed, of "justification by grace through faith because of Christ," and of the infallible inspiration and authority of the Scriptures provided the basis of a common recognition of one another as "brothers and sisters in Christ" and hence for cooperation and service among the two communions wherever conscience would allow.[7] In Packer's view, the statement on justification that Catholics were willing to affirm was sufficiently orthodox for the mutual recognition of a common Christian identity.

The Petrine "Error," Galatians 2:14, Justification by Faith, and Christian Unity

Paul's confrontation with Peter at Antioch, described in Galatians 2:11–21, demonstrates that the truth of justification by faith is fundamental not only for our "vertical" relationship to God in salvation, but also for our "horizontal" relationships across ethnic and racial lines in the fellowship of the visible church. The sixteenth-century Reformers focused on the vertical and soteriological dimensions; today, in the twenty-first century, we need to recover the social implications of this doctrine for the visible unity of the church across racial and denominational divides.

When Peter came to Antioch, Paul stated that he "opposed him to his face." When certain men came from James, Peter withdrew from table fellowship with the Gentile believers in Antioch. By so doing, Paul vehemently stated that Peter was not living "in line with the truth of the gospel" (*ouk orthopodousin pros tēn alētheian tou euangeliou;* literally, "not walking straight with the truth of the gospel"; 2:14). Peter's actions—not merely his cognitive beliefs—were not consistent with the truth of justification by faith. As F. F. Bruce has noted, Peter's actions were, in effect, a statement that the Gentiles' Christian faith was defective, and as such they were not fit company for Jewish Christians at the table. Faith in Christ and baptism in his name were insufficient and "must be supplemented by something else"—Jewish food laws or customs.[8]

"Jesus is not Lord where churches divide along ethnic, tribal, or geographic lines. . . . [A]ll Jesus' followers belong together in worship and table fellowship," states N. T. Wright in his commentary on the exegesis and theology of the letter to the Galatians. "That was the 'truth of the gospel' for which Paul contended in the first century, and it remains the truth of the gospel today."[9]

God's concern for the visible unity of the church is, of course, strongly attested in the New Testament. In his solemn high priestly prayer, Jesus prays that his followers may "be brought to complete unity to let the world know that you have sent me and have loved them even as you have loved me" (John 17:23). Jesus affirms the high value of truth ("Sanctify them by the truth; your word is truth"; John 17:17), but *three* times in this same prayer, he prays for unity (John 17:11, 21, 23). Disunity among his disciples undercuts the credibility of Jesus' life and mission, and the credibility of the Father's love for the disciples.

The apostle Paul sees the reconciliation and visible unity of Jews and Gentiles across ethnic divides as fundamental to God's purposes in the atonement. The death of Jesus on the cross was intended to produce "one new man out of the two," "reconciling both of them to God through the cross" (Eph. 2:15–16) and putting an end to the former hostility. In the same Epistle, the apostle urges believers to be eager to preserve the "unity of the Spirit in the bond of peace" (Eph. 4:3). The basis of unity is the one Lord, one faith, one baptism, and one God and Father shared by all, together with a common life in the Spirit and inclusion in the one body of Christ (Eph. 4:5–6).

Consequently, the apostle is grieved by the disunity of the Corinthians in their table fellowship (1 Cor. 11:17–22). The one loaf they share at the Communion table is meant to signify their unity as members of the same one body (1 Cor. 10:17). As Gordon Fee has noted, this text teaches the unity that should prevail on the *horizontal* and visible level.[10] And as Bishop Lesslie Newbigin stated in the context of efforts toward the reunion of the churches of south India, our modern refusals of table fellowship with other believers "are as scandalous as those that St. Paul had to deal with in Corinth, however reverently we may conduct them."[11]

The foundational confession that united believers in the New Testament and early Christianity was stated by Paul in his Epistle to the Romans this way: "If you confess with your mouth that 'Jesus is Lord' and believe in your heart that God raised him from the dead, you will be saved" (Rom. 10:9). An *ex animo* confession of the Lordship of Jesus as the Messiah and a conviction that God raised him from the dead places one in a state of salvation. In 1 Corinthians 15:3–5, the apostle states the basic Christian *kerygma* that he had himself received and passed along to the Corinthians: "that Christ died for our sins according to the scriptures, that he was buried, that he was raised on the third day according to the scriptures, and that he appeared to Peter, and then to the Twelve."[12] All those who confess this apostolic *kerygma*, or its later formulations in the Nicene and Apostles' Creeds, and who have been baptized, should recognize one another as members of the one body of Christ, and as such welcome one another at the Communion table.

Protestant Barriers to Intercommunion

In this section, we will consider two examples of Protestant objections to intercommunion between Catholics and Protestants: first, that of R. C. Sproul on the basis of a certain understanding of justification as *sola fide*; and second, that of the Missouri Synod Lutheran Churches, on the basis of their specific interpretation of the words of institution of the Lord's Supper.

The prominent conservative Reformed theologian R. C. Sproul has criticized the decision of J. I. Packer and other evangelicals to sign the

1994 "Evangelicals and Catholics Together." In Sproul's view, this joint
Evangelical-Catholic statement of justification falls short by failing to
explicitly affirm justification by faith *alone*. For Sproul, an explicit affirmation of the "aloneness" of faith is essential to the gospel, and its omission
or denial is an act of apostasy which negates recognition of a common
faith between Catholics and Reformation Protestants.[13] He rejects Packer's
view that while *sola fide* may be vital to the *bene esse* (well-being) of the
church, its explicit affirmation is not vital to the *esse* (essence or being) of
a true church.[14]

On this point, Packer rather than Sproul has the better of the argument. The problem with Sproul's position, in the view of this writer, is that
it fails to sufficiently recognize the distinction between faith as a fundamental *disposition* of a person's heart toward God, and that same person's
affirmation of a specific and precise *verbal formulation* of a given *doctrine*
such as justification. As the case of Abraham shows, Abraham was justified
by faith—his heart was disposed to trust in God's promise (Gen. 15:6; Rom.
4:3)—three millennia prior to the precise doctrinal formulation of such
a disposition as *sola fide* by Luther and Melanchthon in the Reformation
period. We are justified by faith—not merely or primarily by intellectual assent to a precise verbal formulation of that faith disposition. The latter (faith
as precise formulation) is consequent to the former (faith as disposition),
and not the reverse. Sproul's insistence that a precise verbal understanding
of a Reformation formulation of *sola fide* is necessary for justification and
salvation would have the peculiar consequence that no "Christian" was in
fact in a state of justification from postapostolic times until Luther rediscovered such a formulation in the sixteenth century![15] This seems like an
all-too-heavy price to pay.

The Missouri Synod Lutheran Church (MSLC) practices "close(d) communion"; that is, they invite to the Communion table only members of
their own denomination or other Lutheran bodies that are in "altar and
pulpit fellowship" with the MSLC[16] and who agree with the church's doctrinal understanding of how Christ is present in the sacrament. The MSLC
holds strongly to a "Real Presence" understanding, in which the "true body
and blood of Christ shed on the cross" are believed to be received "in, with
and under the bread and wine," in an "incomprehensible, spiritual mode of
presence according to which he neither occupies nor yields space but passes
through everything created as he wills."[17] Since in their view, fellowship at
the Lord's Table is meant to be a confession of a "common faith," "it would

not be truthful for those who affirm the Real Presence and those who deny it to join one another."[18]

This restriction on access to the Lord's Table is clearly much more restrictive than the conditions presupposed in New Testament practice, in which the confession of Jesus as Lord, risen from the dead (Rom. 10:9), and repentance and subsequent baptism (Acts 2:38) brought one into communion with other believers.[19] The "common faith" is that which is presupposed in texts such as 1 Corinthians 15:1–3, and its later developments in the Nicene and Apostles' Creeds—and not a detailed explication of a specific understanding of the mode of the presence of Christ in the sacrament. Christ's command to "take and eat" enjoined an *act* of obedience and faith, not a particular theological or metaphysical interpretation of the manner or mode of presence. It would seem that the MSLC position on this matter is a modern analogy to the "Petrine error" at Antioch. Peter, in effect, by his actions was saying that "Gentiles must become like Jews to have table fellowship with us." The MSLC practice of closed communion says, in effect, "Unless you become Missouri Synod Lutheran—even though you are confessing Christians—we cannot have table fellowship with you."

Roman Catholic Barriers to Intercommunion

The Second Vatican Council (1963–65) marked a significant step forward in Catholic-Protestant ecumenical relationships. In *Lumen Gentium* ("Dogmatic Constitution on the Church"), the Roman Catholic Church recognized Protestants, in spite of not professing "the faith in its entirety," as authentically Christian and members of the universal body of Christ:

> The Church recognizes that in many ways she is linked with those who, being baptized, are honored with the name of Christian, though they do not profess the faith in its entirety or preserve unity of communion with the successor of Peter. . . . They are consecrated by Baptism, through which they are united to Christ. They also recognize and receive other Sacraments within their own Churches. [W]e can say that in some real way they are joined with us in the Holy Spirit, for to them also He gives His gifts and graces.[20]

This statement recognized Protestants, Orthodox, and ancient Oriental Christians as being joined to the Roman Catholic Church by the Holy Spirit, but without sharing in Eucharistic communion, since these other ecclesial bodies did not acknowledge the jurisdictional primacy of the pope, the bishop of Rome.

As already noted in the first section ("Recent Ecumenical Discussions") above, the 1999 "Joint Declaration on the Doctrine of Justification" from the Lutheran World Federation and the Catholic Church had, in light of the doctrinal consensus achieved, removed the mutual doctrinal condemnations issued in the sixteenth century. In the October 2016 joint commemoration of the Reformation in Lund, the parties recognized that they were "freed by grace to move towards the communion to which God continually calls us,"[21] and recommitted themselves to "move from conflict to communion . . . as part of the one Body of Christ, into which we are incorporated through Baptism."[22]

Nevertheless, barriers to intercommunion still exist on the basis of Roman Catholic canon law on the administration of the sacraments. Canon 844 of the *Code of Canon Law* states that "Catholic ministers administer the sacraments licitly to Catholic members of the Christian faithful alone, who likewise receive them licitly from Catholic ministers alone."[23] Non-Roman Catholic Christians who do not acknowledge the primacy of the bishop of Rome, and who consequently are not in full communion with the Roman Catholic Church, cannot consequently under normal circumstances be invited to a Catholic Eucharist.

There is a certain irony here. By insisting on the recognition of the primacy of Peter as a condition of communion, the Roman Catholic Church is in effect repeating the "Petrine error" of Peter at Antioch: adding conditions other than a confession of faith in Jesus Christ as Lord and Savior and the reception of Christian baptism as the basis of table fellowship.

Since Vatican II and later ecumenical documents acknowledged other Christians as truly members of the one body of Christ, acknowledging the validity of non-Catholic baptisms, and expressing a desire to remove the remaining barriers to intercommunion, it seems theologically inconsistent for the Roman Catholic Church not to actually do so. By so doing, Catholics and Protestants would be giving to the world a meaningful sign of visible unity. If Catholic theology can recognize a Protestant *baptism* as valid, and recognize Protestant Christians as members of the body of Christ, then why can they not recognize the Protestant Eucharist—and the ministers who celebrate it—as valid as well?

Conclusion and Practical Implications

In conclusion, it has been argued that the doctrine of justification by faith, in light of Galatians 2:11–14, is not only foundational for a believer's individual acceptance before God, but also for the visible, social unity of the church to be demonstrated in fellowship at the Communion table. Both Protestants and Catholics, in their different ways, have fallen into the "Petrine error" of adding conditions for intercommunion beyond those specified in the New Testament.

Protestants have done this either by adding to the basic reality of saving faith as a *disposition* a requirement for a refined, precise verbal *articulation* of that disposition (e.g., Sproul) or by adding to the conditions for Communion the requirement for a precisely articulated belief in the mode of Christ's presence at the supper (e.g., the Missouri Synod Lutheran Church).

Roman Catholics, on the other hand, have insisted and continue to insist on submission to the primacy of the bishop of Rome and acceptance of "Real Presence" in the sacrament understood in terms of transubstantiation. Both forms of the "Petrine error" add extraneous conditions for intercommunion beyond those specified in the New Testament: confession of faith in Jesus Christ as Lord and Savior, risen from the dead, and the reception of Christian baptism.

While Protestants cannot change Roman Catholic canon law, they can reform their own practices in the light of Scripture, and when Communion is celebrated, invite to the table not only members of their own denominations and churches but all who confess Christ—including Roman Catholic and Orthodox members of the one body of Christ. To do so would be in keeping with the spirit of *sola scriptura* of the Reformers. Such a movement toward a visible unity, healing the brokenness and divisions of an earlier era, would be a most fitting way to remember and practice the meaning of justification by faith and to truly celebrate the Reformation—five hundred years later.

NOTES

Introduction

1. For more on this subject see, Berndt Hamm, *The Early Luther: Stages in a Reformation Reorientation*, Lutheran Quarterly Books (Minneapolis: Fortress Press, 2017), 59–84.

2. Martin Luther, *Two Kinds of Righteousness* (1519); *D. Martin Luthers Werke: Kritische Gesamtausgabe* (Weimarer Ausgabe), 73 vols. (Weimar: H. Böhlau, 1883–1993); *Luther's Works: American Edition*, vols. 1–30, ed. Jaroslav Pelikan (Saint Louis: Concordia, 1955–76); vols. 31–55, ed. Helmut Lehmann (Minneapolis: Fortress, 1957–86); vols. 56–82, ed. Christopher B. Brown (Saint Louis: Concordia, 2009ff.); hereafter cited as *LW* with volume and page numbers; *WA* 2:147, 8–9; *LW* 31:298.

3. For more on this subject, see Gordon L. Isaac, *Prayer, Meditation, and Spiritual Trial: Luther's Account of Life in the Spirit* (Peabody, MA: Hendrickson Publishers, 2017), 71–78.

4. Stephen Ozment, *The Age of Reform 1250–1550* (New Haven: Yale University Press, 1980), 381.

Chapter 1

1. For an account of Luther and sixteenth-century printing, see Andrew Pettegree, *Brand Luther* (New York: Penguin Press, 2015).

2. For a good discussion of this, see Eric W. Gritsch and Robert W. Jenson, *Lutheranism: The Theological Movement and Its Confessional Writings* (Philadelphia: Fortress Press, 1976).

3. Ibid., 3.

4. Lutherans routinely refer to four *sola*s, leaving out *soli Deo gloria* ("to God alone be glory"), even though Luther quite often ended his treatises with this phrase. It may be done in opposition to the Reformed tradition that usually adds the fifth *sola* and whose theology promotes the sovereignty of God through the doctrine of double predestination, a doctrine Lutherans do not affirm. Perhaps it is in opposition to the motto of the Roman Catholic Ignatius of Loyola, *Ad maiorem Dei*

gloriam ("To the greater glory of God"). There might have been another reason that was obvious in the nineteenth century when the *solas* were first put into use: Since all theology and, indeed, all of life is to be lived to the glory of God, it is not distinctive to the Reformation. For statistics on the use of these phrases in Luther, see Timothy Wengert, "A Note on '*Sola Scriptura*' in Luther's Writings," *Luther Bulletin* 20 (2011): 21–31.

5. For recent discussion of the *sola scriptura* formulation, see Johannes Zachuler, "Luther's Principle of *sola scriptura* in Recent Ecumenical Discussion," in *Luther Refracted: The Reformer's Ecumenical Legacy*, ed. Piotr J. Malysz and Derek R. Nelson (Minneapolis: Fortress Press, 2015), 249–74, and responses by Anna Case-Winters and Paul R. Hinlicky in the same volume.

6. Niels Henrick Gregersen and Jan-Olav Hendrickson, "The Inclusiveness of the Exclusive Sola-Articles," *Dialog* 55:3 (2016): 185–87.

7. *D. Martin Luthers Werke: Kritische Gesamtausgabe* (Weimarer Ausgabe), 73 vols. (Weimar: H. Böhlau, 1883–1993); hereafter cited as *WA* with volume, page, and line. *Luther's Works: American Edition*, vols. 1–30, ed. Jaroslav Pelikan (Saint Louis: Concordia, 1955–76); vols. 31–55, ed. Helmut Lehmann (Minneapolis: Fortress, 1957–86); vols. 56–82, ed. Christopher B. Brown (Saint Louis: Concordia, 2009ff.); hereafter cited as *LW* with volume and page numbers. *Lectures on Romans* (1515/16), *WA* 56:273; 3–9; *LW* 25:260–61.

8. *Disputation against Scholastic Theology* (1517), *WA* 1:226, 14–15; *LW* 31:12.

9. Ibid., *WA* 1:226, 16; *LW* 31:12.

10. *D. Martin Luthers Werke: Briefwechsel* 18 vols. (Weimar: H. Böhlau, 1906–61); hereafter cited as *WA Br* with volume, page, and line; *WA Br* 1:88, 24; *LW* 48:38.

11. *WA Br* 1:99, 8; *LW* 48:42.

12. *Avoiding the Doctrines of Men* (1522), *WA* 10/2:73, 15–16; *LW* 35:132.

13. *On the Bound Will* (1525), *WA* 18:606, 29; *LW* 33:26.

14. *The Lectures on Romans* (1515/16), *WA* 46:414, 15–19; *LW* 25:405.

15. *A Brief Instruction on What to Look for and Expect in the Gospels, WA* 10/1:13.4–6; *LW* 35:120.

16. Ibid., *WA* 10/1:12.17–13.2; *LW* 35:120.

17. On this point, see Oswald Bayer, *Martin Luther's Theology: A Contemporary Interpretation*, trans. Thomas H. Trapp (Grand Rapids: Eerdmans, 2008), 68–94.

18. *Lectures on Galatians* (1531/35), *WA* 40/1:119; *LW* 26:57–58.

19. Luther refuses to ground the authority of Scripture on any theory outside the material content of the text. For a contrast of this to good portions of modern American evangelicalism, see Mary Worthen, *Apostles of Reason: The Crisis of Authority in American Evangelicalism* (Oxford: Oxford University Press, 2014).

20. *D. Martin Luthers Werke: Tischreden*, 6 vols. (Weimar: H. Böhlau, 1912–21), 2:244, 36–245; *LW* 54:165.

21. *Prefaces to the Old Testament* (1523/45), in *D. Martin Luthers Werke: Deutsche Bibel*, 12 vols. (Weimar: H. Böhlau, 1906–61), 8:12, 1–8; *LW* 36:236.

Chapter 2

1. Gal. 1:3; 1 Cor. 1:3; 2 Cor. 1:2; Rom. 1:7; Phil. 1:2; Eph. 1:2; cf. Col. 1:2. I thank Prof. Scott Manetsch from Trinity Evangelical Divinity School for a critical and constructive reading of this paper.

2. For Luther's works, cf. Martin Luther, *D. Martin Luthers Werke. Weimarer Ausgabe*, 73 vols. (Weimar: Böhlau, 1883–1993), hereafter cited as *WA* with volume, page, and line; Martin Luther, *Luther's Works*, 55 vols. (Minneapolis / St. Louis: Fortress / Concordia, 1955–86), hereafter cited as *LW* with volume and page numbers; also *Martin Luther's Basic Theological Writings*, ed. Timothy F. Lull and William R. Russell, 3rd ed. (Minneapolis: Fortress, 2012).

3. Cf. Heiko A. Oberman, *The Dawn of the Reformation: Essays in Late Medieval and Early Reformation Thought* (Grand Rapids: Eerdmans, 1982), 1–125; Steven Ozment, *The Age of Reform 1250–1550: An Intellectual and Religious History of Late Medieval and Reformation Europe* (New Haven, CT: Yale University Press, 1980), 233–35; see further monographs on (late) medieval nominalism and scholasticism, in particular Gabriel Biel, Thomas Aquinas, Augustine, and other seminal theologians who directly and indirectly influenced Luther. Cf. Markus Wriedt, *Gnade und Erwählung: Eine Untersuchung zu Johann von Staupitz und Martin Luther*, Veröffentlichungen des Instituts für Europäische Geschichte Mainz, Abteilung Religionsgeschichte 141 (Mainz: Zabern, 1991); see the summaries of Mark Mattes, "Luther on Justification as Forensic and Effective," in *The Oxford Handbook of Martin Luther's Theology*, ed. R. Kolb, I. Dingel, and L. Batka (Oxford: Oxford University Press, 2014), 264–73, 268–69; John M. G. Barclay, *Paul and the Gift* (Grand Rapids: Eerdmans, 2015), 97–102; Dietrich Korsch, "Glaube und Rechtfertigung," in *Luther Handbuch*, Dritte, neu bearbeitete und erweiterte Auflage, ed. A. Beutel (Tübingen: Mohr Siebeck, 2017), 418–28.

4. Steven Ozment, *The Age of Reform 1250–1550: An Intellectual and Religious History of Late Medieval and Reformation Europe* (New Haven, CT: Yale University Press, 1980), 234.

5. Cf. Korsch, "Glaube und Rechtfertigung," 418–20.

6. Cf. Martin Brecht, *Martin Luther. Vol. 1: His Road to Reformation, 1483–1521*, trans. J. L. Schaaf (Philadelphia: Fortress, 1985); Bernhard Lohse, *Martin Luther's Theology: Its Historical and Systematic Development*, trans. R. A. Harrisville (Minneapolis: Fortress, 1999), 85–95; Martin Brecht, "Luthers neues Verständnis der Buße und die reformatorische Entdeckung," *Zeitschrift für Theologie und Kirche* 101 (2014): 281–91; Dietrich Korsch, "Die religiöse Leitidee," in *Luther Handbuch*, Dritte, neu bearbeitete und erweiterte Auflage, ed. A. Beutel (Tübingen: Mohr Siebeck, 2017), 115–21; Korsch, "Glaube und Rechtfertigung," 420.

7. *WA* 55/1 (Glossen), II (Scholia); *LW* 10–11.

8. *WA* 57; cf. *LW* 27: 153–410. During Luther's lifetime, six editions of Luther's lectures on Galatians were published, five in Latin and one in German. His commentary of 1531/1535 is the more mature version.

9. *WA* 57:97b–238b; *LW* 29:109–241.

10. *WA* 56–57; *LW* 25.

11. For the late date see Ernst Bizer, *Fides ex auditu. Eine Untersuchung über die Entdeckung der Gerechtigkeit Gottes durch Martin Luther*, Dritte Auflage (Neukirchen-Vluyn: Neukirchener Verlag, 1966).

12. *LW* 34:327–38; *WA* 54:179–87.

13. *LW* 8:192; *WA* 44:719.

14. *LW* 31:3–16; *WA* 1:233–38.

15. *LW* 72; *WA* 1:629–33.

16. Cf. Oswald Bayer, *Martin Luther's Theology: A Contemporary Interpretation*, trans. T. H. Trapp (Grand Rapids: Eerdmans, 2008), 48–57, who emphasizes the fifty theses of 1518 as the reformational breakthrough; cf. Oswald Bayer, *Promissio. Geschichte der reformatorischen Wende in Luthers Theologie*, Zweite Auflage (Darmstadt: Wissenschaftliche Buchgesellschaft, 1989), 164–202. Korsch, "Die religiöse Leitidee," 118, finds the emphasis on the word of God that liberates in the Ninety-Five Theses.

17. On Luther's understanding of grace, see Paul Althaus, *The Theology of Martin Luther*, trans. R. C. Schultz (Philadelphia: Fortress, 1966), 224–50; Otto Herrmann Pesch, *Theologie der Rechtfertigung bei Martin Luther und Thomas von Aquin. Versuch eines systematisch-theologischen Dialogs* (Mainz: Grünewald, 1967); Theobald Beer, *Der fröhliche Wechsel und Steit. Grundzüge der Theologie Martin Luthers*, 2 vols. (Einsiedeln: Johannes-Verlag, 1980); Leo Scheffczyk, "Zur Gnadenlehre Luthers," in *Luther und die Folgen für die Geistes- und Naturwissenschaften*, ed. A. Graf von Brandenstein-Zeppelin and A. von Stockhausen (Weilheim-Bierbronnen: Gustav-Siewerth-Akademie, 2001), 297–310; Stephen J. Chester, *Reading Paul with the Reformers: Reconciling Old and New Perspectives* (Grand Rapids: Eerdmans, 2017), 148–55.

18. *LW* 44:21–114; *WA* 6:202–76 (printed version); 9:229–301 (manuscript version).

19. Barclay, *Paul and the Gift*, 98.

20. *LW* 26:213; *WA* 40/1:343.

21. Barclay, *Paul and the Gift*, 101.

22. *LW* 31:297–306; *WA* 2:145–52.

23. *LW* 7:351–52; *WA* 7:54–55. On Luther's view of the Christian life in *The Freedom of a Christian*, see Andreas Stegmann, *Luthers Auffassung vom christlichen Leben*, Beiträge zur historischen Theologie 175 (Tübingen: Mohr Siebeck, 2014), 313–29.

24. *LW* 26:288; *WA* 40/1:448.

25. *LW* 26:277; *WA* 40/1:437.

26. *LW* 26:278; *WA* 40/1:433.

27. *LW* 26:281; *WA* 40/1:439.

28. *LW* 26:284; *WA* 40/1:434.

29. Johannes Schwanke, "Luther's Theology of Creation," in *The Oxford Handbook of Martin Luther's Theology*, ed. R. Kolb, I. Dingel, and L. Batka (Oxford: Oxford University Press, 2014), 201–11, here 210.

30. *WA* 30.1:241–425 (Vorrede/Preface 264–81); Article I on creation (247–48). Cf. Robert Kolb and Timothy Wengert, eds., *The Book of Concord: The Confessions of the Evangelical Lutheran Church* (Minneapolis: Fortress, 2000), 345–75; for Article I, see ibid., 354–44. See also *Martin Luther's Basic Theological Writings*, ed. Timothy F. Lull and William R. Russell, 3rd ed. (Minneapolis: Fortress, 2012), 322–39, here 327.

31. *LW* 8:39; *WA* 44:607. The lectures on Genesis 45 were delivered in 1545.

32. Barclay, *Paul and the Gift*, 103; for the following point, see ibid.

33. *LW* 35:117–24, quotation ibid., 119–20; *WA* 10.1:1, 8–18 (introduction to the Christmas postil).

34. Cf. Korsch, "Glaube und Rechtfertigung," 425; for the following, see ibid., 425–26.

35. *WA* 7:12–38 (Latin 49–73); *LW* 31:343–76; the English translation follows the Latin text. The quotation is from *LW* 31:362; *WA* 7:32–33, 62.

36. *Thesen für die Promotionsdisputation von Hieroymus Weller und Nikolaus Medler. 11 September 1535*; *WA* 39.1:44–53; there are 71 theses *de fide* (44–48) and 87 theses *de lege* (48–53). *LW* 34:109–32 (*Theses Concerning Faith and Law*).

37. *LW* 34:112–13; *WA* 39/1:47 (*de fide* 52–54).

38. *LW* 31:39–40; *WA* 1:353–54 (*ex theologia*).

39. Kevin J. Vanhoozer, *Biblical Authority after Babel: Retrieving the Solas in the Spirit of Mere Protestant Christianity* (Grand Rapids: Brazos, 2016), 53.

40. Martin Luther, *D. Martin Luthers Werke: Briefwechsel*, 18 vols. (Weimar: H. Böhlau, 1906–61).

41. Martin Luther, *D. Martin Luthers Werke: Tischreden*, 6 vols. (Weimar: H. Böhlau, 1912–21).

42. Martin Luther, *D. Martin Luthers Werke: Deutsche Bibel*, 12 vols. (Weimar: H. Böhlau, 1906–61).

43. *WA DB* 1–12; September Testament 1922 (New Testament), complete Bible 1534.

44. *WA DB* 7:1; *LW* 35:365.

45. *WA* 35:455–57; *LW* 53:283 ("Our God He Is a Castle Strong").

Chapter 3

1. Parts of the article have been published in adapted form in Gwenfair Walters Adams, "Shock and Awe: The Reformers and the Stunning Joy of Romans 1–8," *Journal of Evangelical Theological Society* 61, no. 2 (2018). Used with permission.

2. Martin Brecht, *Martin Luther: His Road to Reformation, 1483–1521*, trans. James L. Schaaf (Minneapolis: Fortress, 1985), 71.

3. Brecht, *Martin Luther*, 74.

4. Quoted and translated by Roland Bainton, *Here I Stand* (1950; repr., Nashville: Abingdon Press, 2013), 25.

5. Quoted by Graham Tomlin in *Luther and His World: An Introduction* (Oxford: Lion Hudson, 2013), 20.

6. Brecht, *Martin Luther*, 74.

7. Martin Luther, *Praefatio Iesu Christi, LW* 10:7. *Luther's Works: American Edition*, vols. 1–30, ed. Jaroslav Pelikan (Saint Louis: Concordia, 1955–76); vols. 31–55, ed. Helmut Lehmann (Minneapolis: Fortress, 1957–86); vols. 56–82, ed. Christopher B. Brown (Saint Louis: Concordia, 2009ff.).

8. Bernhard Lohse, *Martin Luther's Theology: Its Historical and Systematic Development* (Minneapolis: Fortress Press, 1999), 51.

9. Lohse, *Martin Luther's Theology*, 52.

10. *LW* 10:145; italics added.

11. Brecht, *Martin Luther*, 75.

12. Ibid., 79.

13. *LW* 25:181.

14. Martin Luther, *In Epistolam Pauli ad Galatas* (n.p.: 1520), 41; digital copy online at books.google.com.

15. Martin Luther, *Works of Martin Luther*, vol. 1; excerpt trans. C. M. Jacobs (Philadelphia: A. J. Holman, 1915), 40.

16. Ibid., 43.

17. *LW* 42:13.

18. Martin Luther, *Works of Martin Luther with Introductions and Notes*, vol. 2; excerpt trans. C. M. Jacobs (Philadelphia: A. J. Holman, 1915), 164.

19. Martin Luther, *On the Babylonian Captivity of the Church*, trans. Albert T. W. Steinhaeuser in *Works of Martin Luther with Introductions and Notes* (Philadelphia: A. J. Holman Company, 1915), 195.

20. Ibid., 199.

21. Ibid., 199–200; italics added.

22. Martin Luther, "On the Freedom of a Christian" in Henry Wace and C. A. Buchheim, eds., *First Principles of the Reformation or the Ninety-Five Theses and the Three Primary Works* (London: John Murray, 1883), 117.

23. Ibid., 118.

24. Ibid., 127.

25. Martin Luther, *Brief Instruction on What to Look for and Expect in the Gospels; LW* 35:118.

26. Ibid., 119.

27. Martin Luther, *Commentary on the Epistle to the Galatians* (1535), trans. Theodore Graebner (Grand Rapids: Zondervan, 1949), 48–49.

28. Ibid., 91.

29. Ibid., 252, 301.

30. Ibid., 142.

31. Martin Luther, *Commentary on Galatians*, ed. John Prince Fallowes (Grand Rapids: Kregel, 1979), 129–30.

32. Martin Luther, *A Commentary on Paul's Epistle to the Galatians*, trans. Erasmus Middleton (London: Mathews and Leigh, 1807), 245.

33. Ibid., 281; author adaptation.

34. Ibid.

35. Ibid., 282.

36. Ibid., 301; author adaptation.

37. Martin Luther, *The Complete Sermons of Martin Luther*, vol. 5 (Grand Rapids: Baker Books: 2000), 79.

38. Paul Althaus, *The Theology of Martin Luther* (Minneapolis, MN: Fortress Press, 1966), 83.

39. Martin Luther, *Avoiding the Doctrines of Men; LW* 35:132.

40. Sermon on John 3:16–21, quoted in *What Luther Says*, ed. Ewald M. Plass (St. Louis, MO: Concordia, 1959), 147.

41. Martin Luther, *Sermons on the Gospel of John*, quoted in ibid., 187.

42. Philip Melanchthon, "History of the Life and Acts of Dr Martin Luther," in *Luther's Lives: Two Contemporary Accounts of Martin Luther*, ed. Thomas D. Frazel (Manchester: Manchester University Press, 2002), 38.

Chapter 4

1. In the present article, *tôrâ* will refer to the Hebrew word for "law," *Tôrâ* the Five Books of Moses (i.e., the Pentateuch), and "Torah" the broad concept that forms the central theme in Psalm 119.

2. Erik H. Herrmann, "Preface to the Wittenberg Edition of Luther's German Writings," in *Pastoral Writings*, ed. Mary J. Haemig, The Annotated Luther 4 (Minneapolis: Fortress, 2016), 482.

3. In Hebrew poetry, a line is the basic unit of text that can consist of a single colon (i.e., monocolon) or more cola (i.e., bicola, tricola, etc.), and a group of consecutive lines that share a common theme or idea form a strophe. In Psalm 119, the strophes are formed around the common letter of the alphabet at the start of the line.

4. David N. Freedman, *Psalm 119: The Exaltation of Torah*, Biblical and Judaic Studies 6 (Winona Lake, IN: Eisenbrauns, 1999).

5. Ibid., 22–23.

6. Armin Lange, "The Significance of the Pre-Maccabean Literature from the Qumran Library for the Understanding of the Hebrew Bible," in *Congress Volume Ljubljana 2007*, ed. André Lemaire, supplement to *Vetus Testamentum* 137 (Leiden: Brill), 213–17.

7. In a similar manner, "law" is also the term that leads a group of five terms that refer to Torah in the opening line (verse 7) of the second strophe of Psalm 19, another Torah psalm.

8. All biblical quotations in this chapter are from ESV; all brackets and italics added.

9. The tripartite sections of the Hebrew canon of the Old Testament are *Tôrâ* (Law), *Nəḇîʾîm* (Prophets), and *Kətûḇîm* (Writings).

10. Gordon J. Wenham, *Psalms as Torah: Reading Biblical Song Ethically* (Grand Rapids: Baker Academic, 2012), 78; italics added.

11. Kent A. Reynolds, *Torah as Teacher: The Exemplary Torah Student in Psalm 119*, supplement to *Vetus Testamentum* 137 (Leiden: Brill, 2010), 106.

12. Ibid., 58.

13. Ibid., 88.

14. Ivana Procházková, "The Torah within the Heart, in the Feet, and on the Tongue: Law and Freedom in Psalm 119 from the Perspective of Cognitive Linguistics," *Communio Viatorum* 54, no. 1 (2012): 16–37.

15. Herrmann, "Preface to the Wittenberg Edition of Luther's German Writings," 482.

16. Ibid., 477.

17. Ibid.

18. The most recent treatise on the subject is Gordon L. Isaac's *Prayer, Meditation, and Spiritual Trial: Luther's Account of Life in the Spirit* (Peabody, MA: Hendrickson Publishers, 2017).

19. Hermann, "Preface to the Wittenberg Edition of Luther's German Writings," 481.

20. Ibid., 482.

21. Ibid., 476.

22. Wenham, *Psalms as Torah*, 78.

Chapter 5

1. Martin E. Marty, *Martin Luther* (New York: Viking Penguin, 2004), 18–19.

2. For more on Luther's approach to the spiritual life, see Gordon L. Isaac, *Prayer, Meditation, and Spiritual Trial: Luther's Account of Life in the Spirit* (Peabody, MA: Hendrickson Publishers, 2017).

3. Much of my analysis of Genesis is based on Meredith G. Kline, *Kingdom Prologue: Genesis Foundations for a Covenantal Worldview* (Eugene, OR: Wipf and Stock, 2006).

4. All scriptural quotations taken from NIV (2011), unless otherwise indicated.

5. For a comprehensive exploration of the dangers of these reductionistic approaches and a full-orbed alternative, see George C. Hammond, *It Has Not Yet Appeared What We Shall Be: A Reconsideration of the Imago Dei in Light of Those with Severe Cognitive Disabilities*, Reformed Academic Dissertations (Phillipsburg, NJ: P & R Publishing, 2017).

6. Note the lack of the phrase "God said, 'Let . . .'" that introduces the other days.

7. Peter Toon, *From Mind to Heart: Christian Meditation Today* (Grand Rapids: Baker, 1987), 73–75.

8. For a detailed discussion of Jesus' consistently high view of Scripture and the nature of biblical inspiration in general, see Benjamin Breckinridge Warfield, *The Inspiration and Authority of the Bible* (Philadelphia: Presbyterian and Reformed, 1948).

Chapter 6

1. See Robert Kolb, *Martin Luther and the Enduring Word of God: The Wittenberg School and Its Scripture-Centered Proclamation* (Grand Rapids: Baker Academic, 2016).

2. Cited in Henry Zecher, "The Bible Translation That Rocked the World," *Christian History* (April 1992).

3. For the role of translation in mission history, see Lamin Sanneh, *Translating the Message: The Missionary Impact on Culture* (Maryknoll: Orbis Books, 1989), especially ch. 2.

4. Lamin Sanneh, *Whose Religion Is Christianity? The Gospel Beyond the West* (Grand Rapids: Eerdmans, 2003), 99.

5. See Timothy George, "The Priesthood of All Believers," *First Things* (October 31, 2016).

6. See Jason G. Duesing, *Adoniram Judson: A Bicentennial Appreciation of the Pioneer American Missionary* (Nashville: Broadman & Holman Academic), 2012.

7. See Andrew F. Walls, *The Cross-Cultural Process in Christian History: Studies in the Transmission and Appropriation of Faith* (Maryknoll: Orbis Books, 2002); and Sanneh, *Translating the Message.*

8. Thousands of Christian groups broke off from the Protestant fold and consider themselves "Independent." This includes the African Independent Churches, the house churches in China, and groups such as the Vineyard in the United States. On the phenomenon in the United States, see Brad Christerson and Richard Flory, *The Rise of Network Christianity: How Independent Leaders Are Changing the Religious Landscape* (New York: Oxford University Press, 2017).

9. See Gina A. Zurlo, "Demographics of Global Evangelicalism," in *Evangelicals around the World: A Global Handbook for the 21st Century*, ed. Brian C. Stiller, Todd M. Johnson, Karen Stiller, and Mark Hutchinson (Nashville: Thomas Nelson, 2015), 34–47.

10. For example, see Martin E. Marty, *Protestantism: Its Churches and Cultures, Rituals and Doctrines, Yesterday and Today* (New York: Holt, Rinehart & Winston, 1972), xi.

11. Ibid., 13.

12. Note that Jason Mandryk's *Operation World* (Carlisle: Paternoster Press, 2010) utilizes a broader definition of "Evangelical" based on theological criteria. He estimated that there were 546 million Evangelicals worldwide in 2010.

13. Derived from Todd M. Johnson, "Counting Pentecostals Worldwide," *Pneuma* 36 (2014): 265–88.

14. Most scholars have moved to a "multiple origins" theory of the birth of modern Pentecostalism, emphasizing early activity outside the Western world. See Allan Anderson, et al., eds., *Studying Global Pentecostalism: Theories and Methods* (Berkeley: University of California, 2009), especially ch. 1, "Varieties, Taxonomies, and Definitions," 22.

15. Vinson Synan documents this early history and its links to the Holiness tradition in *The Holiness-Pentecostal Movement in the United States* (Grand Rapids: Eerdmans, 1972).

16. See Todd M. Johnson and Gina A. Zurlo, eds., *World Christian Database* (Leiden: Brill), accessed July 2016.

Chapter 7

1. Supersessionism, or Replacement Theology, is the belief that the church has superseded Israel as God's chosen people. This act stripped the Jewish people of their divine inheritance and has often led to forms of anti-Semitism from the Christian church and culture.

2. See Gen. 28:13–15; 35:9–15; Exod. 3:7–8; 32:13; Lev. 26:42–45; Num. 32:11–12; Deut. 1:8; 4:30–31; 9:23–29; 34:4; 1 Chron. 16:15–17; 2 Chron. 20:6; 2 Kings 13:22–25; Ps. 47:10; 105:6–11; Isa. 41:8; 51:1–2; 55:3; 61:8; Jer. 32:10; Ezek. 16:60; 20:5–6; 33:24; Neh. 9:7–8.

3. See the forthcoming volume by a number of scholars on Supersessionism: Stanley Porter and Alan E. Kurschner, eds., Walter C. Kaiser Jr., "The Christian Church: Built on the Foundation of the Abrahamic, Davidic and New Covenants"; esp. my footnote 7 interacting with Chris Wright in "A Christian Approach to Old Testament Prophecy Concerning Israel," *Jerusalem Past and Present in the Purposes of God*, ed. P. W. L. Walker (Cambridge: Tyndale House, 1992), on the word *eternal*.

4. Philip E. Hughes, "The Olive Tree of Romans XI," *Evangelical Quarterly* 20 (1948): 26.

5. See Walter C. Kaiser Jr. "The Promised Land: A Biblical-Historical View," *Bibliotheca Sacra* 138 (1981): 303–05, where I argue that Israel's northern border is *Naha el-Kabir*, "The Great River," which today forms the boundary between Lebanon and Syria in the north, just south of the modern coastal hamlet Sumra.

6. Oswald T. Allis, *God Spoke by Moses* (Nutley, NJ: Presbyterian and Reformed, 1958), 72.

7. The Reformation grew out of Martin Luther's nailing his Ninety-Five Theses to the door of the Wittenberg Church on October 31, 1517. However, in Zurich, Switzerland, others date the beginning of the Reformation to Huldrych Zwingli's birthday on January 1, 1519; for it was on this date that the new pastor of Zurich announced his intention to abandon his method of pulpit ministry, from that time on, of using the traditional lectionary and to use in his preaching a new model of preaching expositional sermons chapter by chapter beginning with the book of Matthew. While Martin Luther at first embraced evangelizing the Jewish people, he was later disappointed over their lack of acceptance of the gospel. Luther then embraced Replacement Theology, along with the Roman Church and several of the leaders in the Protestant Reformation. In fact, Luther took the replacement idea even further in a radical anti-Jewish book *The Jews and Their Lies*. It was so inflammatory that it later became the basis for much of Adolph Hitler's rhetoric against the Jewish people.

8. Francis Turretin, *Institutes of Elenctic Theology* (repr., Phillipsburg, NJ: P & R, 1992–94); 2:163.

Chapter 8

1. Archibald M. Hunter, *Introducing the New Testament*, 3rd ed. (Philadelphia: Westminster, 1972), 124; and others cited by Arthur G. Patzia, *New International Biblical Commentary: Ephesians, Colossians, Philemon* (Peabody, MA: Hendrickson, 1990), 128.

2. The translation is by Ford Lewis Battles, *Calvin: Institutes of the Christian Religion*, ed. John T. McNeill, 2 vols., The Library of Christian Classics (Philadelphia: Westminster, 1960).

3. Bible references are author's translation if not otherwise indicated.

4. E.g., Eph. 2:11–13; 3:1; 4:17–18.

5. E.g., Eph. 4:1.

6. The article in Eph. 2:8 before "grace" refers back to "grace" in 2:5. See also Harold W. Hochner, *Ephesians: An Exegetical Commentary* (Grand Rapids: Baker, 2002), 340.

7. Neuter *touto* in Eph. 2:8 refers to the entire earlier phrase, "the act of being saved by grace conditioned on faith on our part." Archibald Thomas Robertson, *Word Pictures in the New Testament: The Epistles of Paul*, vol. IV (Nashville: Broadman, 1931), 525.

8. Eph. 2:10, 15; 3:9; 4:24; Col. 1:16; Rom. 1:20.

9. John Calvin, *Sermons on the Epistle to the Ephesians* (1562; repr., Edinburgh: Banner of Truth Trust, 1973), 165.

10. F. F. Bruce, *The Epistles to the Colossians, to Philemon, and to the Ephesians*, The New International Commentary on the New Testament (Grand Rapids: Eerdmans, 1984), 291.

11. A. T. Robertson, *A Grammar of the Greek New Testament in the Light of Historical Research* (Nashville: Broadman, 1934), 893.

12. Eph. 4:24; 5:9; 6:14.

13. E.g., Eph. 5:1–2; Rom. 1:17; 3:5, 21–22, 25–26.

14. Bruce, *Ephesians*, 286, 289.

15. Eph. 1:6–8; 2:4–5, 7–8; 4:7.

16. E.g., Lev. 1:3–4, 10; 2:1; 3:1; 22:18–25; Num. 18:9; Deut. 12:11; Heb. 5:1.

17. Gen. 24:53; 32:13–15, 18, 20–21; 43:11, 15, 25–26.

18. Eph. 1:7; 2:1; 5:2.

19. Heb. 9:12–14.

20. E.g., Rom. 2:17–23; 1 Cor. 3:21; Gal. 6:13.

21. E.g., Rom. 5:2; 2 Cor. 5:12; 7:14; 9:2; 10:8, 13; 11:16, 30; 12:6; Phil. 3:3.

22. Robertson, *Grammar*, 600, 604–5.

23. Robertson, *Grammar*, 926–35, divides the subjunctive into futuristic, volitive, and deliberative uses.

24. *Calvin's Commentaries: Ephesians-Jude* (Wilmington, DE: Associated Publishers and Authors, n.d.), 1951.

25. Calvin, *Sermons*, 163.

26. Calvin, *Commentaries*, 1951.

27. Robertson, *Epistles of Paul*, 525; *Grammar*, 605. Cf. Daniel B. Wallace, *Greek Grammar Beyond the Basics: An Exegetical Syntax of the New Testament* (Grand Rapids: Zondervan, 1996), 376.

28. Patzia, *Ephesians*, 185.

29. E.g., the Carthusians. *Luther's Works, vol. 57: Sermons IV*, ed. Benjamin T. G. Mayes (St. Louis: Concordia, 2016), 38–40.

30. N. T. Wright also defines "good works" as "the public face of the church in the world, about Christians shining in the world as lights in a dark place." *Justification: God's Plan & Paul's Vision* (Downers Grove: IVP Academic, 2009), 169, 171.

31. John MacPherson, *Commentary on St. Paul's Epistle to the Ephesians* (Edinburgh: T. & T. Clark, 1892), 203.

32. Hoehner, *Ephesians*, 349.

33. Lynn Cohick, *Ephesians*, New Covenant Commentary Series (Eugene, OR: Cascade, 2010), 68.

34. Frederick Danker, Walter Bauer, William Arndt, and F. Wilbur Gingrich, *Greek-English Lexicon of the New Testament and Other Early Christian Literature*, 3rd ed. (Chicago: University of Chicago Press, 2000), 390.

35. "Good" (*kalos*) "work" (*ergon*) is also used in the Gospels to describe the woman anointing Jesus before his death (Matt. 26:10; Mark 14:6).

36. See also 1 Tim. 5:10; 2 Tim. 2:21–22 ("good works" include righteousness, faith, love, peace, and prayer); 3:17 (the goal of Scripture is "good works"); Titus 1:16; 2 Cor. 9:8 (good works refers to giving to the needy).

37. See also Eph. 4:22–24; 5:3–5, 15.

38. Eph. 1:5; 2:6–7, 13, 18–19; 5:1, 5, 15–17.

39. See Eph. 5:4, 20.

40. *Dōron* comes from *didōmi*, "I give." Henry George Liddell and Robert Scott, *A Greek-English Lexicon*, rev. Henry Stuart Jones, 9th ed. (Oxford: Clarendon, 1940), 465.

Chapter 9

1. John Webster, *Holiness* (Grand Rapids: Eerdmans, 2002), 87.

2. George Hunsinger pointedly remarks of this tendency, "A basic distinction between what happened *in nobis* once for all and what then went on to happen gradually was the hallmark of the traditional Protestant view. What happened once for all we may conveniently designate as 'justification' and what then happened gradually as 'sanctification.' Under the category of sanctification the idea of soteriological gradualism, a process of salvation happening in us by degrees had been restored to prominence in traditional Protestantism. Later traditional Protestantism

typically came to see sanctification as the 'completion' of justification and eventually as its virtual replacement." George Hunsinger, "What Karl Barth Learned from Martin Luther," in *Disruptive Grace: Studies in the Theology of Karl Barth* (Grand Rapids: Eerdmans, 2002), 298.

3. John Calvin, *Institutes of the Christian Religion*, III.17.9. Calvin continues, "By faith alone not only we ourselves but our works as well are justified. Now if this works righteousness depends upon faith and free justification and is effected by this it ought to be included under faith and be subordinated to it, as effect to cause so far is it from having any right to be raised up either to destroy or becloud justification of faith."

4. Louis Berkhof, *Systematic Theology* (Grand Rapids: Eerdmans, 1939) 532; Charles Hodge, *Systematic Theology*, vol. 3 (repr., Grand Rapids: Eerdmans, 1982), 238–44.

5. Hodge, *Systematic Theology*, 213.

6. Ibid., 226.

7. Ibid., 230.

8. Berkhof follows Hodge in this manner but is more careful to guard against the obvious conflict between moral progress and works righteousness. He writes, "Sanctification is a moral or re-creative work changing the inner nature of man. Sanctification calls for the co-operation of man, but is always on guard against works righteousness." Berkhof, *Systematic Theology*, 529. It is less than clear, though, how moral progress that comes about by the cooperation of the human agent does not lead to works righteousness.

9. Hodge, *Systematic Theology*, 230.

10. Ibid., 244. A speculative hypothesis would be to suggest that Hodge has resolved the interpretive tension between Paul and James by taking his clues about justification from Paul and the clues about sanctification from James. This solves the tension by simply locating the domains over which they address to different spheres.

11. Ibid., 238.

12. Berkhof concurs with Hodge at this point: "All humans will appear before the final judgment. The sins of believers will be manifest as pardoned in Christ. There will nonetheless be different degrees of heaven enjoyed by those who are pardoned. These degrees will be determined by what is done in the flesh." Berkhof, *Systematic Theology*, 732.

13. Calvin, *Institutes*, III.14.10.

14. Martin Luther, *Werke. Weimarer Ausgabe* 34/1, 267. As quoted in Webster, *Holiness*, 73.

15. Calvin, *Institutes*, III.14.9.

16. It should be noted in passing that Augustine's legacy on this point seems somewhat mixed as interpreted by the Protestant traditions. Calvin writes, "Augustine gives two reasons why he dared not vaunt his works before God; because if he has anything of good works, he sees in them nothing of his own; and secondly because these are also overwhelmed by a multitude of sins. From this it comes about that his

conscience feels more fear and consternation than assurance. Therefore he would like God to look upon his good deeds only that recognizing the grace of his own call in them he may finish the work he has begun." Calvin, *Institutes*, III.14.20.

17. G. C. Berkouwer, *Faith and Sanctification* (Grand Rapids: Eerdmans, 1969), 75.

18. Why would it be any less true of sanctification than justification that, as Bruce McCormack writes, "clothed with Christ's righteousness . . . they are declared innocent even though as yet, in themselves they are nothing of the sort." "*Justia Aliena: Karl Barth in Conversation with the Evangelical Doctrine of Imputed Righteousness,*" in *Justification in Perspective: Historical Developments and Contemporary Challenges*, ed. Bruce McCormack (Grand Rapids: Baker, 2006), 173.

19. Berkouwer discusses the different routes that Luther and Calvin took to reach this conclusion and seems hesitant to suppose that either of them held it consistently. See especially ch. 4, "The Origins of Sanctification," 71–97, in *Faith and Sanctification* for his discussion of Luther and Calvin on the simultaneity of sin and sanctification. By contrast, George Hunsinger, "A Tale of Two Simultaneities: Justification and Sanctification in Calvin and Barth," in *Conversing with Barth*, ed. John McDowell and Mike Higton (London: Ashgate, 2004), 68–89, argues that Luther and not Calvin was consistently committed to the simultaneity of sin and sanctification.

20. This insistence gives pause to all triumphalism of the church. From within the Reformed tradition, Gabriel Fackre cautions, "The Lutheran emphasis upon simultaneity—simultaneously just and sinful, simultaneously sanctified and sinful—sobers the reformed impulse that sin persists in every sanctifying move forward." See Fackre, "Sovereignty and Sanctification: Reformed Accents in Ecumenics," in *Reformed Theology: Identity and Ecumenicity*, ed. Wallace Alston and Michael Welker (Grand Rapids: Eerdmans, 2003), 279.

21. Webster, *Holiness*, 81.

22. Berkouwer, *Faith and Sanctification*, 84. He goes on to write, "The continued dependence on it [the forgiveness of sins] must—both in pastoral counseling and in dogmatic analysis—be laid bare, emphasized and kept in sight. Only thus can we keep at bay the spectre of haughtiness."

23. Calvin does write in curious ways about the infusion of holiness and seems to attribute certain praiseworthiness to good works performed after justification. "When we hear mention of our union with God, let us remember that holiness must be its bond; not because we come into communion with him by virtue of our holiness! Rather, we ought first to cleave unto him so that, infused with his holiness, we may follow wither he calls." Calvin, *Institutes*, III.6.2.

24. There are undoubtedly Protestant traditions that embrace the medical metaphors as applied to divine grace. Calvin himself gave credence (inconsistently in my mind) to interpreting grace as a form of medicine that over time heals the soul of sin. "Not only does Christ cleave to us by an invisible bond of fellowship, but with a wonderful communion, day by day, he grows more and more into one body with us, until he becomes completely one with us." Calvin, *Institutes*, III.2.24.

25. This follows Berkouwer's comment, "Faith is not a point of departure for a fresh emission of power or a human function or potency producing other effects, but of faith as true orientation toward the grace of God and as the life which flourishes on this divine grace, on the forgiveness of sins." *Faith and Sanctification*, 27.

26. I take this to be George Hunsinger's driving concern in commenting on Luther: "We are not saved by reduplicating his (Christ's) spirituality which Luther would have denounced as a new form of the law, but by the miraculous exchange where he has died in our place as sinners so that we might be clothed in his righteousness by grace and live through his body and blood in eternal fellowship with God. Our salvation is thus permanently anchored not in a repeatable but in an unrepeatable event, not in an event that takes place *in nobis*, but in one that has taken place *extra nos*. Since we are given a share in this event by grace through faith, having been baptized into Christ's very death (Rom 6:3), the substance of our salvation, and not just the source, is Christ himself and Christ alone." Hunsinger, "What Karl Barth Learned from Martin Luther," 285.

27. Calvin writes, "Partial righteousness (of the believer) is a fiction. No other righteousness than the complete observance of the law is allowed in heaven." *Institutes* III.14.13.

28. Calvin, *Institutes*, III.17.8.

29. The New Perspective on Paul literature has been helpful in the reminder that neither Israel's possession of the Torah nor their obedience serve as grounds for their covenant relation to God. The ultimate ground of Abraham and his descendants' covenant relations with God is God's reconciling love in Jesus Christ.

30. Simon Gathercole makes this argument at length in *Where Is Boasting?: Early Jewish Soteriology and Paul's Response in Romans 1–5* (Grand Rapids: Eerdmans, 2002), 232–47.

31. Commenting on the paradox of sin and grace in Luther, Hunsinger comments, "Despite the sin which clings to us so closely wrote Luther, yet grace is sufficient to enable us to be counted entirely and completely righteous in God's sight because his grace does not come in portions and pieces separately like so many gifts, rather it takes us up completely into its embrace for the sake of Christ our mediator and intercessor, and in order that the gifts may take root in us. "What Karl Barth Learned from Martin Luther," 297.

32. John Webster writes, "The polarization of freedom and obedience that is endemic in modern anthropology is part of the pathology of the modern spiritual history of the self. In the freedom given to me in Christ, I am bound to God's grace." *Holiness*, 94.

33. Michael Horton remarks, "In causal and metaphysical grammars justification and sanctification become a debate over the mechanics of the inner life. In communicative and covenantal grammars justification has to do with the Covenant Lord pronouncing a courtroom verdict upon the servant [Jesus] that issues in a completely new ontological ethic and eschatological orientation including the inner life in its sweep." Horton, *Covenant and Salvation: Union with Christ* (Louisville, KY: Westminster John Knox, 2007).

34. I am grateful to a colleague of mine, Gordon Isaac, in bringing this verse to my attention after which he commented, "Was Paul exaggerating when he said the gospel was the power of God unto salvation? Maybe what he really meant to say was that the gospel is the power of God for salvation provided one does not forget the law. Maybe he just wasn't clever enough to say that the real ordering is not law and gospel; it is gospel and then law."

35. By contrast Berkhof writes, "The necessity of good works must be maintained over against the Antinomians who claim that since Christ not only bore the penalty of sin, but also met the positive demands of the Law, the believer is free from the obligation to observe it." *Systematic Theology*, 543.

36. This is not to claim that the authors of the New Testament depicted the law as equivalent to wisdom. The "law," with some exceptions in the New Testament, referred to the Mosaic Law and was most often a reference to the Sinai Covenant. Wisdom, on the other hand, was much less historically tied down by the New Testament writers. Its referent was also far more ambiguous, though not thereby any less consequential. For two different treatments of law and wisdom in the hands of the New Testament writers, see Eckhard J. Schnabel, *Law and Wisdom from Ben Sira to Paul* (Tubingen: Mohr Siebeck, 1985), and C. Marvin Pate, *The Reverse of the Curse: Paul, Wisdom and the Law* (Tubingen: Mohr Siebeck, 2000).

37. This is Bernhard Lohse's term in depicting Luther's view of the law in the life of the Christian. See Lohse, *Martin Luther's Theology: Its Historical and Systematic Development*, trans. Roy A. Harrisville (Minneapolis: Fortress Press, 1999).

38. Cf. Roland Murphy, "The Personification of Wisdom," in *Wisdom in Ancient Israel*, ed. John Day, Robert P. Gordon, and H. G. M. Williamson (Cambridge University Press, 1995), 222–33.

39. Leora Batnitzky, reflecting on Franz Rosenzweig's work on idolatry, writes, "The root of idolatry is a misunderstanding about the ways in which meaning is created and human identity is constituted." Batnitzky, *Idolatry and Representation* (Princeton: Princeton University Press, 2000), 6.

40. Tim Keller, *Counterfeit Gods* (New York: Dutton, 2009).

41. Cf. Richard Lints, "Imaging and Idolatry: The Sociality of Personhood and the Ironic Reversals of the Canon," in *Personal Identity in Theological Perspective*, ed. Richard Lints, Michael Horton, and Mark Talbot (Grand Rapids: Eerdmans, 2006), 204–25.

42. Ephesians 1:18 uses the phrase "the eyes of your heart" in just this fashion.

43. So Meredith Kline writes, "To be the image of God is to be the son of God." *Images of the Spirit* (Grand Rapids: Eerdmans, 1980), 35.

44. One of the chief consequences of worship is the love of neighbor. The summary of the law in Matthew 22 connects the love of God with the love of neighbor on the grounds that the latter is *like* the former.

45. A necessary reminder is that the disobedience of believers results not in condemnation but in dissatisfaction, which is itself a sign that God's redeeming work is not yet finished in believers. That dissatisfaction is also a reminder of the present condition of the human heart wherein believers sometimes "do not do the good

[they] want, but the evil [they] do not want," even as their "members wage war with each other" (Rom. 7:19, 22).

Chapter 10

1. "Sermon before Lent, Paul's Praise of Christian Love, I Corinthians 13," in *Complete Sermons of Martin Luther*, ed. Nicholas Lenker (Grand Rapids: Baker Books, 2000), 4:1.125.

2. For a historic overview of early Lutheran views on the law, see Lowell C. Green, "The 'third use of the law' and Werner Elert's Position," *Logia* 22 no. 2 (2013): 27–33.

3. *Luther's Works: American Edition*, vols. 1–30, ed. Jaroslav Pelikan (Saint Louis: Concordia, 1955–76); vols. 31–55, ed. Helmut Lehmann (Philadelphia/Minneapolis: Fortress, 1957–86); vols. 56–82, ed. Christopher B. Brown (Saint Louis: Concordia, 2009ff.). Hereafter cited as *LW* with volume and page numbers. "The Freedom of a Christian" (1520), *LW* 31:361.

4. "The Heidelberg Disputation" (1518), *LW* 31:41.

5. John Calvin, *The Institutes of the Christian Religion*, ed. John T. McNeill, trans. Ford Lewis Battles, Library of Christian Classics, vols. 20 and 21 (Louisville, KY: The Westminster Press, 1967), cited by book, chapter, and paragraph; II.7.12.

6. Ibid., III.3.6.

7. Ibid., III.14.3.

8. H. Richard Niebuhr, *Christ and Culture* (New York: Harper & Row, 1951), 1–44.

9. For an overview of Luther's use of these terms, see Joel Bermann, *Wholly Citizens: God's Two Realms and Christian Engagement with the World* (Minneapolis: Fortress Press, 2017), 4.

10. "An Open Letter Concerning the Hard Book Against the Peasants" (1525), *LW* 46:69.

11. Ibid., 70.

12. Bermann, 109.

13. For a helpful discussion of thinkers who attempt to make the link between Luther and Nazism and a critique of such assertions, see George W. Forell, *Faith Active in Love: An Investigation of the Principles Underlying Luther's Social Ethics* (Minneapolis: Augsburg Press, 1954), 16–43. See also, Uwe Siemon-Netto, *The Fabricated Luther: Refuting Nazi Connections and Other Modern Myths*, 2nd ed. (St. Louis: Concordia, 2007).

14. *Institutes*, II.2.13.

15. Ibid., IV.20.2.

16. Ibid., IV.20.3.

17. John Calvin, *The Three Forms of Unity: The Reformed Church of the United States Subordinate Doctrinal Standards* (Grand Rapids: The Publications and Promotions Committee of the Reformed Church of the US, 2010). "Article 36 The

Civil Government" of the Belgic Confession (1561) was modified by the Christian Reformed Church in 1938 and 1985 in order to set forward what it judged to be a more biblical statement on the relationship between church and state.

18. Ernst Troeltsch, *The Social Teachings of the Christian Churches*, vol. 1 (New York: Harper & Row, 1960), 335.

19. *Schleitheim Confession*, trans. and ed. John H. Yoder (Scottsdale, PA: Herald Press, 1973), 11–12.

20. Ibid., 15.

21. The best-known expression of a modified Anabaptist model in recent time is John Howard Yoder, *The Politics of Jesus* (Grand Rapids: Eerdmans, 1994).

22. See, for example, J. Daryl Charles, *Retrieving the Natural Law: A Return to Moral First Things* (Grand Rapids: Eerdmans, 2008), and J. Budzisaewski, *Written on the Heart: The Case for Natural Law* (Downers Grove, IL: InterVarsity Press, 1997). The latter wrote his work while still a Protestant and later converted to the Roman Catholic Church.

23. Thomas De Aquino, *St. Thomas Aquinas Summa Theologica: Complete English Edition in Five Volumes*, vol. 1 (repr., Notre Dame: Christian Classics, 2000), pt. 1–11, Q. 91, art 1.

24. Richard McBrien, *Catholicism* (Minneapolis: Winston Press, 1981), 151.

Chapter 11

1. Louis Berkhof, *Systematic Theology*, 4th ed. (Grand Rapids: Eerdmans, 1941), 433.

2. Ibid., 434.

3. Berkhof, *Systematic Theology*, 434.

4. John Calvin, *Institutes of the Christian Religion*, II.2.15: "Therefore, in reading profane authors, the admirable light of truth displayed in them should remind us, that the human mind, however much fallen and perverted from its original integrity, is still adorned and invested with admirable gifts from its Creator. If we reflect that the Spirit of God is the only fountain of truth, we will be careful, as we would avoid offering insult to him, not to reject or condemn truth wherever it appears. In despising the gifts, we insult the Giver. How, then, can we deny that truth must have beamed on those ancient lawgivers who arranged civil order and discipline with so much equity? Shall we say that the philosophers, in their exquisite researches and skillful description of nature, were blind? Shall we deny the possession of intellect to those who drew up rules for discourse, and taught us to speak in accordance with reason? Shall we say that those who, by the cultivation of the medical art, expended their industry in our behalf were only raving? What shall we say of the mathematical sciences? Shall we deem them to be the dreams of madmen? Nay, we cannot read the writings of the ancients on these subjects without the highest admiration; an admiration which their excellence will not allow us to withhold. But shall we deem anything to be noble and praiseworthy, without tracing it to the hand of God? Far from us be such ingratitude; an ingratitude not chargeable even

on heathen poets, who acknowledged that philosophy and laws, and all useful arts were the inventions of the gods. Therefore, since it is manifest that men whom the Scriptures term carnal, are so acute and clear-sighted in the investigation of inferior things, their example should teach us how many gifts the Lord has left in possession of human nature, notwithstanding of its having been despoiled of the true good."

5. Calvin, *Institutes*, II.3.3. In commenting on Romans 2:15, Calvin writes that such Gentiles "prove that there is imprinted on their hearts a discrimination and judgment by which they distinguish between what is just and unjust, between, what is honest and dishonest. John Calvin, *Commentary on Romans*. Accessed February 13, 2017 from https://www.ccel.org/ccel/calvin/calcom38.i.html.

6. From the Synod of Dordrecht (November 13, 1618–May 9, 1619), Third and Fourth Head: Article 4. "There remain, however, in man since the fall, the glimmerings of natural light, whereby he retains some knowledge of God, or natural things, and of the difference between good and evil, and shows some regard for virtue and for good outward behavior. But so far is this light of nature from begin [*sic*] sufficient to bring him to a saving knowledge of God and to true conversion that he is incapable of using it aright even in things natural and civil. Nay further, this light, such as it is, man in various ways renders wholly polluted, and hinders in unrighteousness, by doing which he becomes inexcusable before God." Accessed February 13, 2017, from http://www.sacred-texts.com/chr/syndort.htm.

7. Richard J. Mouw, "He Shines in All That's Fair: Culture and Common Grace," *The 2000 Stob Lectures* (Grand Rapids: Eerdmans, 2001), 9.

8. Berkhof, *Systematic Theology*, 436–37.

9. Cornelius Van Til writes: "In this world the sinner does many 'good' things. He is honest. He helps to alleviate the sufferings of his fellow men. He 'keeps' the moral law. . . . [Depravity] is one of *principle*, not one of full expression. If the natural man fully expressed himself as he is in terms of the principle of ethical hostility to God that dwells within his soul, he would then be a veritable devil. Obviously he is often nothing of the sort. He is not at all as 'bad as he may be.' . . . [Human] depravity is absolute only in principle." Cornelius Van Til and K. S. Oliphint, *Common Grace and the Gospel*, 2nd ed., including the complete text of the original 1972 ed. (Phillipsburg, NJ: P & R, 2015), 226.

10. "The main concern for Calvinists about general revelation, natural law, natural theology, and similar notions is that they can lead to a categorical endorsement of the moral and rational capacities of human beings in general. Either the radical effects of the fall are denied outright, or they are acknowledged and then quickly modified by the idea of a prevenient grace, an across-the-board upgrading of our original fall state, so that some significant segment of our shared human consciousness has been repaired and our depravity is no longer in effect." Mouw, 92.

11. Mouw, 15.

12. Mouw writes: "If unredeemed persons . . . exhibit the 'internal' motives that we recognize as the work of the Spirit in the lives of the elect, here too the Holy Spirit must be at work, since 'the work of the Holy Spirit consists in leading all creation to its destiny, the final purpose of which is the glory of God.'" Mouw, 44.

13. Berkhof, *Systematic Theology*, 436.

14. John Jefferson Davis, *Meditation and Communion with God: Contemplating Scripture in an Age of Distraction* (Downers Grove, IL: IVP Academic, 2012), 38.

15. Berkhof, *Systematic Theology*, 437.

16. All Scripture is from the New International Version.

17. Berkhof, *Systematic Theology*, 437.

18. Ibid., 445.

19. "God our Savior, who wants all people to be saved and to come to a knowledge of the truth" (1 Tim. 2:4). Herman Bavinck, "For Man God Is the Supreme Good: Calvin and Common Grace," *The Princeton Theological Review* 7(3), 437–65. Retrieved February 10, 2017, from https://www.monergism.com/thethreshold/sdg /pdf/bavinck_commongrace.pdf. Barnhouse writes: "Why is God so good toward the lost? He declares that the purpose of the riches of his goodness, forbearance and longsuffering is to lead man to repentance; and he further declares that man does not know the object of God's goodness. Is this not a further picture of the state of man by nature? Can it not be seen that the dark ignorance of unbelief has brought a further fruit of ignorance of the grace of God? You are in good health? Why does God permit it? The answer is that he wants you to turn to him and acknowledge his goodness and accept the riches that he has for you. You have other blessings that come from the common grace of God. The purpose of such riches is to cause you to turn about-face and come to Him for further blessing." D. G. Barnhouse, "God's Wrath," *The Book of the Revelation*, vol. 2 (Grand Rapids: Eerdmans, 1953).

20. Mouw, 50.

21. "The supralapsarian insists that God first decreed that there would be a certain group of elect human beings and another group of reprobates; only then did God decide to make all of this happen by creating the world and permitting the fall into sin. Thus the decree of election and reprobation was prior to, or 'supra,' the decision to permit the fall. Infralapsarians propose a different sequence: first God decided to create the world; then God decided to permit the fall; only after these decrees did the divine decision occur with regard to election and reprobation. Thus God's electing and reprobating purposes were subordinate to, or 'infra,' the decision to create a world that would come to be plagued by sin." Mouw, 54.

22. Ibid., 68.

23. Ibid., 84.

24. For welfare in VanDrunen, see David VanDrunen, *Living in God's Two Kingdoms: A Biblical Vision for Christianity and Culture* (Wheaton, IL: Crossway, 2010), 92. Plantinga offers a useful definition of *shalom*: "In the Bible *shalom* means universal flourishing, wholeness, and delight—a rich state of affairs that inspires joyful wonder as its Creator and Savior opens doors and welcomes the creatures in whom he delights." Cornelius Plantinga, *Educating for Shalom: Our Calling as a Christian College*. Retrieved from https://calvin.edu/about/who-we-are/our-calling .html?dotcmsredir=1 4/27/17.

25. Jacques Derrida, "Letter in 'L'Affaire Derrida: Another Exchange,'" *The New York Review of Books* (March 25, 1993), 65.

26. Mouw, 99.

27. Jonathan T. Pennington, *Heaven and Earth in the Gospel of Matthew* (Grand Rapids: Baker, 2007), 298.

28. Ibid., 330.

29. Mouw, 101.

30. Stark, R. (1991). "Epidemics, Networks, and the Rise of Christianity," *Semeia* 56 (159–75): 166.

31. Tertullian, *Apology* 39, http://www.tertullian.org/articles/reeve_apology.htm 2/9/17.

32. They brought "the whole gospel for the whole man." M. I. M. Causton, *For the Healing of the Nations: The Story of British Baptist Medical Missions, 1792–1951* (London: Kingsgate, 1951), 28.

33. Ibid., 169.

34. B. J. Allen and C. A. Mason, *A Crusade of Compassion for the Healing of the Nations: A Study of Medical Missions for Women and Children* (West Medford, MA: The Central Committee on the United Study of Foreign Missions, 1919), 16. "The sacredness of human life is a conception peculiar to Christianity; to vindicate that conception and to establish it is essentially the aim of the Battalion of Life [i.e., medical missions]."

35. Causton, 32.

36. "All Christians are truly of the spiritual estate, and there is no difference among them, save of office alone. . . . A cobbler, a smith, a peasant, every man, has the office and function of his calling, and yet all alike are consecrated priests and bishops, and every man should by his office or function be useful and beneficial to the rest, so that various kinds of work may all be united for the furtherance of body and soul, just as the members of the body all serve one another." Martin Luther (1520), *To the Christian Nobility of the German Nation*. Retrieved June 15, 2017, from https://sourcebooks.fordham.edu/mod/luther-nobility.asp.

37. Mouw, 40.

38. Abraham Kuyper, J. J. Ballor, S. J. Grabill, and N. D. Kloosterman, *Wisdom & Wonder: Common Grace in Science & Art* (Grand Rapids: Christian's Library Press, 2011), 46.

39. Ibid., 53.

40. Ibid., 55.

41. Elizabeth Barrett Browning, *Aurora Leigh*, 7th book, 5th ed. (London: Chapman and Hall, 1860), 304.

42. David VanDrunen, *Living in God's Two Kingdoms: A Biblical Vision for Christianity and Culture* (Wheaton, IL: Crossway, 2010), 15.

43. Ibid., 14–15.

44. Ibid., 69.

45. Ibid., 95.

46. "Certain Christian traditions . . . have tended to look at this world simply as evil and to find no inherent value in cultural activities (perhaps justifying them only

insofar as they are necessary for feeding our families or providing opportunities for evangelism)." Ibid., 124.

47. Ibid., 166.

48. VanDrunen offers us three fences in our work with unbelievers: "First, Christians should pursue cultural activities not with a spirit of triumph and conquest over their neighbors but with a spirit of love and service toward them" (124). "Second, the New Testament calls us to critical engagement with human culture" (126). "Third and finally, the New Testament calls us to engage in cultural activities with a deep sense of detachment from this world and of longing for our true home in the world-to-come" (126). While believers "will be engaged in the affairs of human culture . . . they will not . . . treat them as if they were of ultimate importance" (67). Ibid.

49. Mouw, 69. "The vulnerability of infralapsarians lies in their insistence that, since creation and providence are independent of the program of redemption, individuals have a certain dignity apart from the decrees of election and reprobation."

50. Ibid., 73. We don't want "'limp-wristed theology' that appropriates psychological themes in order to cater to the needs of a generation of self-actualizers. . . . In a society that emphasizes the limitless possibilities of the individual self, it comes as a strange freshness to be confronted by an unfathomable God, indifferent to the petty, self-conscious needs that consumes us."

51. In conclusion, we do not know why God showers his grace indiscriminately or what his plans are. That is a mystery. Like Job, we are incapable of explaining God's plans: "Who is this that obscures my plans with words without knowledge?" (Job 38:2). As Mouw notes, "Properly understood, common grace theology is an attempt to preserve an area of mystery regarding God's dealings with humankind." Ibid., 90.

Chapter 12

1. The first part of this paper is an elaboration of a previous article: Paul Martindale, "A Muslim Christian Dialogue on Salvation: The Role of Works," *Evangelical Missions Quarterly* 46, no. 2 (January 2010): 69–71.

2. Dialogue meeting with several churches in Malden, Massachusetts, and the Moroccan American Civic and Cultural Association (June 8, 2008).

3. "So also faith by itself, if it does not have works, is dead" (James 2:17). "For as the body apart from the spirit is dead, so also faith apart from works is dead" (James 2:26).

4. Abd-al-Rahman Azzam, *The Eternal Message of Muhammad*, trans. Caesar E. Farah (New York: Mentor Books, 1964), 77ff.

5. Ibid., 78.

6. Hammudah Abdalati, *Islam in Focus* (Indianapolis: American Trust Publications, 1975), 32.

7. See, for example, Rom. 8:18–23.

8. Reinhold Seeburg, *Textbook of the History of Doctrines*, trans. Charles E. Hay, 2 vols. in 1 (Grand Rapids: Baker, 1954), 341–44.

9. Samuel P. Schlorff, "Muslim Ideology and Christian Apologetics," *Missiology* 21/2 (April 1993): 175.

10. Qur'an 22:65. Quotes from the Qur'an in this chapter are taken from the English translation by Majid Fakhry, *An Interpretation of the Quran: English Translation of the Meanings; A Bilingual Edition* (New York: New York University Press, 2004).

11. This formula gives the impression that salvation is the culmination of redemption at the time of judgment. However, salvation refers to the entire process of redemption, beginning with God's election of the believer before the foundation of the world and ending with the glorification of the believer in heaven post judgment.

12. John Piper, *The Future of Justification: A Response to N. T. Wright* (Wheaton, IL: Crossway, 2007), 110.

13. From the Thirty-Nine Articles of the Church of England in 1571. Quoted in Piper, 113–14.

14. "For we are his workmanship, created in Christ Jesus for good works, which God prepared beforehand, that we should walk in them" (Eph. 2:10 ESV).

15. Craig Keener, *The IVP Bible Background Commentary: New Testament* (Downers Grove, IL: InterVarsity Press, 1993), 544.

Chapter 13

1. Thomas Schreiner defends Luther, invoking Joseph Fitzmyer: "Such a translation isn't an imposition on the text, but represents the meaning of the verses in context. The famous Roman Catholic scholar Joseph Fitzmyer agrees." See Thomas Schreiner, *Faith Alone: The Doctrine of Justification* (Grand Rapids: Zondervan, 2015), 44. But Fitzmyer actually says, "The criteriological principle that it [*sola fides*] thus became is understandable in systematic theology and creates no difficulty, but one will look in vain for such a use of it in the Pauline writings themselves; *it is a theological extension of Paul's teaching that presses beyond what he states.*" Joseph A. Fitzmyer, *Romans: A New Translation with Introduction and Commentary*, Anchor Yale Bible 33 (New Haven: Yale University Press, 2008), 362; emphasis added. It sounds more like Fitzmyer is saying that it may not be an imposition on the theology, but it is an imposition on the text.

2. Edward Leigh, *Critica Sacra: Or Philological and Theological Observations upon All the Greek Words of the New Testament* (London: Printed for A. Miller for Thomas Underhill, 1650), 210.

3. See the entries in, e.g., John Parkhurst, *A Greek and English Lexicon to the New Testament* (London: Printed by F. Davis, for G. G. and J. Robinson, 1798), 536; Henry George Liddell, Robert Scott, and Franz Passow, *A Greek-English Lexicon Based on the German Work of F. Passow* (Oxford: University Press, 1848), 1186; Henry George Liddell, Robert Scott, Henry Stuart Jones, and Roderick McKenzie, *A Greek-English Lexicon* (Oxford: Clarendon Press, 1996); Johannes P. Louw and Eugene Albert Nida, *Greek-English Lexicon of the New Testament: Based on Semantic Domains* (New York: United Bible Societies, 1996); Johan Lust, Erik Eynikel, and Katrin Hauspie, *A Greek-English Lexicon of the Septuagint: Revised*

Edition (Deutsche Bibelgesellschaft: Stuttgart, 2003); Horst Robert Balz and Gerhard Schneider, eds., *Exegetical Dictionary of the New Testament* (Grand Rapids: Eerdmans, 1990–1993); Walter Bauer, Frederick W. Danker, William Arndt, and F. Wilbur Gingrich (BDAG), *A Greek-English Lexicon of the New Testament and Other Early Christian Literature*, 3rd ed. (Chicago: University of Chicago Press, 2000); Franco Montanari, ed., *The Brill Dictionary of Ancient Greek* (Leiden : Brill, 2015).

4. See Francis I. Andersen, *Habakkuk: A New Translation with Introduction and Commentary*, Anchor Yale Bible 25 (New Haven: Yale University Press, 2008), 211: "The Old Greek interpretation has resolved the ambiguity of *ʾĕmûnâ* in the right direction, away from man to God. By translating 'his *ʾĕmûnâ*" as "my *pistis*,' LXX correctly identified the *ʾĕmûnâ* as God's faithfulness." Cf. Anderson, *Habakkuk*, 215: "As ascribed to a human being, *ʾĕmûnâ* describes reliability in carrying out a task, steadfastness in relationships, being worthy of someone else's trust." It should be noted that of the numerous occurrences of the Hebrew expression found in Hab. 2:4 (*bēʾĕmūnā**), many directly speak of "working . . . faithfully" in ways that strongly suggest that in Hebrew there was certainly no opposition between working and acting in faith[fulness]. Cf., e.g., 2 Kings 12:16; 22:7; 2 Chron. 19:9; 31:18; 34:12; Ps. 33.

5. Richard B. Hays, *The Faith of Jesus Christ: The Narrative Substructure of Galatians 3:1–4:11* (Society of Biblical Literature, 1983; repr., Grand Rapids: Eerdmans, 2002).

6. See, e.g., N. T. Wright, "Romans and The Theology of Paul," in *Pauline Theology III*, ed. David M. Hay and E. Elizabeth Johnson (Minneapolis: Fortress, 1995), 37n9 and his numerous references to *pistis*/faith in his other writings. See also Douglas A. Campbell, *The Deliverance of God: An Apocalyptic Rereading of Justification in Paul* (Grand Rapids: Eerdmans, 2009), 640–48, 839–41.

7. David Bentley Hart, *The New Testament: A Translation* (New Haven, CT: Yale University Press, 2017); hereafter DBH.

8. Michael F. Bird and Preston M. Sprinkle, eds., *The Faith of Jesus Christ: Exegetical, Biblical, and Theological Studies* (Peabody, MA: Hendrickson, 2010). See also the brief overview of the history of the debate and James D. G. Dunn's argument for the traditional interpretation and translation ("faith in Christ"). James D. G. Dunn, "Once More, ΠΙΣΤΙΣ ΧΡΙΣΤΟΥ," appendix 1, in Hays, *The Faith of Jesus Christ*, 249–71. For a brief defense of the traditional (objective genitive) view, see also Moisés Silva, "πιστεύω, πίστις," in the *New International Dictionary of New Testament Theology and Exegesis*, 5 vols. (Grand Rapids: Zondervan, 2014), 3:768–9.

9. Matthew W. Bates, *Salvation by Allegiance Alone: Rethinking Faith, Works, and the Gospel of Jesus the King* (Grand Rapids: Baker Academic, 2017), 88.

10. Bates, *Salvation by Allegiance Alone*, 205n5.

11. Bates, *Salvation by Allegiance Alone*, 92. This is in contrast to the classic Reformation construct of *notitia* (knowledge), *assensus* (intellectual agreement), and *fiducia* (trust).

12. Thomas Schreiner, "Saved by 'Allegiance' Alone? On a New Attempt to Revise the Reformation," in *Themelios* (2018), https://www.thegospelcoalition.org/reviews/salvation-by-allegiance-alone.

13. Kelly M. Kapic, "Do We Need a New Word for 'Faith'?," *Christianity Today* 61.6 (July-August 2017), 90.

14. See Bates, *Salvation by Allegiance Alone*, 124: "Question: If our salvation depends solely on allegiance to Jesus as Lord, how can I be sure that I have been loyal enough?"

15. A foreignizing translation is one that leaves clear traces of the linguistic and cultural differences between the source text and its translated version. See Lawrence Venuti, *The Translator's Invisibility: A History of Translation* (New York: Routledge, 2018), xiii and passim.

16. For the concept, see Daniel B. Wallace, *Greek Grammar beyond the Basics: Exegetical Syntax of the New Testament* (Grand Rapids: Zondervan, 1996), 119–21; though Wallace himself supports the subjective genitive view (114–16).

17. N. T. Wright, "Paul and the Faithfulness of God," 2 vols., *Christian Origins and the Question of God* 4 (Minneapolis: Fortress, 2013), 968.

18. N. T. Wright, "Whence and Whither Pauline Studies in the Life of the Church?" in *Jesus, Paul and the People of God: A Theological Dialogue with N. T. Wright*, ed. Nicholas Perrin and Richard B. Hays (Downers Grove, IL; IVP Academic, 2011), 271.

19. Teresa Morgan, *Roman Faith and Christian Faith*: Pistis *and* Fides *in the Early Roman Empire and Early Churches* (Oxford: Oxford University Press, 2015).

20. Ibid., 273.

21. Ibid., 290.

22. Ibid., 273.

23. Ibid., 6.

24. Ibid., 53.

25. Ibid., 273. One wonders why Morgan mentions only those two options, since human faithfulness to Christ and Christ's faith in God are also viable.

26. Ibid., 272.

27. See, e.g., Deut. 7:9; Ps. Sol. 14:1; John 3:16; 1 Cor. 4:17; Gal. 2:20; 5:6; Eph. 1:15; 3:17; 6:21; Col. 1:4, 7; 4:7, 9; 1 Thess. 3:6; 2 Thess. 1:3; 1 Tim. 1:14; 6:2; 2 Tim. 1:13; 2:22; Titus 2:2; Philem. 1:5; James 2:5; 1 Pet. 1:8; 1 John 3:23; 4:16; 5:1; 3 John 1:5; Jude 1:20; Rev. 1:5; 2:19. Cf. 1 Macc. 7:8; 3 Macc. 3:10; 5:44; Sir. 6:14–16; 27:16–17; John 16:27; Titus 3:15; James 2:23.

28. See, e.g., Deut. 7:9 (where that pattern is reversed); Ps. Sol. 14:1; John 3:16; 1 Cor. 4:17; Gal. 2:20; Eph. 6:21; Col. 1:7; 4:7, 9; 1 Tim. 6:2; James 2:5; 1 John 4:16; Jude 1:20.

29. Louw and Nida, *Greek-English Lexicon of the New Testament*, 446.

30. See my discussion of Gal. 2:20 in *The Presence and Function of Scripture in Galatians 1 and 2*, WUNT 2.102 (Tübingen: Mohr Siebeck, 1998), 210–12. Here I argue that Paul may be playing with the possibilities of both a messianic and an ecclesiocentric interpretation of Hab. 2:4, so that in one case it would be Christ who lives by his faithfulness, and on the other, as Paul says, "I live by faith in" (or by the faithfulness of) "the Son of God, who loved me."

31. Morgan, *Roman Faith and Christian Faith*, 273–74.

32. That is, their believing in him, which, as BDAG reminds us often includes the "implication of total commitment to the one who is trusted" (BDAG, 817).

33. A key point being that various forms of early Judaism were all committed to a theology of grace, but "grace" did not mean the same thing to everyone who used the word. See John M. G. Barclay, *Paul and the Gift* (Grand Rapids: Eerdmans, 2017).

34. Unfortunately, Luther himself may have contributed to this tendency in his proposed distinction in Scripture between what he calls "an abstract or an absolute faith," when justification is being discussed, and "a concrete, composite, or incarnate faith," when faith is described as something that acts. See his discussion in his *Lectures on Galatians* (1535), *LW* 26:264–66.

35. Matthew Bates, in Jim West, "A Multi-part Interview with Matthew Bates on His New Book, Part Three," https://zwingliusredivivus.wordpress.com/2017/09/08/a-multi-part-interview-with-matthew-bates-on-his-new-book-part-three.

36. Bates, in an interview with Tavis Bohlinger, "Defending 'Allegiance Alone': Part 3 of Bates' Hot Seat Interview," Logos Academic Blog, https://academic.logos.com/defending-allegiance-alone-part-3-of-bates-hot-seat-interview.

37. Ceslas Spicq, "*pistis,*" *Theological Lexicon of the New Testament* (Peabody, MA: Hendrickson, 1994), 3:110.

38. Moisés Silva, "πιστεύω, πίστις," in *New International Dictionary of New Testament Theology and Exegesis*, 5 vols. (Grand Rapids: Zondervan, 2014), 3:760.

Chapter 14

1. Olivier Riaudel, "*Fides qua creditur* et *Fides quae creditur:* Retour sur une distinction qui n'est pas chez Augustin," *Revue théologique de Louvain* 43 (2012): 169–94; see esp. 174–79.

2. Ibid., 183 (author's translation).

3. Much of the material in this chapter from this point forward is adapted from Donald Fairbairn and Ryan Reeves, *The Story of Creeds and Confessions* (Grand Rapids: Baker Academic, forthcoming), esp. chs. 1, 2, and 4. Used by permission of Baker Publishing Group.

4. This and all subsequent biblical quotations are from the ESV.

Chapter 15

1. A. J. Gordon, *The First Thing in the World: or, The Primacy of Faith* (Fleming H. Revell, 1891), 26.

2. Henry Drummond, *The Greatest Thing in the World* (London: Hodder & Stoughton, 1880). The tension over faith and love is found as early as the Reformation. Luther's lectures on Galatians are an interesting engagement with the issue. See Martin Luther, *Lectures on Galatians 1535 Chapters 1–4*, ed. Jaroslav Pelikan and Walter Hansen, *Luther's Works* (Saint Louis: Concordia, 1963): 26:88–92, 160, 168. In contrast, Roman Catholics asserted that faith needed to be completed or formed by love, *charitata formata*. The tension was between "faith alone" and "faith as the

foundation but love needed to be added." Luther, addressing the Catholic position argues, "In this way they prefer love to faith and attribute righteousness, not to faith but to love. . . . Therefore when they do not attribute righteousness to faith except on account of love, they are attributing nothing at all to faith." *Luther's Works*, 26:269. I am indebted to my colleague Gordon Isaac for this historical insight regarding the ongoing debate over faith and love.

3. Gordon, 13.

4. See the James Pott & Co. edition of *The Greatest Thing in the World* (New York: James Pott & Co., 1891), flyleaf.

5. Scott M. Gibson, *A. J. Gordon: American Premillennialist* (Lanham, MD: University Press of America, 2001), 70, 200–203.

6. Gordon, 25–26.

7. Greg R. Scharf, *Let the Earth Hear His Voice: Strategies for Overcoming Bottlenecks in Preaching God's Word* (Phillipsburg: P&R, 2015), 23.

8. Scharf, 24.

9. James Muilenburg, "Faith Comes by Preaching," *Union Seminary Quarterly Review* 15:1 (1959): 17.

10. Charles Cameron, "The Holy Spirit in the Life of Faith," *Evangel* 24:3 (Autumn 2006): 88.

11. Louis Berkhof, *Systematic Theology* (Grand Rapids: Eerdmans, 1941), 506.

12. William E. Hordern, "The Primacy of Faith," *The Christian Century* 77:47 (November 1960): 1370.

13. Harold J. Koelpin, "The Doctrine by Which the Church Either Stands or Falls: Justification by Grace through Faith," *Logia* 26:1 (Epiphany 2017): 43.

14. Scharf, 29.

15. Ibid., 34.

16. Ibid., 40.

17. Franz Arnold, "The Act of Faith, a Personal Commitment," *Lumen Vitae* 5:1 (January-March 1950): 253.

18. Millard J. Erickson, *Christian Theology* (Grand Rapids: Baker, 1985), 930.

19. Berkhof, 497.

20. Lawrence A. Castagnola, S.J., "Preaching and Personal Faith," *Pastoral Life* 26:42 (September 1968): 502.

21. Jerry Bridges, *The Discipline of Grace: God's Role and Our Role in the Pursuit of Holiness* (Colorado Springs: NavPress/Tyndale, 2006), 59.

22. Arnold, 251–52.

23. Haddon W. Robinson, *Biblical Preaching: The Development and Delivery of Expository Messages* (Grand Rapids: Baker, 2014), 5. Robinson defines preaching as the following: "Expository preaching is the communication of a biblical concept, derived from and transmitted through a historical, grammatical, and literary study of a passage in its context, which the Holy Spirit applies to the personality and experience of the preacher, then through the preacher, applies to the hearers."

24. Castagnola, 502.

25. Scharf, 45.

26. Emeric A. Lawrence, "Faith in the Word of God," *Worship* 37:3 (Autumn 2006): 183.

27. Scharf, 45.

28. Kathryn A. Kleinhans, "Keep the Faith, for Christ's Sake!," *Dialog* 52:3 (Fall 2013): 182–85.

29. Castagnola, 501.

30. Martin J. Lohrmann, "Luther on Faith, Love, and Sermon Preparation,"*Currents in Theology and Mission* 43:4 (October 2016): 10.

31. Eugene H. Peterson, *Working the Angles: The Shape of Pastoral Integrity* (Grand Rapids: Eerdmans, 1987), 2.

32. Lohrmann, 10, quoted in Fred W. Meuser, *Luther the Preacher* (Minneapolis: Augsburg, 1983), 41.

33. Scharf, 41.

34. John R. W. Stott, *Between Two Worlds: The Art of Preaching in the Twentieth Century* (Grand Rapids: Eerdmans, 2017), 69.

35. Lawrence, 180–81.

36. Scharf, 31–32.

37. Erickson, 938.

38. William E. Hill, Jr., "Men of Faith," *Presbyterian Journal* 26:42 (February 14, 1968): 7.

39. Gary M. Simpson, " 'Faith Alone'—*Primus Inter Pares:* Welcome to the Banquet," *Dialog* 52:3 (Fall 2013): 179.

40. Arnold, 251.

Chapter 16

1. Cf. Francis Brown, S. R. Driver and Charles A. Briggs, *A Hebrew and English Lexicon of the Old Testament* (Oxford: Oxford University Press, 1952), 52–53.

2. Cf. William Holladay, *A Concise Hebrew and Aramaic Lexicon of the Old Testament* (Grand Rapids: Eerdmans, 1971), 20 ("view s.thg as reliable, believe").

3. Faith is important not only for life in Christ but also for world history. For example, in the past, God's judgment of Canaan depended on one thing: the faith, or lack of faith, of the land's inhabitants. The counterexample of Rahab shows the same (Heb. 11:31). God's final judgment of the world depends on the same principle (cf. Luke 18:8, "However, when the Son of Man comes, will he find faith on the earth?"). Because faith, or lack of it, is so fundamental to human welfare, it becomes important to understand clearly what faith is.

4. So Paul, as he contrasts this present life with that to come, says, "We . . . know that as long as we are at home in the body we are away from the Lord. For we live by faith, not by sight [εἴδους]" (2 Cor. 5:6–7). That is, our true life is not according to what we see in the world around us but according to faith in—our amening of—what is unseen.

5. The Spirit sustains the created order by uninterrupted acts of recreation from, as it were, nanosecond to nanosecond, and this sustaining process is arguably analo-

gous to God's own aseity. Cf. the argument in Jeffrey Jay Niehaus, *God the Poet: Exploring the Origin and Nature of Poetry* (Wooster, OH: Weaver, 2014), ch. 1.

6. For a discussion of righteousness in the Bible and ancient Near East as conformity to a standard, and the consequent idea that biblical righteousness is conformity to the standard of God's nature, cf. Jeffrey J. Niehaus, *Biblical Theology: The Special Grace Covenants; New Testament*, vol. 3 (Wooster, OH: Weaver, 2017), 349–70.

Chapter 17

1. All scriptural quotations are taken from the NRSV, unless otherwise indicated.

2. Cf. Richard J. Bauckham, *Jesus and the God of Israel: God Crucified and Other Studies on the New Testament's Christology of Divine Identity* (Grand Rapids: Eerdmans, 2009), 1–59, on 1 Cor. 8:6, ibid., 26–30, 97–104. On God's personified wisdom in the biblical and Jewish sapiential tradition that provided christologically relevant terminology, see Eckhard J. Schnabel, *Law and Wisdom from Ben Sira to Paul: A Tradition Historical Enquiry into the Relation of Law, Wisdom, and Ethics*, WUNT 2/16 (Tübingen: Mohr Siebeck, 1985), 236–64; Hermann von Lips, *Weisheitliche Traditionen im Neuen Testament*, WMANT 64 (Neukirchen-Vluyn: Neukirchener Verlag, 1990), 290–317; Larry W. Hurtado, *Lord Jesus Christ: Devotion to Jesus in Earliest Christianity* (Grand Rapids: Eerdmans, 2003), 123–26.

3. Cf. Gordon D. Fee, "Toward a Theology of 1 Corinthians," in *Pauline Theology II: 1 & 2 Corinthians*, ed. D. M. Hay (Minneapolis: Fortress, 1993), 37–58, 41–42.

4. David Dungan, *The Sayings of Jesus in the Churches of Paul* (Philadelphia: Fortress, 1971), 83–131; David Wenham, *Paul: Follower of Jesus or Founder of Christianity?* (Grand Rapids: Eerdmans, 1995), 144–47, 156–59, 192–93, 242–49.

5. Cf. Biörn Fjärstedt, *Synoptic Tradition in 1 Corinthians: Themes and Clusters of Theme Words in 1 Corinthians 1–4 and 9* (Uppsala: Teologiska Institutionen, 1974), 138–50; Wenham, *Paul*, 129–36.

6. Cf. Dungan, *Sayings of Jesus*, 1–80; Fjärstedt, *Synoptic Tradition*, 66–94; Wenham, *Paul*, 190–200.

7. See 1:10; 3:1–3; 4:14, 16; 5:4–5, 7–8; 6:1, 4, 6–7, 18, 20; 8:9, 13; 10:24; 11:33–34; 12:14.

8. For this background and for Paul's response in 1 Cor. 1–4, see Bruce W. Winter, *Philo and Paul among the Sophists*, SNTSMS 96 (Cambridge: Cambridge University Press, 1997), 113–202; Bruce W. Winter, *After Paul Left Corinth: The Influence of Secular Ethics and Social Change* (Grand Rapids: Eerdmans, 2001), 31–43.

9. If 1 Cor. 4:6 is regarded as decisive for understanding the divisions in the Corinthian church, then there were only two groups: a Paul group and an Apollos group. It seems that there was no "Messiah group"—Paul describes the exclusive attachment to Jesus Messiah in 3:21–23 as a corrective over against all other attachments. Cf. Wolfgang Schrage, *Der erste Brief an die Korinther*, 4 vols., EKK 7 (Zürich / Neukirchen-Vluyn: Benziger / Neukirchener Verlag, 1991–2001), 1:136, 143–47; Hans-Christian Kammler, *Kreuz und Weisheit. Eine exegetische Untersuchung zu 1 Kor 1,10–3,4*, WUNT 159 (Tübingen: Mohr Siebeck, 2003), 7–14.

10. Thus most commentators; see recently, Schrage, *Korinther*, 1:369. Andreas Lindemann, *Der Erste Korintherbrief*, HNT 9/1 (Tübingen: Mohr Siebeck, 2000), 124, thinks that a sexual relationship of the man with his biological mother is possible.

11. Cf. John K. Chow, *Patronage and Power: A Study of Social Networks at Corinth*, JSNTSup 75 (Sheffield: Sheffield Academic Press, 1992), 139–40; Andrew D. Clarke, *Secular and Christian Leadership in Corinth: A Socio-Historical and Exegetical Study of 1 Corinthians 1–6*, AGAJU 18 (Leiden: Brill, 1993), 85–88; Winter, *After Paul Left Corinth*, 53–57; David E. Garland, *1 Corinthians*, BECNT (Grand Rapids: Baker, 2003), 162–63.

12. Gaius, *Institutiones* 1.63.

13. Cf. Max Kaser, *Das römische Privatrecht. Erster Abschnitt: Das altrömische, das vorklassische und klassische Recht*, Zweite, neubearbeitete Auflage, HdA X/3.3.1 (München: Beck, 1971), 316; Jane F. Gardner, *Women in Roman Law and Society* (London / Bloomington: Croom Helm / Indiana University Press, 1986), 126.

14. Pseudo-Demosthenes 59.122; quoted in Robin Waterfield, *Demosthenes: Selected Speeches*, A New Translation (Oxford: Oxford University Press, 2014), 344.

15. Plutarch, *Moralia* 140B; cf. 142C–D, 144A.

16. Cf. James N. Adams, "Words for Prostitute in Latin," *Rheinisches Museum für Philologie* 126 (1983): 321–58.

17. Musonius Rufus, *Discourses* 12.64; Dio Chrystostom, *Orationes* 7.133–152.

18. Cf. Bettina Eva Stumpp, *Prostitution in der römischen Antike*, Antike in der Moderne (1998; repr., Berlin: Akademie, 2001), 286.

19. LSJ s.v. *melō* A.III.1; the translation "never mind" (BDAG s.v. *melei* 2; NRSV "do not be concerned about it") is reminiscent of a Stoic inner peace undisturbed by external circumstances, which is not Paul's concern here; in several papyri the Greek term is used with the connotation of emotional involvement that indicates an intensive preoccupation with something or someone; cf. Peter Arzt-Grabner and Ruth Elisabeth Kritzer, *1. Korinther*, Papyrologische Kommentare zum Neuen Testament 2 (Göttingen: Vandenhoeck & Ruprecht, 2006), 276.

20. Interpreting *mallon chrēsai* as expressing a contrast to the previous state-ment and supplying *tē eleutheria* ("your freedom"); thus NIV: "If you can gain your freedom, do so"; also ESV, GNB, NASB, NLT, RSV; see Schrage, *Korinther*, 2:139–40; Eckhard J. Schnabel, *Der erste Brief des Paulus an die Korinther*, 3. Auflage, Historisch-Theologische Auslegung (Wuppertal: R. Brockhaus, 2014), 391–93. Dif-ferently, some scholars and translations interpret v. 21b as a continuation of v. 21a in the sense of v. 20, supplying *tē douleia* ("your slavery"); cf. NRSV: "Even if you can gain your freedom, make use of your present condition now more than ever"; Anthony C. Thiselton, *The First Epistle to the Corinthians*, NIGTC (Grand Rapids: Eerdmans, 2000), 553–59.

21. Cf. Helmut Merklein, *Der erste Brief an die Korinther*, 3 vols., Ökumenischer Taschenbuchkommentar zum Neuen Testament 7/1–3 (Gütersloh / Würzburg: Mohn / Echter, 1992–2005), 2:249; Garland, *1 Corinthians*, 461.

22. Cf. Richard E. Oster, "When Men Wore Veils to Worship: The Historical Context of 1 Corinthians 11.4," *NTS* 34 (1988): 481–505; David W. J. Gill, "The

Importance of Roman Portraiture for Head Coverings in 1 Corinthians 11.2–16," *TynBul* 41 (1990): 245–60; Winter, *After Paul Left Corinth*, 120–41; Bruce W. Winter, *Roman Wives, Roman Widows: The Appearance of New Women and the Pauline Communities* (Grand Rapids: Eerdmans, 2003), 77–96. For women see Judith Lynn Sebesta, "Symbolism in the Costume of the Roman Woman," in *The World of Roman Costume*, ed. J. L. Sebesta and L. Bonfante, Wisconsin Studies in Classics (Madison: University of Wisconsin Press, 1994), 46–53; Susan E. Wood, *Imperial Women: A Study in Public Images, 40 B.C.–A.D. 68*, Mnemosyne Sup 194 (Leiden: Brill, 1999), 159.

23. For *kephalē* meaning "prominence," cf. Richard S. Cervin, "Does Κεφαλή Mean 'Source' or 'Authority Over' in Greek Literature? A Rebuttal," *Trinity Journal* 10 (1989): 85–112; Cervin, "Κεφαλή"; Andrew C. Perriman, "The Head of a Woman: The Meaning of κεφαλή in I Cor. 11:3," *JTS* 45 (1994): 602–22; Thiselton, *First Epistle to the Corinthians*, 812–22.

24. Cf. Otfried Hofius, "Herrenmahl und Herrenmahlsparadosis. Erwägungen zu 1Kor 11,23b-25 [1988]," in *Paulusstudien* (Tübingen: Mohr Siebeck, 1994), 203–40, 216–23; Matthias Klinghardt, *Gemeinschaftsmahl und Mahlgemeinschaft. Soziologie und Liturgie frühchristlicher Mahlfeiern*, TANZ (Tübingen: Francke, 1996), 286–301; Winter, *After Paul Left Corinth*, 143–52.

25. The translation of the phrase *allēlous ekdechesthe* with "wait for one another" (ESV, GNB, NASB, NRSV, RSV) is semantically possible, but less likely, as the context suggests. Both Josephus and the papyri use the verb *ekdechomai* with the connotation "receive as a guest" or "entertain"; cf. Arzt-Grabner et al., *1. Korinther*, 402–3; see Hofius, "Herrenmahl," 221; Garland, *1 Corinthians*, 554–55; Winter, *After Paul Left Corinth*, 151–52.

26. Cf. Schnabel, *Korinther*, 697.

27. Ernst Käsemann, *Perspectives on Paul* (London: SCM, 1971), 116–17.

28. NIV and NRSV render the verb *diermēneuō* as "interpret," ignoring the fact that in the context of the references to *glōssa*, which here means "language," the verb means "translate from one language to another."

Chapter 18

1. Please note that in employing the adjective "Nicaean" rather than "Nicene," I am distinguishing between the Creed and Council of Nicaea of AD 325 and the Nicene Creed of AD 381, which, being an attempt to expand the original creed, added in a doctrine the original council rejected for inclusion. For further information, please see my article "The Need for Caution in the Use of Eternal Birth Language for Jesus Christ in the Early Church and Today," in *Africanus Journal* 10, no. 1 (April 2018): 5–22.

2. *Reasoning from the Scriptures* (Brooklyn, NY: Watchtower Bible and Tract Society, 1989) answers the questions "Is Jesus Christ actually God?" with "Notice that Jesus referred not to himself but to his Father in heaven as 'the only true God' "

(212); "Does John 1:1 prove that Jesus is God?" with "So, then, was John saying that Jesus was God? Obviously not" (213); "Does the Bible teach that each of those said to be part of the Trinity is God?" with "He [the Father] cannot be 'the only true God,' the one 'who alone (is) truly God,' if there are two others who are God to the same degree as he is, can he? Any others referred to as 'gods' must be either false or merely a reflection of the true God" (411), and on and on.

3. This magnificent defense of Nicene orthodoxy against the various heterodox creeds created to overturn it is gathered with other documents by Athanasius in *Select Treatises of S. Athanasius, Archbishop of Alexandria, in Controversy with the Arians* (hereafter *De Synodis*), vol. 1, which is the first half of vol. 8 of *A Library of Fathers of the Holy Catholic Church, Anterior to the Division of the East and West*, trans. Members of the English Church (Oxford: John Henry Parker; J. G. F. and J. Rivington 1842), 73–176. I have also drawn Athanasius's views for this chapter from his *Epistle of S. Athanasius, Archbishop of Alexandria, In Defence of the Nicene Definition*, along with its appendix and a note on "the Nicene Anathema" on pages 1–72 of the same volume.

4. John Henry Cardinal Newman, "Semi-Arians," in *Select Treatises of St. Athanasius in Controversy with the Arians*, vol. 2, 4th ed. (London: Longmans, Green, 1888), 282–84.

5. Athanasius, *De Synodis*, 8:1.2.16.3.98n.

6. Ibid., 8:1.2.17.4.99.

7. Ibid., 8:1.2.17.4.99n. In my estimation, Eusebius was missing the fact that God is an eternal absolute. Absolutes do not have degrees of absoluteness, just as unique does not have degrees of uniqueness. Christ is either equal with God and therefore a full coeternal person of the Godhead, or not equal with God and therefore not God. If only the Father is God, then there would be no Triune Godhead but just the Father. In that light, positing degrees of Godness would seem to be more a pagan idea.

8. Ibid., 8:1.3.49.20, 148–49.

9. Ibid., 8:1.3.49.20, 148–50.

10. Ibid., 8:1.3.51.23, 151.

11. This is a position that appears to me to be a modification of the low Christology of Origen, former overseer of the Church of Alexandria, whose bizarre explanation of the dependence of deity of the Son on the Father was accomplished through constant meditation, according to his *Commentary on the Gospel According to John Books 1–10*. An accessible translation is available from Ronald E. Heine of the Emmanuel School of Religion, published by The Catholic University of America Press of Washington, DC (1989).

12. Eusebius, *The Church History*, trans. Paul L. Maier (Grand Rapids: Kregel, 1999), 3.36, 123.

13. Athanasius, *De Synodis*, 8:1.3.47.18, 147. *The Oxford Dictionary of the Christian Church*, 2nd ed., ed. F. L. Cross and E. A. Livingstone (New York: Oxford, 1974), speculates Ignatius's dates to be circa AD 35–107, but he points out that Origen records him as the second rather than the third bishop of Antioch after Peter; if accurate, that makes him Peter's direct successor (688, col. 2).

14. Athanasius, *De Synodis*, 8:1:3.51.23, 151.

15. J. N. D. Kelly reports, "Who Praxeas was remains a mystery; he is a shadowy figure, and some have identified him ('Praxeas' could be a nickname, meaning 'busy body') with Noetus or Epigonus, or even . . . with Pope Callistus," *Early Christian Doctrines*, 2nd ed. (New York: Harper & Row, 1960), 121. For a brief explanation of Noetus's teaching, see Kelly, 120, or *The Oxford Dictionary of the Christian Church*, 978, col. 2.

16. E. Evan's translation of "Tertullian's Treatise against Praxeas" (130–131) gathered in J. Stevenson, W. H. C. Frend, *A New Eusebius: Documents Illustrating the History of the Church to AD 337*, 3rd ed. (Grand Rapids: Baker, 2013), 188.

17. Hippolytus quoting Zephyrinus in his *Refutation of all Heresies*, cited in Stevenson and Frend, eds., *A New Eusebius*, 167. Hippolytus charges that Pope Zephyrinus was being manipulated by Pope Callistus when he made this claim: "Now Callistus brought forward Zephyrinus himself, and induced him publicly to say 'I know one God, Jesus Christ; nor except him do I know any other that is begotten and susceptible to suffering.' And on another occasion he made the following statement: 'The Father did not die, but the Son.'" J. N. D. Kelly has an interesting discussion on the theology surrounding this heretical statement in his *Early Christian Doctrines*, 123. In *Against Noëtus*, Hippolytus reports, "He alleged that Christ was the Father himself, and that the Father himself was born, and suffered, and died"; also see *A New Eusebius*, 163.

18. Kelly, *Early Christian Doctrines*, 121.

19. Ibid, 122.

20. General Superintendent David K. Bernard of the United Pentecostal Church International also explains that "water baptism" in this church is done "in the name of Jesus Christ" alone rather than in the name of the Trinity. This practice comes from "an appreciation of God's identity." See http://www.upci.org/about/our-beliefs, accessed May 9, 2017.

21. Ibid.

22. Jules Bonnet, *Letters of John Calvin*, vol. 1, trans. David Constable (Edinburgh: Thomas Constable, 1855), 29n3.

23. Ibid., 30.

24. Ibid.

25. Ibid.

26. Ibid., 31.

27. Ibid., 31–32.

28. Ibid., 32.

29. Athanasius, *De Synodis*, 8:1.3.49.20, 148–49. Where does Paul call Christ the "I Am That I Am"? I think Calvin is thinking along the same lines in his *Institutes* when he writes, "Hence, also, that saying of Paul's that Christ was the leader of the people in the wilderness [1 Cor. 10:4]." John Calvin, *Institutes of the Christian Religion*, ed. John T. McNeil, trans. Ford Lewis Battles (Philadelphia: Westminster, 1960), I.13.10.

30. Athanasius, *De Synodis,* 8:1. 3.35.4, 132.

31. The Athanasian Creed is widely available. This version is from *The Book of Concord: The Confessions of the Lutheran Church*, http://bookofconcord.org/creeds .php. It is also available in Philip Schaff, *The Creeds of Christendom* (New York: Harper Brothers, 1877); J. N. D. Kelly, *The Athanasian Creed* (New York: Harper & Row, 1964), and so on. It can even be found for quick reference on Wikipedia: http://en.wikipedia.org/wiki/Athanasian_Creed.

32. Calvin, *Institutes*, I.13.18.

33. Ibid.

34. Ibid., I.10.2.

35. Ibid.

36. Charles Hodge, *Systematic Theology*, vol. 1 (Grand Rapids: Eerdmans, 1968), 467. See a recent discussion of the issue of the self-existence (aseity) not being limited solely to the Father in the Trinity, in Brannon Ellis, *Calvin, Classical Trinitarianism, and the Aseity of the Son* (Oxford: Oxford University Press, 2012).

37. When referencing Christ's command to baptize, Calvin also points out, "For this means precisely to be baptized into the name of the one God who has shown himself with complete clarity in the Father, the Son, and the Spirit. Hence it is quite clear that in God's essence reside three persons in whom one God is known." Calvin, *Institutes*, I.13.16.

38. Ibid., III.13.22.

39. Ibid., I.13.5.

40. Bruce A. Ware, *Father, Son, and Holy Spirit: Relationships, Roles, and Relevance* (Wheaton, IL: Crossway, 2005), 131, 51, 55.

41. Ibid., 51.

42. Ibid., 55.

43. Ibid.

44. See Henry Bettenson and Chris Maunder, *Documents of the Christian Church*, 4th ed. (Oxford: Oxford University Press, 2011), 44.

45. Author's translation.

Chapter 19

1. "Joint Declaration on the Occasion of the Joint Catholic-Lutheran Commemoration of the Reformation" (October 31, 2016), http://saltandlighttv.org/blogfeed /getpost.php?id=72522&language.

2. "Catholic and Lutheran Churches pledge to work for shared Eucharist," http:// cruxnow.com/papal-visit/2016/10/31/catholic-lutheran-churches-pledge-work -shared-eucharist.

3. See http://www.vatican.va/roman_curia/pontifical_councils/chrstuni/docu ments/rc_pc-christuni_doc-31101999_cath_luth-joint-declaration_en.html on; citations are provided to sections of document.

4. "Grace and Justification," *Catechism of the Catholic Church* (Ligouri, MO: Ligouri Publications, 1994), 482: "Justification is not only the remission of sins, but

also the sanctification and renewal of the interior man," citing the Council of Trent (1547), Denziger 1528.

5. This consensus on the "basic truths" of the doctrine of justification is consistent with a proposed distinction (which we will introduce and develop in the sections below), with respect to doctrinal formulations, between a *maximally orthodox* statement and a *sufficiently orthodox* statement. From the perspective of a given ecclesial community in a particular context of discussion, a *maximally orthodox* statement may be deemed necessary to define a denomination's distinctive identity, while a *sufficiently orthodox* statement may be deemed sufficient for the purposes of recognizing other bodies as authentically Christian, or for interchurch cooperation, or even more specifically, for the practice of intercommunion. The concept of "orthodoxy," in other words, may function as a binary concept in one context and as a "graded" concept in another.

6. See https://www.firstthings.com/article/1994/05/evangelicals-catholics -together-the-christian-mission-in-the-third-millennium.

7. J. I. Packer, "Why I Signed It," *Christianity Today* (December 1994), http:// www.christianitytoday.com/ct/1994/december12/4te34a.html?start=4.

8. F. F. Bruce, *The Epistle to the Galatians* (Grand Rapids: Eerdmans, 1982), 133. Similarly, as Frank Matera states in his commentary, "to separate Gentile from Jew on the basis of food laws was to undercut the truth of the gospel." Frank J. Matera, *Galatians* (Collegeville, MN: Michael Glazier / The Liturgical Press, 1992), 90.

9. N. T. Wright, "The Letter to the Galatians: Exegesis and Theology," http:// ntwrightpage.com/2016/07/12/the-letter-to-the-galatians-exegesis-and-theology, 23.

10. Gordon D. Fee, *The First Epistle to the Corinthians*, rev. ed. (Grand Rapids: Eerdmans, 2014), 343.

11. J. E. Lesslie Newbigin, *The Reunion of the Church: A Defense of the South India Scheme* (New York: Harper & Brothers, 1948), 103.

12. C. H. Dodd, in his well-known study of the early Christian preaching, states that the Pauline *kerygma* "is a proclamation of the facts of the death and resurrection of Christ in an eschatological setting which gives significance to the facts. . . . The new age is here, of which Christ, again by virtue of his death and resurrection, is Lord. . . . Paul . . . believed that in essentials his Gospel was that of the primitive apostles." C. H. Dodd, *The Apostolic Preaching and Its Developments* (New York: Harper & Brothers, 1962), 13.

13. R. C. Sproul, *Faith Alone: The Evangelical Doctrine of Justification* (Grand Rapids: Baker Books, 1995), 178.

14. Ibid., 180.

15. Alister E. McGrath, in his comprehensive history of the doctrine of justification, *Iustitia Dei: A History of the Christian Doctrine of Justification*, 3rd ed. (Cambridge: Cambridge University Press, 2005), 229–35, concludes that Luther and Melanchthon's *sola fide* formulation of the doctrine of justification was in fact an example of the development of Christian doctrine, advancing a clearer and sharper distinction between justification (as event) and sanctification (as a process)—a

distinction that had not been present in the tradition from the time of Augustine until the time of Luther in the Latin Church.

16. "Theology and Practice of the Lord's Supper, Part I," www.lcms.org/faqs (May 24, 2017).

17. "LCMS: Frequently Asked Questions: The Lord's Supper/Holy Communion," www.lcms.org/faqs (May 24, 2017).

18. "Theology and Practice of the Lord's Supper, Part I," op. cit., Section 2. Closed Communion [24].

19. Only serious, unrepentant sinning (e.g., 1 Cor. 5:1–5, the case of incest in Corinth) barred a confessing, baptized believer from the Communion table.

20. Walter M. Abbot, S.J., ed., *The Documents of Vatican II* (New York: Corpus Books, 1966), 33–34.

21. "Joint Declaration on the Occasion of the Joint Catholic-Lutheran Commemoration of the Reformation," op. cit., 1.

22. Ibid., 2.

23. *Code of Canon Law*, Can. 844.1, htttp://www.vatican.va/archive/ENG1104/_P2THM. In sections 2 and 3 of Canon 844, some exceptions are permitted; e.g., members of Eastern Churches who "seek such (sacraments) on their own accord and are properly disposed," and for others, in cases of danger of death or "grave necessity" who seek such on their own accord and "manifest Catholic faith in respect to these sacraments and are properly disposed."

List of Contributors

Gwenfair Walters Adams is associate professor of church history and director of the Master of Arts in Spiritual Formation at Gordon-Conwell Theological Seminary.

Roy E. Ciampa is the S. Louis and Ann W. Armstrong Professor of Religion and chair of the Department of Religion at Samford University, and formerly professor of New Testament and chair of the Biblical Studies Division at Gordon-Conwell Theological Seminary.

David A. Currie is dean of the Doctor of Ministry Program and the Ockenga Institute and professor of pastoral theology at Gordon-Conwell Theological Seminary.

John Jefferson Davis is chair of the Division of Christian Thought and professor of systematic theology and Christian ethics at Gordon-Conwell Theological Seminary.

Donald Fairbairn is the Robert E. Cooley Professor of Early Christianity at Gordon-Conwell Theological Seminary and academic dean of the Charlotte Campus.

Scott M. Gibson is the David E. Garland Chair of Preaching and director of the PhD program in preaching at Baylor University, George W. Truett Theological Seminary, and formerly the Haddon W. Robinson Professor of Preaching and Ministry and director of the Haddon W. Robinson Center for Preaching at Gordon-Conwell Theological Seminary.

Dennis P. Hollinger is president of Gordon-Conwell Theological Seminary and the Colman M. Mockler Distinguished Professor of Christian Ethics at Gordon-Conwell Theological Seminary.

Gordon L. Isaac is the director of the ThM Program in Church History and Theology and MA and MAR Programs and the Berkshire Associate Professor of Church History and Advent Christian Studies at Gordon-Conwell Theological Seminary.

Todd M. Johnson is the director of the Center for the Study of Global Christianity and associate professor of global Christianity at Gordon-Conwell Theological Seminary.

Walter C. Kaiser Jr. is president emeritus of Gordon-Conwell Theological Seminary.

Richard Lints is vice president for academic affairs and the Andrew Mutch Distinguished Professor of Theology at Gordon-Conwell Theological Seminary.

Paul T. Martindale is ranked adjunct professor of missions and Islamic studies at Gordon-Conwell Theological Seminary.

Karen Mason is associate professor of counseling and psychology at Gordon-Conwell Theological Seminary and director of the Hamilton counseling program.

Jeffrey J. Niehaus is professor of Old Testament at Gordon-Conwell Theological Seminary.

Seong Hyun Park is dean of the Boston Campus and assistant professor of Old Testament at Gordon-Conwell Theological Seminary.

Eckhard J. Schnabel is the director of the Master of Theology in Biblical Studies Program and the Mary French Rockefeller Distinguished Professor of New Testament at Gordon-Conwell Theological Seminary.

Aída Besançon Spencer is senior professor of New Testament at Gordon-Conwell Theological Seminary.

William David Spencer is ranked adjunct professor of theology and the arts at Gordon-Conwell Theological Seminary.